PENGUIN BOOKS

AYODHYA

Pamulaparti Venkata Narasimha Rao was born in Karimnagar in the erstwhile state of Hyderabad in June 1921. After playing an active part in Hyderabad's independence movement, he served as a Congress minister in Andhra Pradesh and became chief minister of the state in 1971. In 1977, he was elected to the Lok Sabha and went on to hold several cabinet posts under Indira and Rajiv Gandhi, including those of foreign minister and home minister. After Rajiv Gandhi's assassination in 1991, Rao was chosen to lead the Congress party and became the prime minister of India.

Leading a minority government, Rao was the first prime minister from outside the Gandhi–Nehru family to serve out a full five-year term. His premiership is remembered for the liberalization of the Indian economy and the move towards free-market reforms. Rao resigned as Congress president after the party lost the 1996 general elections. He died in December 2004.

PRAISE FOR THE BOOK

'[It is] his best account of the developments which had shaken the entire country . . . Reproduce[s] the governor's report that may give a totally new twist to the Ram Janmbhoomi controversy . . . tries to answer some questions which have remained unanswered, so far, about the most defining political moments of recent times'—*Times of India*

'A sensational book . . . a defence and a testament . . . It is not a confession; it is an affirmation, a declaration of faith in political decency and constitutional propriety'—*India Today*

PENGUIN BOOKS

AYODHYA

Pamulaparti Venkata Narasimha Rao was born in Karimnagar in the erstwhile state of Hyderabad in June 1921. After playing an active part in Hyderabad's independence movement, he served as a Congress minister in Andhra Pradesh and became chief minister of the state in 1971. In 1977, he was elected to the Lok Sabha and went on to hold several cabinet posts under Indira and Rajiv Gandhi, including those of foreign minister and home minister. After Rajiv Gandhi's assassination in 1991, Rao was chosen to lead the Congress party and became the prime minister of India.

Leading a minority government, Rao was the first prime minister from outside the Gandhi-Nehru family to serve out a full five-year term. His premiership is remembered for the liberalization of the Indian economy and the move towards free-market reforms. Rao resigned as Congress president after the party lost the 1996 general elections. He died in December 2004.

PRAISE FOR THE BOOK

'[It is] the best account of the developments which had shaken the entire country . . . [Rao has] provided a report that may give a totally new twist to the Ram Janmabhoomi controversy . . . tries to answer some questions which have remained unanswered, so far, about the most defining political moment in recent times'—*Times of India*

'A sensational book . . . a defence and an assessment . . . It is not a confession; it is an affirmation, a declaration of faith in political decency and constitutional propriety'—*India Today*

AYODHYA

6 DECEMBER 1992

P.V. NARASIMHA RAO

PENGUIN BOOKS
An imprint of Penguin Random House

PENGUIN BOOKS

USA | Canada | UK | Ireland | Australia
New Zealand | India | South Africa | China | Singapore

Penguin Books is part of the Penguin Random House group of companies
whose addresses can be found at global.penguinrandomhouse.com

Published by Penguin Random House India Pvt. Ltd
4th Floor, Capital Tower 1, MG Road,
Gurugram 122 002, Haryana, India

First published in Viking by Penguin Books India 2006
This edition published by Penguin Random House India 2019

10 9 8 7 6 5 4 3 2

ISBN 9780143442226

Typeset in Sabon by Mantra Virtual Services, New Delhi
Printed at Manipal Technologies Limited, India

www.penguin.co.in

Contents

Publisher's Note

P.V. Narasimha Rao wrote his account of what happened at Ayodhya in 1992 after he stepped down as Prime Minister of India in 1996. For various reasons, he did not publish the long study, supplemented by a number of appendices, in his lifetime. He made revisions to this book till a few days before his death in December 2004. The text of this book is taken from P.V. Narasimha Rao's papers that came to hand after his death, collated in consultation with Shri Rao's family. The book is being published posthumously, in accordance with the author's wishes.

Chronology of Major Events Related to Ayodhya

1528	Mosque built in Ayodhya, which Hindus believe to be the birthplace of Shri Ram, by Mir Baqi, a noble in Emperor Babur's court.
1855	Records of a battle in Ayodhya.
1859	British administration erects fence to separate places of worship, allowing the inner court to be used by Muslims and the outer court by Hindus.
1885	Suit filed praying for permission to erect a temple on outer court close to mosque; suit denied.
1934	Communal riots over use of the disputed structure.
23 December 1949	Ram Lalla idols are installed in the RJM–BM. Lock put on the structure by orders of the magistrate under Section 145 Cr. PC.
January 1950	Two title suits filed by Gopal Singh Visharad and Paramhans Ramachandra. Interim injunction orders passed by Civil Judge to allow pooja and not to remove idols.

3 March 1951	Civil Judge confirms interim injunction order.
26 April 1955	High Court confirms interim injunction order dated 3 March 1951.
1959	Title suit filed by Nirmohi Akhara.
1961	Title suit filed by Sunni Central Waqf Board.
1984	Vishwa Hindu Parishad begins campaign to build a Ram temple at Ayodhya.
1 February 1986	Order passed by District Judge for opening locks of the RJB–BM and allowing pooja by devotees.
February 1986	Prominent Muslim leaders decide to form Babri Masjid Action Committee.
July 1988–November 1989	Discussions held by Buta Singh, Union Home Minister, with various parties relating to RJB–BM issue.
1989	Title suit filed by D.N. Agarwal. Original title suits transferred to High Court and consolidated for being taken up together.
14 August 1989	Order passed by High Court for maintenance of *status quo* of disputed property.
October–November 1989	*Pujan shilas* (bricks) brought from all over the country to Ayodhya.
9 November 1989	*Shilanyas* of the proposed Ram

	temple performed at a site agreed between various sides as being undisputed.
February 1990	*Kar seva* at RJB–BM.
July–October 1990	Negotiations during the government of V.P. Singh.
September–October 1990	Advani's rath yatra.
19 October 1990	The Ramjanmabhoomi–Babri Masjid (Acquisition of Area) Ordinance, 1990 promulgated to acquire the disputed shrine and its adjoining area.
23 October 1990	The Ramjanmabhoomi–Babri Masjid (Acquisition of Area) Withdrawal Ordinance 1990 promulgated to cancel the earlier Ordinance.
30 October 1990	*Kar seva* at RJB–BM. Some devotees climb the domes of RJB–BM, damage them and hoist saffron flags. Some damage also done to compound walls of RJB–BM. The situation is brought under control quickly by the Central and State Governments, led by V.P. Singh and Mulayam Singh Yadav respectively.
2 November 1990	Use of force at Ayodhya leads to death of some people. Riots in many parts of the country follow.
9 December 1990	Attempt to blow up shrine.
December 1990–February 1991	Negotiations during the government of Chandra Shekhar.

June 1991	General elections. BJP government formed in UP. Congress government headed by P.V. Narasimha Rao comes to power at the Centre.
7, 10 October 1991	Notifications for land acquisition issued by Government of UP. This is followed by demolition of certain structures on acquired land.
25 October 1991	High Court passes order in writ petitions, *inter alia,* allowing Government of UP to take possession of acquired land but prohibiting permanent construction.
31 October 1991	Some people attack the structure and cause some damage to its walls.
2 November 1991	Meeting of National Integration Council. CM's assurances. Unanimous resolution passed.
15 November 1991	Supreme Court passes order noting CM's assurances to NIC and High Court's order of 25 October 1991 and directing compliance with these.
December 1991 onwards	Removal of various security measures.
February 1992	Construction of boundary wall (Ram Diwar) started in Ayodhya.
March 1992	42.09 acres of land acquired in 1988 and 1989 handed over by UP Government to RJB Nyas for Ram Katha Park.

March–May 1992	All other structures on acquired land demolished.
May 1992	Extensive digging and levelling operations. (High Court refuses to stay these operations.)
9 July 1992	Construction of concrete platform commenced.
15 July 1992	High Court prohibits undertaking or continuing construction activity.
July 1992	Contempt petitions filed in Supreme Court. (Some petitions had been filed earlier also.)
23 July 1992	Supreme Court prohibits construction activity of any kind. P.V. Narasimha Rao's meeting with religious leaders.
26 July 1992	Construction activity stops.
27 July 1992	P.V. Narasimha Rao's statement in Parliament.
August–September 1992	Ayodhya Cell set up in PMO. P.V. Narasimha Rao's meetings with various leaders.
October 1992	Two meetings between VHP and BMAC in resumed negotiations.
23 October 1992	Meeting for study of archaeological material between VHP and BMAC nominees.
30 and 31 October 1992	Dharam Sansad/KMDM meetings. Announcement made for resumption of *kar seva* on 6 December 1992.

8 November 1992	Third and last meeting between VHP and BMAC.
23 November 1992	NIC meeting boycotted by BJP. Unanimous resolution passed. Government of India makes submissions before Supreme Court following its directive on 20 November 1992.
24 November 1992	CPMFs stationed at places near Ayodhya by Central Government.
26 November 1992	Supreme Court passes order regarding Ayodhya.
27, 28 November 1992	Affidavits/assurances given by Government of UP. Supreme Court passes order classifying that *kar seva* would be symbolic and not entail construction. Court appoints Observer.
6 December 1992	Date of *kar seva*. RJB–BM attacked and demolished by *kar sevaks*. Idols removed and reinstalled. A wall and shed erected on 6 and 7 December. President's Rule imposed in UP. UP Assembly dissolved.
Night of 7-8 December 1992	CPMFs take control of RJB–BM area.
December 1992	BJP brings no-confidence motion against P.V. Narasimha Rao's government in Parliament; the motion is defeated.
27 December 1992	Central Government decides to take over RJB–BM site.

7 January 1993	Acquisition of Certain Area at Ayodhya Ordinance issued. Core question of dispute referred to Supreme Court by President of India.
January 1993	Bomb blasts, thought to be orchestrated in retaliation to the Babri Masjid demolition, rock Mumbai; thousands die in the resultant communal riots.
24 December 1994	Supreme Court passes judgment on Ayodhya incident, holds Kalyan Singh's government responsible.
1998	BJP comes to power at the Centre.
2002	BJP withdraws from its commitment to build a Ram temple at Ayodhya. VHP sets deadline of 15 March to begin construction of temple. *Kar sevaks* from across the country converge on Ayodhya. Compartment of Sabarmati Express carrying *kar sevaks* burns down in Godhra, Gujarat, killing a number of people. Thousands die in communal riots in Gujarat following the incident. Meanwhile, three High Court judges begin hearings to determine who owns the disputed site.
2003	Archaeological Survey of India begins a court-ordered survey to find out whether a temple to Ram existed on the disputed site. The survey says there is evidence of a temple beneath the mosque; Muslims dispute the

findings. A court rules that seven Hindu leaders should stand trial for inciting the destruction of the Babri Masjid in 1992.

2004	Congress government comes to power at the Centre after six years of BJP rule. Leader of the Opposition L.K. Advani says his party has an unwavering commitment to building a Ram temple at Ayodhya.
5 July 2005	Six heavily-armed terrorists make an attempt to storm the high-security makeshift Ram temple at Ayodhya. The attack is thwarted and all terrorists killed by security forces.

MAP OF RAMJANMABHOOMI–BABRI MASJID

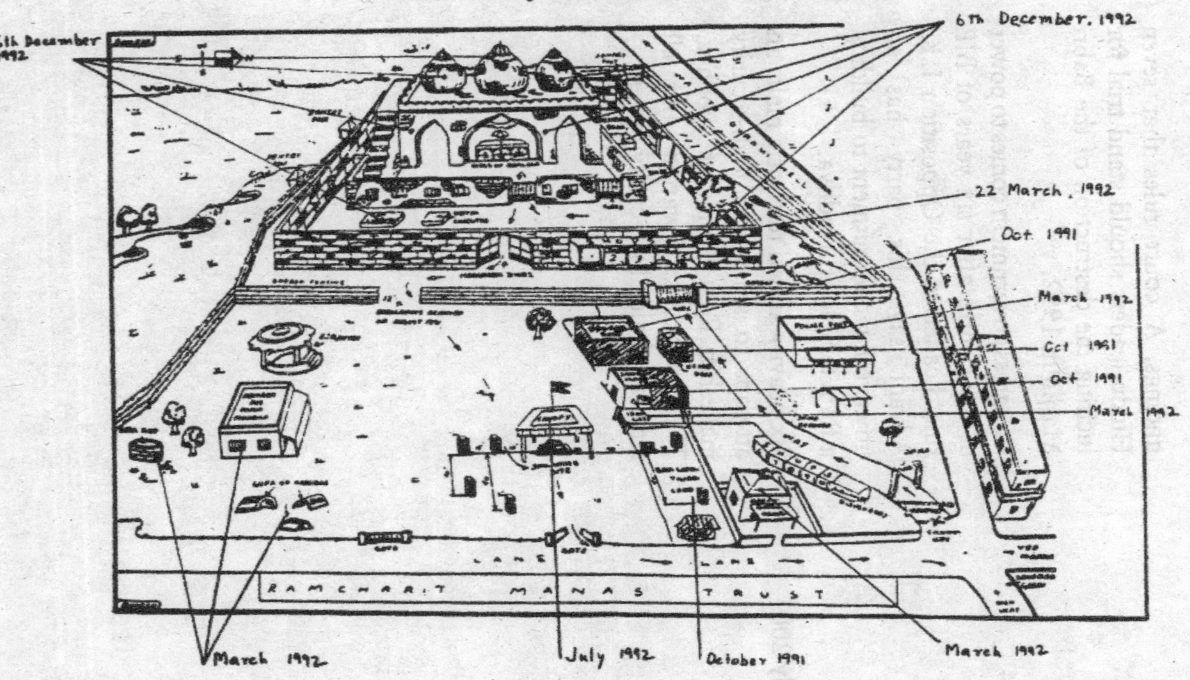

Sketch showing structures in RJB–BM complex in July 1991 and their progressive demolition

Introduction

Conquerors throughout history have treated the conquered humiliatingly, and with varying degrees of barbarity. Women, slaves and property of all kinds were captured as of right and the conqueror became their lord and master by virtue of the conquest. Religious bigotry, where it manifested itself, led to forcible conversions, desecration of religious monuments or the conversion of the conquered into the conqueror's religion. In his arrogance of power, man sought to change the shape of God by force of arms.

The alleged construction of the Babri Masjid on the exact spot where a Ramjanmabhoomi temple had stood, whose authenticity is still to be established, is said to fall under one of these acts of conquest which, even in its present form of controvert belief, has left its trail of bitterness and violence for about 500 years and threatens to be a tragic shadow looming over the history of modern India right into the twenty-first century, as a misfit that will not go, as an anachronism that will always bewilder our own future generations and many abroad.

At a distance of several years from the unfortunate demolition of the Babri structure, but without the emotional pressure of raw passions, or the convenience of rationalization by hindsight, this book attempts to examine the broad factual, Constitutional, judicial, legal and political aspects of the events that culminated in the tragedy of 6 December 1992. It is not intended as an exercise in self-righteousness or justification of anything done or not done then; it attempts only to give a true sequence of happenings and points out certain practical grey spots in the language and provisions of the Constitution. It highlights the importance—indeed inevitability—of trust and good faith in a federal structure where opposing political parties legitimately elected to office on divergent platforms at the Centre and in a state are required to harmonize their policies and actions in the national good. Above all, it emphasizes the essence of a complete separation of religious matters from political issues, campaigns and policies—particularly aimed at short-term electoral benefits.

2

Ramjanmabhoomi–Babri Masjid

The Ramjanmabhoomi–Babri Masjid (RJB–BM) story is about half a century old. Apart from the protracted litigation spanning the period, some important events mark decisive stages in the story. When I took over as Prime Minister of India in June 1991, I inherited the following important events in the history of the RJB–BM at Ayodhya, viz.

1949: Appearance of the idols in the structure,
1986: Opening of the locks and commencement of the pooja,
1989: *Shilanyas*,
1990: First attempt at demolition of the Babri structure and the State Government's successful effort to save it, and
1991: Efforts of Chandra Shekhar's government to find an amicable solution by mutual discussions.

Each of these significant stages in the history of the RJB–BM is dealt with in detail in the subsequent chapters.

*

Ayodhya, situated in northern India, is a township in district Faizabad of Uttar Pradesh (UP). It has long been a place of holy pilgrimage because of its mention in the epic *Ramayana* as the place of birth of Shri Ram. The structure commonly known as Ramjanmabhoomi–Babri Masjid was erected as a mosque by one Mir Baqi in Ayodhya in AD 1528. It is claimed by some sections that it was built at the site believed to be the birth spot of Shri Ram where a temple had stood earlier. This resulted in a long-standing dispute.

There was a minor battle in this part of Ayodhya (Kot Ram Chandra) in 1855 which resulted in a large number of casualties. A three-man inquiry report of this incident is available on the records of the East India Company (and a copy is in the National Archives).

At some stage during the history of the RJB–BM structure, a portion of its outer compound was occupied by Hindu structures of worship, viz. Ram Chabutra and Kaushalya Rasoi where the idol of Ram Lalla had stood. The presence of these structures is marked in court documents relating to a suit filed by one Mahant Raghuvir Das of Ayodhya in 1885. These structures were in existence till 6 December 1992. There are indications that these structures were considerably older but the evidence on this point is not conclusive. Some survey records of 1807-14 have come to notice in which the disputed site has been marked as 'Yanmasthan', i.e. Janmasthan.

The dispute entered the civil legal arena for the first time with the filing of the above referred suits by Mahant Raghuvir Das registering case no. 61/280 of 1885 praying for permission to re-erect a temple on the said platform (Ram Chabutra), situated in the outer courtyard adjacent to the mosque. The said suit was dismissed on the ground that it would be against the public policy and peace to allow a temple to be constructed so close to a mosque. It is also established that the dispute between Hindus and Muslims over this structure led to communal riots in 1934 in which the structure suffered some damage, which was later repaired.

A controversy was raised before the Supreme Court about the use of the disputed structure as a mosque after the said riot in 1934, i.e. between the years 1934 and 1949. The Supreme Court has noted that: 'One version is that after some disturbance in 1934 the use of the disputed structure as a mosque has been stopped from 1934 itself and not merely from December 1949. The other side disputes the alleged disuse of the mosque for prayer upto December 1949.' The stand of the UP Government (during Congress regime) in the suits was that 'the place was used as a mosque till 1949.'

3

Ayodhya 1949: Idols Move into the Mosque

On 23 December 1949, in the dead of night, a group of men set in motion a chain of events that were to become most contentious in independent India. On that cold night, a bag containing water from the Saryu river, idols of Ram Lalla and a copper urn moved towards the Babri Masjid from the Ram Chabutra.

The two dozen odd policemen posted at the shrine paid no attention to the stealthy movements of that shadowy group, who entered the poorly guarded precincts of the shrine by scaling the boundary wall between the inner and the outer courtyard. With the light of a lantern, a few of them washed the floor of the *sanctum sanctorum* and placed the idol on a sacred piece of cloth. They reverentially covered it with another piece of cloth and lit incense sticks in front of it.

It was only when the group broke into chants of '*Prakat kripala, Deen dayala*' that there was a flurry of activity among the policemen outside. It was past 3.30 a.m. No one knows till today why the authorities were not informed right away, but Ramdeo Dubey, the station officer of Ayodhya police station, hardly a kilometre away from the site, reached the site by 7 a.m. the following morning, probably on a routine inspection. The FIR lodged by him said:

> At about 7 a.m. when I reached Janam Bhoomi, I came to know from Constable (No. 7) Mata Prasad who was on duty, that 50-60 persons in the night have entered into the mosque by breaking the lock and scaling the wall and installed an idol of Sri Ramchandraji there. They have also written on the wall inside and outside, the words 'Sita Ram' etc. by geru and yellow colour. Constable Hans Raj who was on duty at that time told them not to act in this manner but they did not listen to him. The PAC which was posted there was also called but by that time they had already entered into the mosque.

This was lodged under sections 147/448/295 of the Indian Penal Code against Mahant Abhiram Das, Sudershan Das, Ram Sakai Das and some fifty others whose names were not known.

By then, all of Ayodhya was buzzing with reports about the divine appearance of the idol. This was interpreted as having established that the site was indeed the Ram Janmabhoomi. Announcements were made throughout the countryside about the miraculous appearance. The state administration was bewildered, unable to act as people began to swarm to the shrine. By afternoon, the crowd had swelled to 5,000.

Worship of these idols after their placing inside the structure was started on a big scale from the next morning. In view of the enraged feelings between Hindus and Muslims of the locality, the City Magistrate, Faizabad, Guru Datt Singh, passed an order imposing a ban under section 144, and after publication of the report of the Additional District Magistrate and other information, the proceedings under section 145 were undertaken. The premises were attached and handed over to the Receiver, Chairman of the Municipal Board, Faizabad, by the order of the magistrate under section 145. Obviously, these preliminary steps under criminal law were taken mainly to maintain the status quo and avert any breach of peace locally. This is borne out by the fact that at

2.30 p.m. on the same day the Deputy Inspector General (DIG) Police reached the spot. He handed over a written message from the Chief Secretary to the District Magistrate, K.K.K. Nayar, which read:

> 1. The aim of our policy is to maintain status quo. Changes can be brought about by mutual consent of the two communities; but the position cannot be allowed to be altered by force or by subterfuge.
> 2. To ensure the policy you can use force (to the minimum necessary) if required.
> 3. Sensational use of force such as firing should be avoided to the utmost intent if possible so that side issues are not raised subsequently; the same objection would not apply to large scale arrests.
> 4. The actual handling of the situation is entirely left to your choice.
>
> Bhagwan Sahay
> 23.12.49

The dispute entered the arena of civil litigation in 1950 when two title suits were filed by Gopal Singh Visharad and Paramhans Ramchandra in the court of the Civil Judge, Faizabad, which were registered as Regular Suit No. 2 of 1950 and No. 25 of 1950. These consisted of an application praying for an interim injunction restraining the opposite parties, i.e. the State and Muslims from removing the idols from their present place in the disputed structure and not to close the entry to the place and not to put any impediment in pooja, darshan etc.

On the application of Gopal Singh Visharad the Civil Judge, Faizabad passed the following order on 16 January 1950: 'Issue notices. Issue interim injunction in the meanwhile as prayed. The defendant should also be informed that a temporary injunction has been issued ex-parte.'

On an application for clarification/modification of the said interim order, the court passed the following order on 19 January 1950: 'The parties are hereby restrained by means of temporary injunction to refrain from removing the idols in question from the site in dispute and from interfering with pooja etc. as at present carried on. The order dated 16.1.1950 stands modified accordingly.'

The latter order was confirmed by the court in the form of an interim injunction on 3 March 1951 after hearing the parties. The interim injunction was subsequently confirmed by the High Court vide its order dated 26 April 1955.

In the year 1959, a third suit was filed by Nirmohi Akhara describing the structure as Shri Ram temple and claiming title over the same. This was numbered as Regular Suit No. 26 of 1959. Thereafter, in the year 1961, the Sunni Central Waqf Board, UP also filed a title suit claiming the structure to be Babri Masjid belonging to it, which was numbered as Regular Suit No. 12 of 1961. All these suits were consolidated vide order of the Civil Judge making the Sunni Central Waqf Board's suit as the leading case.

The Hindu idols thus continued inside the disputed structure since 1949. Worship of these idols by Hindus also continued without interruption since 1949 and the structure was not used by the Muslims for offering prayers since then. The controversy remained at a low ebb till 1986.

*

This protracted five hundred-year dispute on a single shrine inevitably left its ravages on the psyche of the concerned communities—as it was bound to. It had remained at a low profile for a long time, but certain overtones appeared with the advent of Independence. The two were not visibly connected, but it was not possible to assert that they had no nexus whatsoever either. It was a religious issue no doubt, but the long-standing tension, compounded by the horrendous events that characterized the Partition days, manifested itself at the earliest. Around two and a half years after Independence was perhaps the time that the concerned persons thought good enough for something overt to happen.

It is on record that both the then Central and the State Governments felt the reverberations of Ram Lalla's '*prakat*' (manifestation) phenomenon in December 1949. The way it swayed thousands of people in the locality was ominous enough to bode something serious for the political ambience. The Indian Constitution was not yet promulgated, but its central idea of secularism was firmly embedded in the leaders' minds. And Mahatma Gandhi's assassination had not faded—nor was it likely to fade—from public memory for quite some time.

It is reported that when some Muslim leaders, including Maulana Hussain Ahmed Madani, Maulana Abdul Azad and Maulana Hifzur-Rehman Seoharvi, brought the matter to Prime Minister Jawaharlal Nehru's notice, the latter issued instructions for the removal of the idols from the mosque immediately. The UP Chief Minister Pt. Gobind Ballabh Pant and the State Home Minister Lai Bahadur Shastri were both seized of the matter at once. A high-level meeting of senior officers took place at Lucknow on 24, 25 and 26 December 1949 and a decision to shift the idols from the mosque back to the Ram Chabutra was taken and communicated to the Deputy Commissioner to ensure this. The government took a serious view of the incident and an explanation was called for from the local authorities.

This seems to have triggered an unusual, yet not unexpected response, considering the possible circumstances prevailing in Ayodhya and the surrounding villages in those days. The response of the local officials, perhaps represented by the Deputy Commissioner, Faizabad, contained not only the explanation called for, but also an expression of a grievance at not being appreciated by the higher echelons of government for the very delicate and difficult work he was doing under trying circumstances. The full text of the letters from the Deputy Commissioner is given below:

Deputy Commissioner's House
Faizabad
December 26, 1949

My dear Bhagwan Sahay,

Yesterday the Commissioner on return from Lucknow said that in the course of conversation with him, you were pleased to ask:

1. Why district authorities did not take precautions to prevent the planting of the idol in the mosque;
2. Why the idol was not being removed.

In the afternoon Deputy Inspector General on return from Lucknow said that it was asked again why the idol was not removed on 23rd in the morning when the crowd was not too big to resist effectively.

Perhaps I have merely to narrate the facts which will themselves answer these questions.

Installation of the idol was carried out in the night between 22nd and 23rd instant. It was an act of which there was no forewarning. The last CID report which I received regarding Ayodhya affairs reached me on the 22nd. Neither in that report nor in any previous report was it ever indicated that there was a move to install an idol in the mosque either surreptitiously or by force. Neither through official nor through non-official channels we ever received any report of such a move with the exception that during Naunh Path there was a rumour that the mosque would be entered on Poornmasi Day, but that attempt was not made.

I must also mention that none of the Muslims who met me in this connection and who must also have met higher authorities in government ever said that there was a move for installing an idol either forcibly or clandestinely in the mosque.

Their complaints always referred to dismantling of tombs in the open grounds outside the temple. In fact, the act was as much a surprise to them as to anybody else, as a deputation of Muslims consisting of Rahmat Hussain Vakil, Himayat Ullah Kidwai Vakil, Anisur Rehman and others admitted before me only yesterday. One of the deputationists Anisur Rehman, however, said that on 21st instant in the evening shortly after Govind Sahai Ji and Sita Ram Shukla had addressed a meeting in Ayodhya, which local Hindus tried to break up, some persons held a meeting at the same place at which a master from Maharaja High School Ayodhya declared that Hindus should install an idol in the mosque and also prevent Muslims from praying Friday prayer (23rd was a Friday). The CID report of the meeting made no reference to the alleged speech and Narendra Prasad, CID group officer, is now thinking out a falsehood. When I asked Anisur Rehman why he did not promptly bring the matter to my notice, he said that he had not considered it necessary to do so since a CID officer himself was present. To me also it appears that Anisur Rehman himself could never have believed that this mischief was likely to happen for otherwise he would straightaway have rushed to the local authorities and informed them.

In this connection I would also mention that Akshaya Kumar Brahmchari who has been a staunch protagonist of the Muslim point of view in this controversy and who accompanied Muslims to meet higher authorities in Lucknow and elsewhere also never suspected that such a step was ever likely. He admitted so to me on 23rd instant when he visited the spot with me; and I believe he himself never said anywhere that such a step was in contemplation.

I must also point out that Abhiram Das, the sadhu who headed the crowd which was responsible for this act, is neither a mahant nor in any sense a leader. His name did not even come to prominent notice in this connection. The speeches made by leaders including Baba Raghava Das never advocated violence and were not actionable. There was therefore no question of our taking any steps either to arrest the leaders or to start any proceedings against them. And in any case the arrest of the leaders would not in my view have prevented this mischief by a small body of determined persons who depend on the immense public sympathy in support of this cause. While the arrests would not have prevented this crisis they could conceivably have precipitated it in some form.

The mosque can be entered only through the temple premises and so is accessible at all times. Further the temple premises are occupied at all hours. And the mosque is deserted all the time except for one hour during Friday prayers. To prevent determined Hindus from getting into the mosque either by force or in secret, the mosque would have to be permanently policed with a force which must cost the exchequer thousands of rupees a month. Although this controversy led to many riots in the past 36 years according to local tradition and tremendous holocausts in lives, I do not believe that there was any decision to police the mosque permanently. Surely, if permanent policing was a remedy, government, who could not have been unaware of the controversy that has raged for centuries over this and other disputed shrines in the province, would not have failed to provide permanent police force for this purpose. And in the absence of any such arrangement, local authorities who had no information from any source whatever that such mischief as this was contemplated could not have made out a case before government for the policing of a deserted and almost unused mosque permanently at a tremendous cost to the taxpayer.

And I would also respectfully inquire if government could think of policing this and other similar disputed shrines, such as those in Benares, Mathura etc. on a permanent basis to prevent such mischief. And if government do not decide to do so, would the district authorities be held responsible for any future site of mischief in these places, of however unexpected or unsuspected a character.

Why the idol is not being removed, and why it was not removed on 23rd morning, are facile questions to ask. The removing of the idol by force is possible, though at some cost, with the police force now available. Removal surreptitiously at night against weaker resistance is also possible. But to attempt such a removal without careful consideration of consequences would in my view have been a step of administrative bankruptcy and tyranny. The short-term reaction on public tranquillity can be guarded against with the force now available though it was not possible on 23rd with our limited resources. Even now I doubt if we can do much if communal riot flares up in places remote from headquarters. But the reactions short-term and long-term on government prestige and position are matters on which I am entitled to no opinion and on which I must expect government to make up their minds before I take any action. The removal of the idol in haste by me, if carried out, might instead of solving the problem have created a bigger one for government and for this I could not in loyalty to government have essayed without clear orders from government.

Even today I cannot imagine the manner in which the removal can be carried out. If it is to be done according to religious sanction I could not find a qualified Hindu priest willing to stake life and salvation in the act. If it is to be done anyhow or by anybody, the resulting hostility from all sections of the Hindu public may be tremendously embarrassing to government and I should be told clearly that government are prepared to face it.

In my view I acted with the utmost discretion in not precipitating a greater crisis than the one which has overtaken us and in proceeding cautiously at every stage.

Lastly I must say that any consideration of small local precautions which might or might not have prevented the crisis in the particular form in which it has precipitated itself seems to ignore completely the immense reality of this problem which in Ayodhya has led to so many riots and to the loss of hundreds of lives. The problem is one to be faced squarely and while local precautions might alter the nature or timing of the crisis, it is bound to arise for want of a real solution which no amount of evasion can put off for long; and with the advent of freedom people are much less inclined to obey local authority or to give up an old and defeated cause.

I trust my plain speaking will not be misunderstood for it has been dictated by the necessity of correcting wrong impressions. District authorities who, without the advantage of support from public men of any cause, have faced a difficult situation with the limited resources at their disposal and done their best to preserve public peace, administrative prestige and government policy certainly deserve better recognition that this.

Yours sincerely,
K.K.K. Nayar, ICS

Shri Bhagwan Sahay, ICS
Chief Secretary to UP Government
Lucknow

The next day Nayar again wrote to the Chief Secretary:

Deputy Commissioner's House
Faizabad,
December 27, 1949

My dear Bhagwan Sahay,

This is in continuation of my D.C. No. 301/C regarding Ayodhya affairs.

The Commissioner returned from Lucknow and gave me and the Superintendent of Police the outline of a scheme for removing the idol from the mosque surreptitiously to Janmabhoomi temple outside the mosque. The scheme was discussed yesterday before Commissioner, DIG, SP and myself and later in the evening before IG, DIG (PAC), SP and myself. It was discussed again this morning by all of us.

The idea of the removal of the idol is not one which I can agree with or wish to carry out on my initiative for it is fraught with the gravest danger to public peace over the entire district and must lead to a conflagration of horror unprecedented in the annals of this controversy. The district is aflame and it is reported that licence-holders for firearms have promised support with their arms in a fight against police and officers if it becomes necessary. It will be no easy or quick matter to collect arms from all licencees in the district to prevent such a sanguinary outcome. The Hindus with no exception that I know of, are behind the demand for keeping the idol on site, however disunited they may be on the propriety of the act which led to the present situation, and are ready to kill and die in this cause. The depth of feeling behind the movement and the desperate nature of their resolve and vows in support of it should not be underestimated or pooh-poohed. When the storm breaks out it may be possible to quell riots within municipal limits with the force at our disposal hut firing will have to be resorted to in certainty and many lives will be lost not only from the firing but also in repercussive fulmination over the entire district. Today rumour is rife that the removal of the idol is being contemplated and Hindus are reported to have resolved to attack Muslim habitations and burn and pillage. If this happens it will not be possible to protect the lives of the Muslims in all the places where the storm breaks out, nor would it be possible to protect even my officers or their property. I have so far failed to find any Hindu even among Congressmen who is ready to support the move for the removal of the idol.

With the feeling in this state a step of this character would be like setting a lighted match to a powder magazine and I certainly cannot contemplate the results with equanimity or feeling of justification.

I shall also be unable to find in the district a Hindu, let alone a qualified priest, who will be prepared on any inducement to undertake the removal of the idol. Kripal Singh and I are at our wits' end to find a person who could do this for us if it becomes necessary. No person in the district is likely to be ready for this errand, for his life and property will thereafter be forfeit in the eyes of the entire Hindu population. We suggested that the Hindu Commissioner, IG and DIG help us by getting a man from outside who would be able to do this, as our resources are limited in the district in which the situation excludes all hopes of success in our quest. But they could not agree to find us the necessary instrument and I doubt if the government itself could find us a suitable one if our resources failed. Further, any attempt on our part to approach a qualified priest is likely to give away the move, if the priest refused, as he most certainly would. And if the removal is carried out anyhow through anybody the storm of indignation and protest which will break will spread beyond the confines of the district and involve not only the officers concerned but also government in ignominy and obloquy.

Government does not seem to have been able to send an Hon'ble Minister to appreciate the situation at first hand and to decide if it could be resolved better by force than by a peaceful solution of compromise.

Government must, I earnestly request, listen to my voice and accept that any attempt to adopt a solution involving the use of force in the present state of intense and desperate feeling is bound to lead to terrible happenings.

The Superintendent of Police agrees fully with this and we are of the considered view that on our initiative we cannot think of resorting to force in the hope of cowing down the Hindus without spread of violence and pillage.

The question now remains as to what is to be done on the present situation. The installation of the idol in the mosque has certainly been an illegal act, and it has placed not only local authorities but also government in a false position. We have to see how the position can be retrieved as far as possible without such terrible cost and sacrifice. I have a solution to offer for the government's consideration.

The mosque should be attached and both Hindus and Muslims should be excluded from it with the exception of the minimum number of pujaris. I am attempting to reduce the number of pujaris from three to one without creating another impasse. The pujari could offer puja and bhog before the idol which could continue inside. The pujari or pujaris will be appointed by order of magistrate. The parties will be referred to the civil court for adjudication on rights. No attempt will be made to hand over possession to the Muslims until the civil court, if at all, decrees the claim in their favour.

The solution is open to the criticism that it perpetuates an illegal possession created by force and subterfuge and that it does not immediately restore the *status quo* which existed before the illegal act. But it has the following merits that are worth careful consideration:

1. If the civil court decided the dispute in favour of Hindus, a terrible amount of suffering, bloodshed, and countrywide reactions would have been avoided.
2. During the pendency of the civil proceedings it may be possible (I sincerely hope it will be achieved) to reach a compromise of some kind. The Muslims, of whom a small number are even now of this way of thinking, could be induced to give up the mosque voluntarily in return for another mosque built for them at no less cost. But if the situation is forced into a riot even these Muslims would afterwards be unwilling to reach this solution. And the situation would continue to be pregnant with the possibility of future riots.
3. If no compromise were reached and finally the civil court decreed the claim in favour of Muslims, the positions which would then result would be no worse than that which now exists and the heat of present reactions would have disappeared by then in some measure.
4. Although government might be accused of not having the *status quo* immediately they have a perfectly legal and valid excuse that the matter of civil rights is before a civil court for decision, that property has been attached by a magistrate who has excluded the general body of Hindus and Muslims and the question of immediately restoring the *status quo* which existed recently was a matter of judicial discretion of the attaching magistrate which government could not lawfully influence or dictate. I must pinpoint in this

> connection that any executive direction from the government to myself or to the attaching magistrate to restore the *status quo* would be illegal, for these proceedings are under law supposed to be taken by the magistrate concerned in judicial discretion and government cannot even for rectifying an illegal position themselves give an illegal direction merely to placate persons whose grievance, however legitimate, was before the courts for judicial consideration.

I would like to add that *status quo* is an ideal objective, but it cannot be allowed to become a fetish to be assuaged with a corban of glory. I have been at the spot all these days and have tackled the situation almost without support. Today the slogan outside is '*Naya anyay karna chhor do, Nayar bhagwan ka pbatak khol do*'. I am facing this odium with equanimity and without complaint. But I have certainly no reason to desire to be soft with the mob which is accusing me daily and which has placed me and the entire administration in extraordinary difficulty. I offer counsel of peace not withstanding all this, not because I feel less keenly than government the magnitude and implications of the position which this illegal act has created, but because I fully believe that its solution must be found without tremendous cost of life and property as also in countrywide reactions on peace and policy.

I would therefore emphasize that the question of removing the idol is not one which the Superintendent of Police and I can agree with or carry out on our initiative. The alternative solution which I propose to government has a fair chance of success in preserving peace and policy. If this solution is not accepted and if the government decides to remove the idol and face the consequences then it is only fair that I having only lost government's confidence in this matter and being of the view that the solution dictated to me is neither correct, necessary, advisable, nor legally justifiable, should not be asked to put it into effect. I would, if the government decided to remove the idol at any cost, request that I be relieved and replaced by any officer who may be able to see in that solution a merit which I cannot discern. For my part, I cannot, in my discretion which is the only legal sanction as I am fully aware of the widespread sufferings which it will entail to many innocent lives.

Yours sincerely,
K.K.K. Nayar, ICS

Shri Bhagwan Sahay, ICS,
Chief Secretary to Government, UP
Lucknow

These letters had the desired effect. The next day, Nayar wrote in the official diary maintained by him at that time: 'Bhagwan Sahay telephoned in the morning to say that he had received my letter and if the situation was as I had reported it should not be forced. At the same time he said that the impression should continue to be publicized that the government could not accept the correctness of the position which has been created. He asked me also to proceed with my solution.'

Significantly, from the very day after the second letter was written, things began moving exactly in accordance with the suggestions contained in it. The shrine was attached under section 145 of the Code of Criminal Procedure on 28 December 1949. The then Chairman of the Municipal Board, Priya Dutt Ram, was appointed Receiver to look after the property, and was asked by the city magistrate to submit a scheme for the management of the property in dispute during attachment.

The Union Minister Vallabhbhai Patel discussed the matter with the Chief Minister at Lucknow and the Prime Minister sent a telegram expressing his concern over the developments. On

9 January 1950 Sardar Patel wrote a letter to Pant saying that any unilateral action based on an attitude of aggression or coercion would not be tolerated. Pant was very worried about the developments in the light of the deteriorating situation. On 13 January he wrote to Sardar Patel that the efforts to set the matter right peacefully were continuing and there was a reasonable chance of success. However, he stressed that things were still in a dangerous state of flux.

4

Ayodhya 1986: The Opening of the Locks

The local people of Ayodhya used to organize a Ram Prakat Utsav (manifestation of Ram day), an anniversary celebration every year to commemorate the memory of the 'appearance' of the idol inside the Babri Masjid, in which a few hundred people would participate. The date for the celebration is decided according to the Hindu calendar. The thirty-fourth anniversary, which was on 4 January 1984, was celebrated with marked enthusiasm because, for the first time, the Hanuman pataka (Hanuman flag) was hoisted on the central dome of the disputed shrine. This news spread like wild fire attracting massive crowds. Significantly a *hawan* was also performed inside the *sanctum sanctorum* for the first time in which almost all Ayodhya's prominent mahants participated. The Rashtriya Swayamsevak Sangh (RSS) leadership then realized the political potential of the issue. Leaders at the RSS headquarters in Jhandewala, Delhi contacted the convener of the year's celebration, Wing Commander (Retd.) Dhirendra Singh Jafa, through RSS activists in Faizabad. This move, however, failed. Three months later a meeting of the Dharm Sansad of the Vishwa Hindu Parishad (VHP) was held at New Delhi on 7 and 8 April 1984, wherein it was decided to start the movement for the 'liberation' of the Ayodhya shrine as well as the Sri Krishna Janam Bhumi at Mathura and the Vishwa Nath shrine at Gyanvapi, Varanasi.

The meeting decided to launch an agitation for the Ayodhya shrine first. A call was issued to open the locked gates of the shrine and a slogan '*Aage badh kar jor se bole: janambhoomi*' was coined. The disputed structure had two locked gates and only the pujaris were allowed inside. The darshan of the idol of Ram Lalla installed in the *sanctum sanctorum* could be had only through the iron grills of the gate which the VHP sought to project as the imprisonment of Ram Lalla. It was further decided to convene the next meeting at Ayodhya on 18 June the same year. At its meeting in Ayodhya the Ram Janmabhoomi Mukti Yagya Samiti (Ram Janmabhoomi liberation front) was formed with Dau Dayal Khanna, a former minister in the UP Congress government, as its convener. There was a sparse attendance of thirty-five saints on the occasion. Moro Pant Pingale and Ashok Singhal were the moving force behind the temple movement since the beginning. Both were veteran RSS leaders.

The next meeting was held again at Ayodhya on 1 July 1984 in which Mahant Avaidyanath of Gorakhnath Peeth, Gorakhpur was declared president, besides Mahant Nritya Gopal Das of the Mani Ram Ki Chawni, Ayodhya and Praramhans Ramchandra of Digambar Akhara as vice president, and Onkar Bhave, Mahesh Narain Singh and Dinesh Tyagi as secretaries of the Samiti.

First Rath Yatra

At its meeting on 11 July 1984, the VHP decided to create public awareness about the temple agitation. A rath yatra of Sri Ram-Janki was begun on 25 September 1984, from Sitamarhi in Bihar (believed to be Sita's birthplace). This was the first motorized rath yatra taken out by the VHP. Its success greatly encouraged the Sangh parivar. Lai Krishna Advani's 10,000-kilometre rath yatra from Somnath in September 1990, the next BJP president Murli Manohar Joshi's 'ekta yatra' in 1991, the repeat of Advani's yatra again in November 1992, four 'janadesh yatras' by the BJP in September 1993, besides the 'shila yatra', 'asthi kalash yatra', 'dharm yatra', etc. were all the product of faith in this course of action.

Passing through many towns in Bihar and UP, the rath yatra reached Ayodhya at 9 p.m. on 6 October 1984. The 1,000-strong procession accompanying it came in buses, cars and jeeps. The administration had made elaborate security arrangements. The next day, a big congregation estimated at between 35,000 to 40,000, including a large number of women and Bharatiya Janata Party (BJP) office-bearers, resolved to liberate' the Ramjanmabhoomi and demanded the opening of the locked gates. There were also about 150 sadhus and sants present at the meeting.

Kalyan Singh had been a supporter since the very inception of the movement and was among the BJP and RSS leaders present at the first congregation. He was then president of the state unit of the BJP. Other prominent BJP and RSS leaders present included Rajendra Kumar Gupta, BJP treasurer Surya Krishna, Raghav Ram Misra, RSS organizer Mithilesh Narayan, Amrendra Narayan and Jagat Narayan Dubey.

The white Matador converted into a rath carrying life-sized idols of Ram and Sita began its 'dharm yatra' from Ayodhya to Lucknow the next day, halting at several places on the way. The routes were illuminated and *aartis* were performed by the local people at various places. In Lucknow, thousands were awaiting the rath since the morning. The rath entered Lucknow around 11 a.m. People had came in to accord a tumultuous reception, with men, women and children offering floral tributes. The rath is particularly symbolic to devout Hindus because they believe it to be the vehicle of the gods.

Addressing a mammoth rally in the afternoon, the VHP leaders reiterated their resolve. This was the biggest ever meeting held in Lucknow. The former Director General of the UP police, Srish Chandra Dixit, was seen for the first time on the dais of a VHP meeting. A VHP delegation also called on the UP Chief Minister, Narayan Dutt Tewari, and handed over a memorandum demanding the liberation of the three sites that had been identified earlier.

From Lucknow, the rath passing through Naimisharnya in Sitapur and Chitrakoot was to reach Delhi. But following the assassination of the then Prime Minister, Indira Gandhi, on 31 October 1984, it was stopped at Ghaziabad.

*

It is quite imaginable that the dispute impacted on the electoral prospects and processes in post-Independence Uttar Pradesh; indeed it would have been surprising if it had been otherwise. It is therefore idle to pretend that political parties did not keep the electoral potential of the issue in mind from time to time in that state.

I have no intention of digressing into party matters and political comments, but in this case it appears to me that several phenomena will remain unexplained unless the main purpose behind these agitations is brought to light. Having participated in the last phase of the independence struggle and being a party to all the post-Independence developments on the power front, I believe I am in a position to unravel the background with coherence and logic. I do not expect universal agreement with my assessment, but the concerned events would need to be interpreted in some other equally plausible manner if my own views are to be considered wrong.

It is natural that in any democratic process, attempts at an orderly change of hands in political power should inevitably occur. It could not have been different in India's case too, obviously. But there was a special difficulty, or convenience, here—according to how one looked at the scene. The first leadership of the Indian Government was thrown up not by Indian democracy simply, but by India's freedom struggle. That one factor made an enormous difference in the attitudes of all political parties in India after Independence—at least for what may be called a long time, considering the duration of political patience without power, imposed on those who were also competent contestants. For a time it looked as though *one* party was going on and on, cornering power election after election—not for its own fault, nor of the other parties.

Both the Congress and Jawaharlal Nehru seemed to have become invincible and irreplaceable, at least at the Centre. Ideologically, the Congress came to occupy a unique position, again unmatched on the whole by any other party. Every Indian could find a place and a benefit for himself or herself in it—regardless of whether he or she in fact got it. On secular and economic programmes, the Congress was unbeatable and could at least formulate schemes, which the people found right, timely and appropriate. And when the Congress itself adopted socialism as its creed and some socialist enthusiasts who had left the Congress at the end of the forties began trickling back into it after the mid-fifties, the stage seemed to be set for anti-Congress politics to lose the last vestige of a positive alternative, making it become more and more negative and dependent on emotionally explosive issues. This was the real tragedy that came to stay; and even today, it remains almost unchanged in substance, whatever the cosmetic changes in actual presentation.

There is one common feature of post-Independence democratic politics in India that needs to be especially noted. After the Constitution of India came into force in 1950, it was naturally expected that its basic postulates such as secularism, equality before law etc. would no longer be violated or even brought into question for any purpose, particularly one connected with the process of political agitation or ascendancy. However, some political parties, in the Opposition, took recourse again and again precisely to mount agitations in violation of these basic principles, to beat the ruling party with. These movements have been mainly of three kinds: separatist, communal and armed struggles. These issues, totally devoid of any Constitutional validity, were launched almost as if the parties launching them had nothing to do with the Indian Constitution. This has been a most regrettable feature of the history of our post-Independence agitations.

Unfortunately, however, most of the ideological questions with emotional potential, which could be conjured up by the parties eager to replace the Congress, had a direct impact on the basic postulates of the Constitution and generally on national integration as mentioned above. In the main, they consisted of two categories:

1. National unity, which came under strain during the Dravidian movement in Tamil Nadu in the mid-sixties and in Punjab on several occasions as per electoral exigencies, as also in the North-East, particularly in Nagaland, with its inspiration coming from outside; and
2. Secularism, which came under strain right from the beginning of the British Government's 'divide and rule' policy and seemed unreal even at the time of Partition. It became a pillar of our Constitution, quite naturally because of the country's tradition and the leaders' conviction. But an out-and-out theocratic state across the border could not but leave some ugly spots on this side as well on our secular face. And some parties found in anti-secularism the potential of a vote-rich issue, preying on the emotional pressures generated by the human tragedies of the Partition days. The idea always seemed to be to polarize the Hindu majority on one side until it fetched electoral victories to them by sheer numbers.

As a result, the same electoral considerations could not be totally ignored in the calculations of other parties as well, even if they did not, in fact, believe in any anti-secularist strategy at all. Then some other parties, for the same reasons, found it convenient to do everything to alienate the minorities—especially the Muslim minority in Uttar Pradesh—from the Congress, combine it with certain castes among Hindus so as to take their total electoral prospect close to a victory-yielding number.

The most desperate situation for the parties opposed to the Congress came through the tragedy of Indira Gandhi's assassination and the massive tally of 415 seats that came to the Congress in the 1984 Lok Sabha election, along with Rajiv Gandhi's Prime Ministership in early 1985. It may be added here that the general impression, right or wrong, was that Indira Gandhi's second stint during 1980-84 as Prime Minister somehow did not exude the promise that had enabled the Congress to sail through the earlier elections with handsome majorities. The Punjab separatist trend that had almost regularly appeared whenever a Congress government came to power in that state earlier, made its appearance this time too, in a big way. Thus Indiraji clearly helped the Congress several times before while alive, but most remarkably this time in death. This was yet another shot in the arm for secularism and a formidable vindication of the country's integration. By the same token, the other parties, at least subconsciously, felt in a way cheated in their long-cherished aspiration to power just when they had begun to find it within sight and beckoning to them in a couple of months' time before Indiraji's assassination in 1984. Howsoever in bad taste this assessment appears when thus expressed, it is difficult to argue that it is not a realistic appraisal.

This was the time when their political desperation, reinforced by complete negativism and anti-Congressism as a creed, got consolidated as perhaps the only 'art of the possible' under the circumstances immediately after Rajiv Gandhi's steamroller majority became a breathtaking spectacle in the Lok Sabha. The only possible card seemed to be the communal one, when Rajiv's youthful and dynamic approach to the plethora of problems made it impossible to match him at his own game. In the circumstances, the Hindu card came in handy not only for the BJP, in whose case it could at least have looked logical, but also for its three-legged race partners who were from several 'secular' parties but had agreed to subordinate their anti-communalism to the commonly forged anti-Congressism in most unequivocal terms. Even after long discussions with friends in these other parties, I must admit that I could not quite grasp the political sagacity in this contradictory approach except in terms of an attempt to snatch power from the Congress, no matter how. I was unable even to see any lasting political strategy in this deliberate *volte face*, assuming that there is, or at any rate there ought to be, a philosophy that dictates strategies and is not dictated by them.

The BJP's (or VHP's, as the case may be) gangajal-carrying campaign seemed to make a dent in the Hindu mind. Ironically, however, Rajiv Gandhi's huge scheme of cleaning up the Ganga at a huge expense for environmental reasons, did not seem to evoke the same response. The reason, in retrospect, looks simple. The environment, which almost everyone has been polluting for centuries, is not the same thing as religion, whose spell of faith has remained indelible on the people's minds for many more centuries. So while a secular programme, infinitely more useful, could not evoke faith, the mere carrying of gangajal (even polluted) swayed millions. I am pretty certain, however, that in that frenzy of faith, many of those millions did not expect to be called upon to switch to a political role and vote for the BJP one fine morning. The nexus was not at all clear to most of them at the time, even while carrying gangajal. Even for the organizers, I am inclined to think that it was a religio-political move, but its exact political fallout was not quite quantifiable at the time. It was the result of a hunch, a leap in the dark, but a leap neverthless, particularly in the total absence of any other potential political card, even one-tenth as effective as the gangajal gimmick, as things stood. It is thus clear to me that the scenario of a five-year 415-member Lok Sabha prospect with Rajiv Gandhi at the helm, drove the BJP (and other non-BJP parties who had pledged to become anti-

Congress first and foremost) to explore and utilize the religious card as a political ploy—for the time being in the case of the non-BJP parties and, of course, as a long-term strategy for the BJP.

*

Before her death, Indira Gandhi had asked to prepare various plans for the development of Ayodhya. The political potential of this emotive issue was not lost on Mrs Gandhi. She wanted to tackle it differently. The people should first be convinced, she felt, that the government was keen to develop this pilgrim city for the benefit of devotees and tourists. Proposals were pushed through rapidly. The Ram Ki Pourhi project, languishing for lack of funds, was given the go-ahead. The hotel of the tourism department at Ayodhya was modernized and officials engaged in the process of giving Ayodhya a facelift. With her death, her plans suffered a setback. Her son took over as Prime Minister and another colleague of his took command of the Ayodhya matter. From then on, a series of disastrous steps followed.

The rath yatra was started again on 23 October 1985. This was on Vijaya Dashami day. One was started in Bihar while six began from UP alone. This played a tempestuous role in arousing the religious sentiments of devout Hindus. Paramhans Ramchandra announced his plan to immortate himself on the next Ram Navami day if the locks were not opened by then.

Initially, the VHP wanted the opening of the locks on the gates of the shrine. But in November 1985, at the second Dharm Sansad held at Udipi, the demand was enlarged to include the handing over of the management of the shrine to Ramanandacharya Shivramacharya, the chief of the Ramanand sampraday. In the third week of December 1985, Ramayana Mela, a government-sponsored annual event, was organized in Ayodhya. Veer Bahadur Singh, who by then had replaced Narayan Dutt Tewari as the Chief Minister of UP, went to Ayodhya on 19 December to inaugurate the mela. A VHP delegation, led by former Justice Shiva Nath Katju, called on the Chief Minister and reiterated the demand for opening the lock of the disputed shrine.

The Opening of the Locks

On 21 January 1986, an application for interim relief in the Regular Suits was filed by one Umesh Chandra Pandey praying for opening of the locks placed on the grill of the *sanctum sanctorum* and for allowing unrestricted pooja, darshan etc. to Hindus and removal of police force from the disputed structure. On 25 January another application was moved by Umesh Chandra Pandey before Munsif Sadar, Faizabad in Regular Suit No. 2 of 1950 praying for the same relief. The application was rejected by Munsif Sadar, Faizabad.

But on 1 February 1986, the District Judge of Faizabad, K.M. Pandey, ordered the opening of the locks. He gave this judgment in an appeal filed on 30 January 1986 by Umesh Chandra Pandey. Applications by Muslims to be impleaded as a party and an opportunity to be heard in the appeal were rejected by the court. The order read as under:

> The appeal is allowed. The respondents are directed to open the locks of the gates 'O' and 'P' forthwith. They shall not impose any restriction or hurdle in the Darshan and Pooja etc. of the applicant and other members of the community in general. However, the respondents are free to make an independent decision to control any law and order problem according to the needs of the situation and to regulate the entry of the pilgrims. Costs of the appeal shall abide the result of the suit.

The district administration is reported to have complied with the court's order in forty minutes.

A writ petition was also filed against the said order of unlocking before the Single Judge of the High Court by the Muslims, being Writ Petition No. 776/1986, Mohd. Hashim vs. State of UP and others. The court passed an interim order in the same on 3 February 1986, the operative portion of which reads: 'Until further orders of the court, the nature of the property in question as existing today shall not be changed.'

The Congress government in UP complied with the orders of the judiciary in relation to a property under court attachment. It would be significant to note that in the petition filed against the order of the District Judge, Faizabad, for opening of the lock, an interim relief application for staying the same was also filed, but this was not accepted by the High Court.

The Congress government, however, tried to defuse the communal tension and to resolve the dispute both through negotiations and persuasions and by expediting proceedings in the suits. Thus, Buta Singh, the then Union Home Minister, personally visited Lucknow and along with the Chief Minister N.D. Tewari, held parleys with various parties to find some amicable solution and to reduce the tension and avert the threat posed by the VHP of undertaking construction of the temple in violation of the court's orders.

As no formula agreeable to both Hindus and Muslims for solving the dispute could be found during these parleys, the Advocate General on behalf of the then Congress government headed by N.D. Tewari, moved before the High Court, Lucknow Bench, an application for transferring the civil suits pending before the Civil Judge, Faizabad to the High Court and consolidating them for expeditious hearing. The High Court was further requested to form a Special Full Bench to ensure early decision through filing of Misc. Case No. 29/1987, State of UP vs. Sunni Central Board of Waqf and others, by the State Government. The application was allowed by the High Court vide its order dated 10 July 1989 and all the suits stood transferred and consolidated with new Nos. (OOS No. 1 to 5 of 1989). A Special Full Bench comprising acting Chief Justice K.C. Agarwal, Justice U.C. Srivastava and Justice S.H.A. Raza was also constituted to hear and decide the suits expeditiously.

*

Until the court order, the temple agitation remained almost a unilateral affair, but the opening of the locks triggered off a great deal of controversy. It sent tremors through the Muslim community. Many described it as a state-managed affair which proceeded with undue haste to pre-empt the VHP plan. Even the Sangh parivar made sarcastic comments on the proceedings and the court order and described it as the result of the announcement of a VHP deadline to launch a large-scale agitation for it. The BJP's thoughts on this deserve mention:

> *The case for opening the locks—a contrast.*
>
> Compare it with the lightning speed with which the case filed by an unknown advocate was heard and disposed of. It is worth recalling the event.
>
> First, an unknown advocate (Umesh Chand Pandey) filed an application on 21st January, 1986, within two days after the sants' ultimatum, in the Munsif court at Faizabad;
>
> Second, on 28th January, 1986, Munsif refused to pass any order;
>
> Third, an appeal was filed forthwith, in the court of District Judge, Faizabad;
>
> Fourth, on 1st February, 1986, i.e. within three days of the Munsif court order, the District Court passed an order directing the government of UP to unlock the gate, and further directed that they shall not impose any restriction or hurdles in the darshan or pooja by the Hindu community.

Fifth, within hours of passing of the above order, the temple was unlocked and even the Doordarshan cameramen were present to cover the occasion which was widely telecast all over India.

How did this case move at this speed? How did the government acquiesce in this case? How did the Faizabad District Court allow the appeal ordering the opening of locks in a matter of two days when the Hindus had been pleading for nearly 37 years? How did the Doordarshan cameras click the opening of the locks within an hour of the court orders? All these questions have only one answer, the government is not against such things and they can, and do, happen. Even the courts respond. So, could it be said that law or the courts are solely responsible for Ramjanambhoomi cases being where they are, or is it the government which wants the cases to remain frozen?

(BJP's White Paper on Ayodhya, page 155, para 1.17, 1.18, 1.19)

Babri Masjid Action Committee Formed

The Babri Masjid Action Committee (BMAC) was formed more or less in the wake of the opening of the shrine gate. On 3 February 1986, an appeal was filed in the High Court by M.A. Siddiqui, an advocate acting on behalf of Mohammed Hashim, challenging the Faizabad District Judge's order on opening the locks. On 6 February 1986, a general meeting of Muslims in Lucknow was fixed, wherein a decision to form the Babri Masjid Action Committee was taken. Maulana Muzaffer Husain Kichhouchhwi was declared president with Azam Khan and Zafaryab Jilani as conveners. Later, other members and office-bearers were nominated. They were all from UP.

The All India Muslim Majlis-e-Mushawarat (AIMMM) took

up the issue at the national level. On the AIMMM call Muslims observed a day of mourning on 14 February 1986, and handed over a memorandum to the Prime Minister, Rajiv Gandhi. On 24 February 1986, the AIMMM held a meeting in which it decided to enlarge the scope of its activities. Ultimately a resolution was passed for constituting a central action committee to be convened by Syed Sahabuddin, a former IFS officer turned politician. This was followed by a flurry of activity in the Muslim community. The following week, Muslim MPs also handed over a memorandum to the Prime Minister expressing their concern over the developments.

The VHP had organized a three day 'Ram Janam Bhumi Mahotsav' in Ayodhya on 19, 20 and 21 April 1986. On Ram Navami day, lakhs of devotees throng the temple town to have a dip in the Saryu. The BMAC had also announced a counter conference in Faizabad on 20 April. As tension had been developing over reports of the meeting by both communities, the administration had banned the Muslim conference from Faizabad. This was the first such conference in Faizabad held by the BMAC in connection with the disputed shrine in which all top Muslim leaders were to participate. The authorities had sealed all entry points to prevent Muslims from reaching Faizabad. Nevertheless, about 10,000 Muslims sneaked into the town and decided to hold the rally. After the evening namaz in the Tashah mosque in Chowk, BMAC volunteers began moving towards the venue of the meeting in Ashfaqullah Colony. The police tried to prevent them. They are reported to have broken the police cordon and even pelted stones. The police resorted to a mild lathi charge and ultimately the move to hold the meeting was foiled. Significantly, the level of participation of local Muslims was poor.

On 23 and 24 December 1986, an All India Babri Masjid Conference was held under the presidentship of Syed Sahabuddin wherein the Babri Masjid Movement Coordination Committee (BMMCC) was formed with him as its convener. The members ended with a call to boycott the official observance of Republic Day, 1987. The call was, however, withdrawn on 24 January following severe criticism by a large cross-section of people. The BMMCC then decided to organize a massive rally at the Boat Club in Delhi.

As the communal situation worsened the Home Ministry assured leaders of the Babri panel that efforts to evolve an amicable solution would be made at the earliest.

Meanwhile, the BMMCC organized a massive rally at the Boat Club on 30 March 1987. It was the biggest ever rally of Muslims in Delhi.

As tensions continued mounting, the Home Minister announced in Parliament that a sub-committee consisting of ministers to suggest steps for the resolution of the dispute would be constituted. This sub-committee made several efforts but all in vain.

On 1 January 1988, the BMMCC decided to organize two Ayodhya marches, one for the leaders on 12 August and the other for the general public on 14 October 1988. The BMMCC also called for defeating the Congress in the by-elections to be held in Allahabad and elsewhere. The Janata Party leader Vishwanath Pratap Singh was contesting from Allahabad against the Congress nominee, Sunil Shastri. V.P. Singh won the elections.

VHP after the Unlocking

Significantly, the unlocking of the shrine came as a bolt from the blue, albeit temporarily, for the VHP as well, because they lost the issue on which their agitation was based. The snide remarks in the BJP White Paper and the suggestion that the District Court's order in a regular appeal (the original suit having been discussed by the Munsif Court earlier, with no suggestion of anyone 'managing' it) was 'Government-managed', clearly reveal their ire at being left without their pet programme. At that time their main demand was for removing the locks. To my mind, the demolition of the mosque or construction of the temple was not on their agenda—yet. Some VHP leaders felt that the credit had gone to Umesh Chandra Pandey. The VHP organized several meetings after the unlocking; but none of them was a success in the emotional sense—the only sense in which they were interested in success. Their rath yatras were also banned following violence at several places. Three raths were grounded at Ayodhya and the VHP tried to defy the ban on 17 June 1986. Rajmata Scindia and Prabhu Dutt Brahmchari came all the way to lead the yatra but the move elicited little response from the local people. Ultimately, 108 sadhus 'courted arrest' inside the Valmiki Ramayan mandir. The Ram Prakat Utsav celebrated after the unlocking hardly attracted any crowd. The same was the case with the three-day Ram Janam Bhumi Mahotsav organized by the VHP in Ayodhya that year.

However, it was on this occasion that the VHP announced its plan to construct a Ram temple at the disputed site. They needed this additional item rather badly at the time. And as if in a new one-up exercise, a new plan to constitute a government-sponsored trust was mooted by the then UP Chief Minister, Veer Bahadur Singh, to take up the responsibility for the construction. The plan contemplated the shifting of the mosque to another place and if this was not possible, the construction of the temple in the area leaving the three domes of the mosque intact. A number of sants in the VHP trust were also included in this trust. Ultimately, the plan was sent to the Prime Minister, Rajiv Gandhi, who gave it to the Home Minister, Buta Singh, to examine its feasibility. This was not cleared.

Meanwhile, not too happy at the poor responses to its various programmes to speed up the agitation, the VHP decided to organize a rally of Hindus on 5 April 1987 at Ayodhya, again coinciding with Ram Navami. This time they resolved to leave no stone unturned to make it succeed.

Even so, the people's response remained far short of anything spectacular. However, the BMMCC's rally at the Boat Club in Delhi on 30 March 1987 attracted a massive crowd of Muslims. After this, in a virtual race of rallies, the Hindus' rally organized in the next month at Ayodhya was also reported to have attracted a huge crowd from various parts of the state. The issue thus jumped the confines of Ayodhya to spill into the country at large—on both sides, as it happened.

In November 1987, the VHP again planned to start a rath yatra from Ayodhya where three raths had been grounded earlier. The VHP leadership was determined to defy the ban but the three sants, Mahant Nritya Gopal Das, Paramhans Ramchandra and Narayanacharya, who were the main pillars of the VHP's agitation in Ayodhya, did not want a confrontation with the government and requested the District Magistrate to shift the grounded raths from Ayodhya to the VHP headquarters at Lucknow under police escort. This pre-empted the VHP's plan. But ultimately after a few months, on 1 February 1989, at the sant sammelan held on the occasion of the Kumbh Mela at Allahabad the announcement was made for laying the foundation stone for temple construction on 10 November. Later, plans were chalked out for the *shila poojan* in various parts of the country.*

The VHP agitation got a further boost when in June 1989, the national executive of the BJP at its meeting held in Palampur reviewed the impact of the Ayodhya movement and felt it had

* An interesting—though intriguing—aspect of the *shilanyas* came to my notice during my election campaign. Some Hindu scholars and astrologers in Nagpur and even some villagers asked me how any auspicious Hindu religious function, like a *shilanyas*, could be held in the middle of the Dakshinayan period, on 10 November. They declared this a sacrilege. However, no date seemed to be taboo, since the election to the Lok Sabha, slated for January/February 1990 then, did not choose to wait for the onset of Uttarayan! Religion thus had to yield place to politics once again in a matter that is well-known to almost every Hindu in the country.

become a sensitive political issue. The meeting decided to support the Ayodhya movement and unequivocally declared that the temple issue was incapable of judicial determination. In its resolution adopted on the occasion, the national executive said:

> The BJP holds that the nature of the controversy is such that it just cannot be sorted out by a court of law. A court of law can settle issues of title, trespass, possession, etc. but it cannot adjudicate as to whether Babar did actually invade Ayodhya, destroy a temple and build a mosque in its place. Even where a court does pronounce on such fact, it cannot suggest remedies to undo the vandalism of history . . .
>
> The National Executive of the BJP regards the current debate on the Ram Janmabhoomi issue as one which has dramatically highlighted the callous unconcern which the Congress Party in particular, and the other political parties in general, betray towards the sentiments of the overwhelming majority in this country—the Hindus . . .
>
> The sentiments of the people must be respected, and Ram Janmasthan handed over to the Hindus—if possible through a negotiated settlement, or else, by legislation. Litigation certainly is no answer.*

The VHP's temple plan began to take shape from 13 July

---

* This was perhaps the first time that the BJP openly questioned the sanctity of the rule of law and the inviolability of the verdict of the courts in this matter. After decades and decades of unquestioning litigation on the basis of rights, politicization of the issue led to another uncertainty regarding the manner in which the issue could be resolved. The BJP virtually said, 'We will abide by the court, provided the court abides by our wish'! To date, this ambiguity does not seem to have been sorted out, whatever some leaders of the BJP may choose to say when it suits them.

1989, when a Bajrang Dal convention was organized in Ayodhya in which about 6,000 volunteers drawn from different states were consecrated to construct the temple. Saryu water, kept in the consecrated pitchers, was sprinkled on the volunteers to enthuse them. Ashok Singhal and S.C. Dixit were also present. Singhal called upon the Bajrang Dal volunteers to go to educational institutions and spread the message among the youth. A sant sammelan was also organized on the occasion and the sants called upon the people to make the *shilanyas* programme scheduled for 10 November a success.

By August 1989, the campaign of the VHP and its allied organizations for construction of a Ram temple on the site of the disputed structure by removing or relocating it, based on their assertion that the site was the birthplace of Shri Ram and a Hindu temple commemorating the same stood there prior to its destruction on Babur's command before the erection of the masjid, gathered strength and momentum. This demand of the VHP found support from BJP and RSS also. The VHP then launched a countrywide movement of collecting consecrated bricks (Ram *shilas*) from all over the country by November 1989 with the avowed purpose of construction of the Ram temple at Ayodhya. No secret was made of the fact that the *garbha griha* or *sanctum sanctorum* of the proposed temple would be located at the site of the central dome of the disputed structure.

By the beginning of August 1989, the atmosphere became surcharged with communal tension in view of the rival campaign by the VHP and its allied organizations on the one hand, and the BMAC on the other, which was further aggravated by the threat of the VHP to start construction on the disputed land that forms the subject matter of the title suits, now referred to the Allahabad High Court, Lucknow Bench. When the State Government tried to forestall the same, a plea was taken by the VHP and allied organizations that while for the original suits the Civil Court had passed orders restraining the defendants from removing the idols and for continuance of pooja, darshan etc. and while this was enlarged by the order of the District Judge, Faizabad in the year 1986, there was no order of the court restraining construction of the temple in the vicinity. As to the interim order of the High Court dated 3 February 1986 referred to above, the further argument was raised that the order passed by the High Court in the writ petition filed by the Muslims against the order of the District Judge could be operative only against the respondents in that writ petition. As the VHP and its allied organizations were not party to the said writ petition, the order of not changing the nature of the property in question did not bind them.

In the circumstances, the State of UP (during the Congress regime) in August 1989, moved an application before the High Court under section 94 read with order 39 rule 1 and 2 of the CPC for grant of injunction, (i) restraining the plaintiffs and the defendants from disturbing the *status quo* and organizing any activity which may bring about confrontation between Hindus and Muslims, and (ii) to ensure that orders passed by the court were strictly enforced and were not breached. The application was disposed of vide order of the High Court dated 14 August 1989. In the order the court referred to the order dated 3 February 1986 passed in the above referred writ petition No. 746 of 1986 and other orders passed in other petitioner / FAFO etc. and issued the following directions:

> However, since in the writ petition (WP No. 746/86), in which order dated 3.2.1986 was passed, only some of the parties to the present suit were arrayed, we consider it necessary in the interest of justice that a similar order is adopted in each of the injunction applications in the present suits, as a result whereof until further orders of the court, the parties to suits No. 1 of 1989 (Regular Suit No. 2 of 1950), 2 of 1989 (Regular Suit No. 25 of 1950), 3 of 1989 (Regular Suit No. 26 of 1959), 4 of 1989 (Regular Suit

No. 12 of 1961) and 5 of 1989 (Regular Suit No. 236 of 1989), shall maintain status quo and shall not change the nature of the property in question.

I understood later that undeterred by the order of the court dated 14 August 1989, the VHP continued with its programme and declared its intention to start construction on a location approximate to plot no. 586 in the vicinity of the disputed structure. The BJP and VHP took the plea that the property in the suit had never been identified on the spot or defined and that it was confined to the inner and outer courtyard of the disputed structure only and that the land outside the outer courtyard was undisputed. When the efforts of both the State and Central Governments and the Union Home Minister Buta Singh failed to persuade the said organizations to withdraw the call, a meeting was held by the Chief Minister, UP on 27 September 1989 with the representatives of VHP during which the Union Home Minister also remained present. In the said meeting all aspects of the situation arising in the wake of the VHP's programme to perform *shilanyas* in different parts of the country and carry the sanctified bricks to Ayodhya for laying the foundation stone of the Ram temple on 9 November 1989, were discussed. Both the governments made it clear that they would not allow any breach of the court's orders in any case, whatever may be the consequences. The governments' efforts were to bind the VHP to the legal process and to confine its programme only to the place where the court's orders regarding the structure and the disputed land were not violated. The negotiations resulted in the signing of an agreement by the VHP representatives and others, viz. Ashok Singhal, Avaidyanath, Mahant Nritya Gopal Das and Dau Dayal Khanna. It was laid down in clause (f) that 'the VHP undertakes to abide by the directions of the Lucknow Bench of Allahabad High Court given on 14 August 1989 to the effect that the parties to the suits shall maintain *status quo* and shall not change the nature of the property in question and ensure that peace and communal harmony was maintained'. After obtaining the said undertaking, the use of sanctified bricks at Ayodhya were agreed to.

*

The Congress government in UP, on many more occasions during the 1984-89 period, clearly showed its concern at the religious polarization that was taking place through the efforts of a thoroughly defeated, and therefore frustrated, BJP. The *shila poojans* and rath yatras and the carrying of gangajal and many such programmes had almost succeeded in hijacking the political process in a direction that threatened to become disastrous for the country. The Congress party naturally thought it had to do something to arrest this trend. It also did not want to lose the 1989 election on account of this new Hindu consciousness wave in UP. The situation was bad enough for the secular political forces, but what proved to be the last straw was the sudden anti-Congress craze that developed and made other secular parties enter into a common cause with the BJP, against the Congress—at any cost. The real measure of this cost became obvious within a few months of V.P. Singh's government taking over at the Centre. But by that time it was too late for V.P. Singh and his party to do anything about it. The BJP went from strength to strength, having earned the necessary clout and respectability from their short-lived friendship and naturally at the expense of both the Congress and the Janata Dal and other secular forces. Thus the readiness to subordinate principles to short-term electoral gains resulted in severely damaging the secular credentials of the country. We do not as yet see any clear signs of recovery from this blow. And in any event, it has compromised the secular credentials of all the erstwhile secular parties—albeit in varying degrees. No party has been able to escape this damage.

5

Ayodhya 1989: The *Shilanyas*

It was 16 October 1989. Around 8 a.m., when I was reading the daily newspapers, I got an unexpected phone call from PM House that I should go to see the Prime Minister around 9.30. I found it a bit unusual in our routine of meetings, but a young Prime Minister, I reasoned, could have umpteen reasons to summon his Foreign Minister any time of night or day, since anything may happen anywhere in the world, demanding our immediate attention. So I reached 7 Race Course Road punctually as asked.

Rajiv was already busy talking to some of his close colleagues, whose exact identity I forget at this distance of time. I knew they were close; so what they were discussing must be important and urgent. And in a few minutes my suspense ended, in a rather unexpected manner.

'You will now deputize for me as head of the Indian delegation at the Commonwealth summit starting tomorrow at Kuala Lumpur,' Rajivji began. 'I'm afraid my own trip is off. We are announcing the dates of the Lok Sabha election today; they're likely to be around the 20th of next month. There's hardly any time and I've to plunge into election work rightaway.'

This wasn't exactly a thunderbolt, since elections to the Lok Sabha were normally expected in January or February 1990 (even March, as some half-prepared candidates hoped), but November 1989 was certainly a date out of the blue, whether forced by stars or leaders. Well, from the Prime Minister's tone, it seemed to me: that was that. I was a pretty prominent member of the CCPA (Cabinet Committee on Political Afairs) but this particular decision seemed to have been made to overfly the CCPA, as I could see. So we dispensed with any discussion that would involve going over the decision again. And in my case, I was anyhow going to accompany the Prime Minister to the summit. So it did not involve any dislocation of my itinerary for the next few days. It did, however, mean a disconcertingly hectic election campaign in Ramtek constituency, which had returned me with a massive margin in 1984, but which I was instinctively finding a bit tougher this time. The feeling was atmospheric, not personal in any sense. The people as well as Congress activists continued to support me as before.

So I flew to Kuala Lumpur in my ill-fitting role of a virtual Prime Minister, as leader of the Indian delegation. And to my utter consternation, I discovered that the security arrangements for the Prime Minister of India were the toughest among all the Heads of State or Governments. As a result, I became an alien to my own long-standing group (we loved to call it a gang) of foreign ministers, without the countervailing advantage of moving anywhere among the Heads, being a total stranger in that exalted company. In the summit meeting, I was slotted at the end of the regular Heads, with no chance whatsoever of getting an opportunity to speak on India's behalf—and there *was* something that India did wish to convey on some important subject of the Agenda. And the most hilarious climax came while visiting the place for the usual retreat when they kept a huge Air Force transport plane at my solitary disposal, with no one else getting admittance into it, even to keep company with me during that one-hour flight. I realized the complete isolation of the head from the body on that occasion, more poignantly than at any time before!

I hurried back to India, maybe a few hours before the time

originally planned, having successfully swapped departure slots with an obliging Prime Minister who at once appreciated my election priority. I hardly met Rajivji for a few minutes to give him an 'all well' report about the summit (which is what it always is anyway) and rushed Ramtek-wards as quickly as the twice-a-week Indian Airlines service could carry me. Thereafter it was all *'Bbaiyo aur bahno!'* round the clock. I forgot all about Ayodhya for the time being.

Well, not quite, though. A few months earlier, the Prime Minister had appointed a Cabinet committee (or was it just another committee?) with me as chairman, to examine the mess that Ayodhya had become and to suggest a neat way out, if possible. I had a hunch that we were under some unstated instruction to forge something at Delhi—to be handed down to Lucknow, obviously. However, even at the committee's first meeting, it became clear that without Lucknow's participation we would have no luck. So we adjourned and requested the UP Chief Minister to join us at the next meeting. I had decided upon this course quite innocently, in the normal course. But somehow the next meeting never materialized and the matter could not be proceeded with further. And I had to leave it at that.

Yet the spectre of Ayodhya had haunted many Congress candidates and functionaries since a couple of years earlier, to make them restless. The systematic politicization of a long-standing religious dispute for the first time mystified and confused us no end. Even while Indiraji was alive, the gangajal processions attracted attention in a large part of the country. We were, by and large, brought up in matters secular (socio-economic, in brief) when thinking of political programmes, both for elections and on the ideological front. A vast majority among us did have our respective religious faiths intact and found no difficulty in maintaining them completely independent from and regardless of our political parties and political thoughts. But the programmes of the BJP after 1985, combined with the strong anti-Congress stance of the other secular parties, further compounded the confusion. It appeared clearly that day after day, the BJP was dictating the nation's agenda and we in the Congress too were in a way pursuing the same agenda in opposing it politically. Most of the religious leaders in the country somehow got subsumed in the BJP outlook, with the result that neither the country's ancient ethos of *sarva dharma sama bhava*, nor its modern Constitutional version of secularism, was projected effectively in non-communal terms. Religiosity and communalism subconsciously (in some cases consciously and deliberately) were made to look almost identical. This was a great tragedy in a country where for centuries on end, *samanvaya* (harmonization) among several strands of thought and faith had remained the main preoccupation among leaders of the evolving society—enveloping, in its stride, numerous historical and political events of conquest and absorption. The BJP's pseudo-religious movement could not have sustained itself on a purely religious plane; it needed a *political* reaction, to flourish politically. I cannot escape the uneasy feeling that we Congressmen (while in government) supplied it with just that. We also let our own religious susceptibilities go by default, with the same subconscious inhibition that any expression of religious sentiment on our part, even if we felt it strongly, would be seen as 'non-secular'. As a result, the BJP became the sole repository and protector of the Hindu religion in the public mind.

It was perhaps this realization during Rajiv Gandhi's regime that made the Congress leadership think of playing a role in the Ayodhya affair. However, what gave rise to an adverse reaction was the overt part the State Government was made to play, rather hurriedly and uncharacteristically, presumably responding to electoral urgencies. The BJP at least had the fig-leaf of a VHP, RSS etc. trumpeting the Hindu demand and sentiment; but in the case of the Congress the Chief Minister of UP and prominent ministers and leaders at the Centre (then close to Rajivji) became active in the competitive programme of 'occupying' Ayodhya.

The jump from total Congress non-involvement to the Congress government's full involvement within a short time quite naturally created different waves in different groups. A very important item of this involvement was the *shilanyas*.

When the locks of the temple gates were opened in 1986, it was done under the order of a competent court. Even then the innuendo that the opening was 'managed' by the Congress government created a good deal of commotion—curiously enough, both in BJP circles and Muslim minds, for obviously different reasons. It had hurt both, in different ways, of course. Whichever way one looked at it, the gist of the matter was that while the BJP was systematically politicizing Ayodhya, other authorities—whether the Congress government or alternatively, the court in its discretion—intervened as a pre-emptive measure to respond to a situation, which the BJP had deliberately created and which threatened to go out of control. It amounted to something like 'meeting the lawless halfway to obviate lawlessness'. The BJP and VHP having thus tasted the facile success of a mild threat in 1986, it would only be surprising if they had not gone on to mount another emotional campaign by 1989, particularly as the Lok Sabha election was fast approaching.

Let me emphasize, once again, that I am not criticizing anything done by anyone at any time. I am only chronicling the events as they happened and trying to look into their background intentions as could be gleaned from the way they came about.

As MP from Ramtek, I had occasion to run into truck processions carrying *shilas* (sanctified bricks) coming from South Indian states along the National Highway that runs across Ramtek Lok Sabha constituency. While I drove along the same highway touring the constituency, many of those driving in the trucks (showing hoardings bearing the names of their district BJP or VHP organizations) happened to recognize me, and would stop the trucks, stop my vehicle too—and chat for a while with me. These stray encounters gave me a pretty clear idea of the depth of sentiment the people had for the construction of the Ram temple at Ayodhya—and incidentally of what we the Congress candidates were to expect in the impending elections when the process of politicizing Ram would be completed as scheduled and inexorably face us.

In point of fact, the decision to allow the VHP to have the *shilanyas* on 10 November (the date already announced by the VHP some months back and which, due to the recent decision to hold the Lok Sabha elections on 22 and 24 November, came dangerously close to the dates of the poll) was taken at the highest level, obviously. I had no knowledge of how it actually happened, being constantly busy with my campaign those days. But the news of the participation of the Union Home Minister Buta Singh gave me a clear enough indication.

*

And now the *shilanyas*. We were in the thick of the 1989 Lok Sabha election campaign when all of a sudden, we came to know about the *shilanyas* having taken place about ten days before the polling day. We were first told that the *shilanyas* was done by the consent of all concerned and that therefore there would be no comparative electoral advantage to any party in the election on that issue. We could not make any sense of the sudden decision to get the *shilanyas* done, except on the sole basis of its being a consensual decision. We felt happy that a very tricky issue had been de-fanged in time and that the election would now be on normal secular lines. But the manner in which the communal forces distorted the picture within the few days before the poll left us dumbfounded. As a result, the Congress lost the votes of both Hindus and Muslims to an extent that became clear only after the counting of votes. The fall from 415 seats in 1984 to 196 in 1989 was too steep for anyone to predict. It meant a clear swing towards the communal slant. UP again led this debacle and the

BJP jumped from 2 seats to 88 in the Lok Sabha.

What we discovered later contained certain details, some of which are given below.

At Lucknow the details of the situation arising from the VHP's plan to perform *shila poojan* (sanctification of bricks) in various parts of the country and the transportation of the sanctified bricks to Ayodhya for the *shilanyas* were discussed. An agreement was arrived at after the VHP gave the following undertakings:

(a) The VHP would give prior intimation to the concerned district authorities about the *shila* procession routes and agree to change the same in case the district authorities so desired in the public interest.

(b) The VHP and its followers would not raise any provocative slogans, which could endanger communal harmony.

(c) As far as possible, the sanctified bricks would be carried in trucks on routes determined beforehand in consultation with the concerned district authorities.

(d) Senior and responsible VHP functionaries would take the responsibility of guiding the procession and would extend full cooperation to the district authorities.

(e) The plot in Ayodhya where the sanctified bricks were to be collected would be decided in consultation with district authorities.

(f) The VHP undertook to abide by the directive of the Lucknow Bench of the Allahabad High Court given on 14 August 1989, to the effect that the parties to the suits would maintain the *status quo* and would not change the nature of the property in question and ensure that peace and communal harmony were maintained.

Dau Dayal Khanna, S.C. Dixit, Mahesh Narain Singh, Onkar Bhave and Dr Suresh Gupta were nominated to coordinate with the UP Government. The signatories on the undertaking were Ashok Singhal, Mahant Nritya Gopal Das and Dau Dayal Khanna. According to reliable sources, the draft of the undertaking was ready before the meeting.

The next day, the district officials and VHP leaders made a joint inspection of the site. The exact location of the *singh dwar* (lion gate) of the proposed temple, where the foundation stone was to be laid, was finalized. The land behind the Amanwa temple was specified for the storage of the Ram *shilas*. In all, eight routes in various parts of the country were specified through which the sanctified bricks were to be transported.

Obviously, the agreement created resentment among the Muslims.

In the second week of October the matter was raised in Parliament where some members alleged that the government had given its land for the laying of the foundation stone. This was, however, denied by Buta Singh.

Members of all the non-BJP parties in the Lok Sabha opposed the *shilanyas* and on 13 October passed a resolution that the government would not permit the *shilanyas* at the disputed site.

On 14 October the *Times of India,* Lucknow, carried a story disclosing for the first time that the plot where the VHP intended to perform the *shilanyas* was *nazul* (government) land. Its plot number was 586. In the remarks column of the *nazul* record it was recorded as a graveyard under the control of Waqf Shahi. It was also disclosed in the *Times* story that the plot behind the Amanwa temple specified for the storage of the sanctified bricks was also government land. (Significantly, the graveyards were disputed in the Babri Masjid–Ramjanmabhoomi case pending before the Special Bench of the Allahabad High Court and an injunction order had been issued on 14 August 1989 to maintain *status quo.*)

The entire plan for the *shilanyas,* therefore, ran into rough weather at that time and the government backtracked. The construction work of the approach road to the plot behind the

Amanwa temple was stopped and the officials refused to allow the storage of the bricks there. The VHP then made its own arrangements and stored the bricks in the Ved mandir complex, 200 metres from the disputed site.

On 15 October V.M. Tarkunde filed a writ petition before the Supreme Court praying for the ban on the *shila poojan* and *shila yatras*. The apex court rejected this on 27 October 1989, on the ground that taking out religious processions was a fundamental right.

Meanwhile, the Lok Sabha elections were announced on 17 October 1989, fixing 22 and 24 November as the polling dates. With this announcement the Ayodhya issue was relegated to the background for a while. While there was no great enthusiasm among the Hindus for the *shilanyas*, the Muslims had taken it very seriously. A secret meeting of the Uttar Pradesh Babri Masjid Action Committee (UPBMAC) leaders was held on 26 October at the Darul Safa residence of the BMAC leader, Azam Khan. Leaders at this meeting decided to take up the matter at the international level and called on members of their community to send telegrams to the UN and Amnesty International after 31 October requesting them to help stop the 'physical and cultural annihilation of Muslims'. Another resolution emphasized the need of the formation of hit squads to counter the 'increasing butchery of Muslims'.

After this conclave, closed-door meetings of Muslims were held in almost all the towns in UP. At some places the meeting decided to intercept the transportation of the *shilas* to Ayodhya in case the government failed to act. At least four incidents of confrontation from the Faizabad villages were reported. A Muslim's shop in Atroulia Bazaar in Azamgarh district was set on fire during a Ram *shila* procession. Similar incidents of violence were reported from other parts of the country as well.

Meanwhile, the Sunni Central Waqf Board and others moved an application before the Special Bench of the Allahabad High Court under order 339, rules 1 and 2 read with section 151 of the

Code of Civil Procedures, praying the court to call upon the State not to permit anyone to enter the contested premises. The applicant further prayed for a direction that no foundation-laying ceremony within 200 yards of the disputed site be allowed. The applicant alleged that the VHP was intending to perform *shila poojan* and if that was permitted it would create law and order problems. It was also alleged that the VHP would demolish the Babri Masjid in the absence of any verdict from the court.

Denying the allegation, the State in its counter affidavit asserted that the government had made arrangements and would make further arrangements for the safety of the disputed structure. The government denied that it had permitted or negotiated with the VHP for the demolition of the shrine.

After hearing the case, the court observed: 'We are unable to find any substance in this application. An injunction can be granted only in respect of the property which is involved in a suit. In the instant case, admittedly, there is no such evidence which leads us to hold that the Babri Masjid is intended to be demolished. On such bald allegations no injunction can be issued. Further, in paragraphs 7 and 8 of the counter affidavit the State has asserted that it will take all possible steps to maintain law and order.' As such, the court rejected the application on 23 October 1989, on the ground that there was no merit in the application.

According to the programme, the sanctified bricks from different parts of the country were to start reaching Ayodhya from 5 November 1989. The *shila* yatra was divided in five routes by the VHP, namely: Brahmavart yatra, Prayagraj yatra, Kashi yatra, Chitrakoot yatra and Gorakhnath yatra. Orders were issued by the government to ensure smooth and peaceful transportation of the bricks.

By this time the consecrated bricks had already started their journey towards Ayodhya from far corners of the country and had started converging in Central UP/Ayodhya. A showdown and confrontation between the two communities became imminent at

Ayodhya. The BMAC leaders also gave a call to prevent any construction activity and to be prepared for any sacrifice for the purpose. It was contended by some that the site of construction chosen by the VHP fell within the restrictive orders of the High Court.

An application for clarification of the order dated 14 August 1989 was moved by the State of UP in OOS No. 4 of 1989. This application and other applications were disposed by the Special Full Bench vide its order dated 7 November 1989. The operative portion of the said order reads as under:

> *Status quo* order, in the circumstances of the present case, injuncted both the parties not to alter or modify the status or condition of the properties in question.
>
> We clarify that the order dated 11.8.1989, was in respect of the entire property mentioned in suit, including plot no. 586, in so far included within the boundary described by the letters EFGH.
>
> It is doubtful that some of the questions involved in the suit are solvable by judicial process.

In order to avoid direct confrontation and bloodshed and deterioration of communal harmony, the VHP was allowed to lay the foundation stone of the proposed temple at a spot in front of the disputed structure which it claimed did not form part of the disputed property. This was done after obtaining a report from the District Officers and the opinion of the Advocate General. According to the report of the local officers and legal opinion made available at that time, the said spot did not form part of the land involved in the litigation. This was generally agreed to by all sides involved in the suit in the interest of peace.

It would be relevant to point out here that while the BJP supported the VHP's stand of constructing a Ram temple on the site of the disputed structure by removing or relocating it, other major political parties generally opposed this demand and took the stand that while a temple should be built, the issue in dispute should be resolved either through negotiations amicably or by decision of the court. The decision to allow the foundation stone to be laid on the land said to be not in dispute but in the vicinity of the disputed structure (the place believed to be the birthplace of Shri Ram by many), was thus in keeping with the stand taken by almost all major political parties of the country.

*

It must be stressed that the permission for *shilanyas* was given on the understanding that it would be symbolic and that no further construction would be raised by the organizations till either a negotiated settlement was found between the representatives of the Muslims and Hindu communities or the position amply clarified by the High Court. The VHP-BJP combine, however, took advantage of the permission and after laying the foundation stone, immediately declared its intention to continue construction work till the temple was completed. The plans of the temple were not made public either, thereby keeping it ambiguous as to whether the temple was meant to be extended towards the disputed structure or not. In the meantime the issue was raised before the High Court by Muslims claiming that the site of the *shilanyas* also fell within the property in suit and, therefore, the construction would constitute a breach of the court orders. In the circumstances, the State Government immediately ordered to stop the construction activities on the site and enforced it with an iron hand, undeterred by the virulent propaganda campaign launched by the VHP and the BJP charging it of appeasing the Muslims and depriving the Hindus of their legitimate right of constructing a Ram temple at the site of his birthplace.

A scathing attack has been made against the Congress government of the time by certain quarters for allowing the *shilanyas,* branding it an act of collusion with Hindu fundamentalists. However, as the above analysis of facts would reveal, the efforts of both the Central Government (headed by Rajiv Gandhi) and the State Government were *bona fide* and motivated by the desire to maintain harmony and mutual goodwill between the two communities. As pointed out above, it was in keeping with the stand generally taken by all major political parties except the BJP, that the temple should be built without disturbing the disputed structure and without violation of the court orders. It would be relevant to point out here that the property in suit had never been demarcated on the spot by the court. Several commissions were issued by the courts for the purpose; they submitted their reports also, but none of them was accepted, for different reasons, by the courts. In the circumstances, only a general idea could be formed about the property in dispute and it could be said that it at least included the walled area. The outer limit of the property in suit was not clear at that time. The government appeared to be trying to defuse a highly explosive situation without violating court orders by way of obtaining a report from the District / Revenue Officers and a legal expert of the stature of the Advocate General of the state. Only when it was reported that the proposed site was not covered by the injunction orders of the court, the government granted permission for laying the foundation stone *only*, that too *symbolically.* The most significant aspect of the decision was that the government's agreement with the VHP at that time secured the safety of the disputed structure and kept it outside the threatened construction activities. Unfortunately, however, the atmosphere of communal confrontation in UP had reached a level where anything whatsoever that was done was seen as either anti-Hindu or anti-Muslim. And doing nothing was not open as an option either, the way emotions were being roused all the time.

The stopping of construction of the temple on the *shilanyas* site by the Congress government thus gave an excellent opportunity to the BJP to exploit the Hindu sentiments and to alienate a large section of the majority community from the Congress party. The United Front comprising of the undivided Janata Dal and the two Communist Parties etc. joined hands with the BJP, though indirectly, in the elections in UP. Seat adjustments were openly made among the BJP, the Janata Dal of Mulayam Singh Yadav and V.P. Singh in the state. It was on the basis of this tacit support from the BJP that Mulayam Singh Yadav was able to form a Janata Dal government in the state, after the Assembly elections in the year 1990.

In Parliament, the Congress emerged as the largest single party but it could not muster an absolute majority. The Janata Dal and Left Front taken together were far behind the Congress party. Then the Janata Dal and the Left Front under the leadership of V.P. Singh joined with the BJP to form a BJP-supported Janata Dal government at the Centre.

This unusual development, however, did not allow the new Central or State Government any breathing time. All that it could achieve in political terms was to prevent Congress governments from coming to power.

The communal situation in the country deteriorated considerably in the year 1990 because of the tensions generated from this dispute. Towards October 1990, a programme for construction of the temple through *kar seva* was announced by the VHP. It was apprehended that this programme would cause damage to the disputed structure and elaborate arrangements for its security were made.

6

Ayodhya 1990: The Crisis Averted

The strategy chalked out by Mulayam Singh Yadav to counter the efforts of the VHP and Hindu fundamentalists was one of confrontation. Indeed there was further communal polarization inevitably.

Direct confrontation with the BJP did not, however, suit the V.P. Singh government at the Centre as it was formed and was continuing with the support of the BJP. It could see that the Ayodhya imbroglio could not be solved purely by a confrontationist approach and that it would be difficult to run the government if tempers continued to run high as they already did. V.P. Singh, therefore, initiated negotiations between the VHP, BJP, RSS and the BMAC and Muslim leaders, which continued throughout the period July to October 1990.

As the deadline set by the VHP to undertake construction on the disputed land, i.e. 30 October 1990 drew nearer, V.P. Singh made attempts to find a mutually agreed formula and promulgated the RJB–BM (Acquisition of Area) Ordinance 1990, on 19 October 1990. The similarity in the substance of this Ordinance with that of the Acquisition of Certain Area at Ayodhya Ordinance 1993, later promulgated by the subsequent Congress government, is striking.

Some leaders of the BMAC, however, opposed the Ordinance tooth and nail and demanded its withdrawal. They said that they would withdraw from the negotiations if this demand was not met.

V.P. Singh had to withdraw the Ordinance on 23 October 1990 by promulgating the RJB–BM (Acquisition of Area) Withdrawal Ordinance, 1990, cancelling the earlier Ordinance.

Even as the leaders of the National Front and its ally BJP were rejoicing over forming their new governments, the Ram Janmabhoomi Mukti Yagya Samiti held its meeting on 11 December 1990 and reiterated its resolve to expedite the construction. The resolution adopted at the meeting rejected any mediation in the talks between the sants and the government. The Samiti, however, was of the view that if necessary, it would talk directly to the government.

The sants' meet at Allahabad on 27 January 1990 was significant in as much as it showed that the sants were unexpectedly vociferous there. The BJP was against creating trouble for the government at this stage by starting the *kar seva*. But the majority of the leading sants did not want to keep the issue in abeyance. Contrary to the wishes of the VHP leaders, the sants pressed to fix a date for beginning the *kar seva*. Ashok Singhal took the path of least resistance. Ultimately, the Kendriya Marg Darshak Mandal (KMDM) took a decision to begin construction from 14 February 1990. In its resolution, the KMDM expressed its anguish over the apathy of the newly elected government towards the construction and warned of dire consequences if it failed to take an appropriate decision.

The resolution also called upon the sants, dharmacharyas and Ram Bhakts to extend their cooperation and send in a list of the *kar sevaks* determined to sacrifice their life for the cause of the temple. The meeting also endorsed the resolution adopted by the Ram Janmabhoomi Mukti Yagya Samiti at its meeting on 11 December 1989 asserting that it would not accept any mediation in the talks between the Samiti and the government.

The VHP chalked out a fourteen-day action plan to be implemented in case the administration decided to prevent them from constructing the temple at the disputed site. According to the plan at least 5,000 volunteers including sants were to court arrest at Ayodhya on 15 February and observe a UP bandh on 16 February. The programme was to continue till 28 February during which time at least one person from each village of the country where *shila poojan* was carried out, was to reach Ayodhya.

After 28 February, there would be a break to consider the further course of action, which included courting arrest at all the district headquarters, state capitals and embassies abroad. Similarly the next action plan for Ayodhya was to be for forty days and the agitation was to continue for the whole year.

The sants' announcement naturally caused a flutter in the Janata Dal government. On getting intelligence and other reports, V.P. Singh is said to have made an offer for a dialogue on the subject and sought the presence of some VHP leaders in Delhi for this. The VHP sent former Justice Deoki Nandan Agarwal, a prominent leader spearheading the temple agitation, to Delhi. He had a detailed talk with V.P. Singh wherein the latter asked for time and requested postponement of the construction. Justice Agarwal did not make any commitment, but returned to Allahabad with the Prime Minister's request.

The sants declined the request to put off construction and reiterated their resolve to begin the *kar seva* from 14 February, but agreed to keep the door open for talks with the government till 6 February 1990. Therefore, 4, 5 and 6 February were fixed for talks at New Delhi.

The sants and VHP leaders had gathered in Delhi since 1 February 1989, where a nine-member VHP committee would meet every day to review developments. The committee comprised Mahant Avaidyanath, Mahant Nritya Gopal Das, Ashok Singhal, Deoki Nandan Agarwal, Vishnu Hari Dalmia, S.C. Dixit, Ghuman Mal Lodha, Swami Chinmayananda and Dau Dayal Khanna.

Then an announcement came from the BMAC for a Faizabad march asking the Muslims to reach there on 13 February, a day before the proposed *kar seva*.

In the first round of discussions, V.P. Singh appealed to the VHP leaders to defer the construction plan in view of the alarming situation in some other parts of the country. The atmosphere at the meeting was quite cordial but nothing came of it. The VHP leaders stuck to their guns. V.P. Singh appealed again and by 7 February, the trio of sants, Mahant Avaidyanath, Swami Chinmayananda and Ramchandra Paramhans were actively persuading the hardliners to soften their stance.

On 8 February 1990, a six-member VHP delegation met with the Prime Minister and assured him of a formal response the next day. Mulayam Singh Yadav warned the VHP that his government would adopt a tough line against its *kar seva* plan.

Notwithstanding the announcement to put off the *kar seva* scheduled for 14 February, security arrangements were made in Ayodhya. Vehicles and people going towards the temple town passed security checks at all entry points and Border Security Force (BSF) and Central Reserve Police Force (CRPF) personnel were posted in strength in and around the shrine.

Though the government was trying for an acceptable settlement, it was clear that both parties were only sparring. The VHP had already announced its programme to be carried out during the four months' time. Even as the VHP and Bajrang Dal had finalized their plan for a thirteen-day Dharm Jagran Yatra from 9 April 1990, the BMAC which had expressed its opposition to this, chalked out a programme of meetings of Muslims in all the state's towns. The State Government made elaborate plans to ensure law and order. The BMAC and the Muslim Majlis leaders were apprehensive that the proposed yatra would trigger communal violence as had happened during the *shila* yatra in October 1989.

Meanwhile, the Shankaracharya of Dwarka Peeth, Swami Swaroopanand Saraswati, entered the picture for a brief while. His active participation in the temple movement began in the last week of March 1990 when he announced 7 May 1990 as the day for re-laying the foundation stone. Swaroopanand was the first to attack the VHP for performing the *shilanyas* at Ayodhya on an inauspicious day, violating procedures laid down in the shastras.

In an exclusive interview, he said that the eminent pandits of Varanasi and Kashi Vidwat Parishad entrusted with the task of finding out an auspicious day for the foundation laying had finally fixed 7 May 1990. He clarified that the present structure would not be demolished before the court verdict. If the court declared it a temple, it would never be demolished but be renovated. But if the court declared it a mosque then the newly formed organization, the Akhil Bharatiya Ram Janma Bhumi Punarudhar Samiti, led by him would reconstruct the temple after demolishing the structure, he said. He claimed that besides the Kashi Vidwat Parishad, the Akhil Bharatiya Dharam Sangh, the Bharat Dharam Mahamandal, Akhil Bharatiya Pandit Mahasabha and several other religious organizations had extended their support to him.

Alleging that the VHP was the front organization of the RSS, the Shankaracharya asserted that its aim was to have the sants and mahants obeying the RSS leadership. Citing a provision from the Constitution of the Ram Janma Bhumi Nyas, he said that to retain power, the Sangh parivar had cleverly inserted a clause which envisages that if the post of secretary or cashier fell vacant it would be filled in accordance with the decision of the executive committee of the VHP. Significantly, other vacancies were to be filled in accordance with the decision of the KMDM.

The Shankaracharya remained in Ayodhya for about a week during the Ram Navami festival, making a considerable dent in the sant community there. Later he toured other places to muster support for his plan and held meetings of dharmacharyas and pandits in Varanasi, Haridwar, Allahabad and elsewhere.

By the end of April 1990, arrangements for the relaying of the foundation stone were completed. But on 30 April, while on his way to Faizabad, the Shankaracharya was arrested in Azamgarh district of UP along with ten of his followers. Later he was taken to Mirzapur and lodged in the Chunar fort. Two separate writ petitions challenging the arrest were filed before the Supreme Court. A division bench comprising Justice Sabyasachi Mukherjee and Justice K.I. Shetty asked the UP Government to explain the reason of the arrest. On 3 May advocates of the Allahabad High Court went on a lightning strike in protest against the Shankaracharya's arrest. On the same day, the BMAC gave a call to Muslims to reach Faizabad and thwart the *shilanyas* bid, but this was withdrawn on 6 May after categorical assurance by the Central and the UP Governments on maintaining *status quo*. On 4 May, the Supreme Court held the arrest legal and there was a furore over this.

The government had made elaborate security arrangements to foil the Shankaracharya's attempt. The leading sants supporting the plan were not allowed to come out of their *asthans* in Ayodhya. The tough steps taken by the Yadav government adversely affected the Shankaracharya's and his followers' plans. However, the district administration finally agreed to allow the followers of the Shankaracharya to assemble at Barasthan complex to court arrest on 7 May. The first batch of seventy-one sants and activists courted arrest around 9 a.m. As the activists came out with four consecrated bricks—Jaya, Nanda, Bhadra and Purna—and proceeded towards the shrine for performing the *shilanyas*, the police immediately took them into custody. Likewise forty-four others courted arrest at the Ved mandir complex where the sanctified bricks were stored by the VHP in 1989. The head priest of this complex, a staunch supporter of the VHP, had switched over to the Shankaracharya's side. The arrested persons were let off in the evening. The head priest of the disputed structure, Baba Lal Das, known for his anti-VHP stand, was also taken into custody.

On 9 May, Swami Swaroopanand was released after a midnight order by the judicial magistrate of Azamgarh. He went to Varanasi where he was accorded a grand reception in the Hanuman Ghat area.

Although the Shankaracharya's plan did not quite materialize as intended, it created waves. The four months given to V.P. Singh to find an amicable solution had lapsed. With the VHP's obdurate stand that it would not wait for the court orders to begin construction and the government's stand that it would abide by the court orders, the possibility of an amicable solution receded. The VHP strategists realized that something should be done but they felt that the circumstances were not in their favour. Unlike in the past, the government was bent upon thwarting them this time. For the first time the VHP had to engage in a direct confrontation with the government.

A section of the VHP leadership favoured starting the *kar seva* from 30 October 1990 or 1 November, both auspicious days. But some prominent sants opposed a further delay of five months and wanted a date in July. Fixing so remote a date would be considered by the people as another ploy to delay the construction and it was felt that since the temple movement was already organized all over the country, two months' time should be enough. There was also disagreement over the programme coinciding with the religious fairs at Ayodhya. While 30 October was the day of *parikrama* (circumambulation) of Ayodhya, it was the Kartik Purnima on 1 November. Both attract lakhs of people. VHP strategists felt that during these fairs it would not be possible for the government to prevent activists from reaching the temple town and mingling among the devotees. Besides, the government could not impose a curfew during a fair. However, the sants had always been against agitational programmes coinciding with the fairs at Ayodhya. The fairs are the main source of livelihood for the sants and others in Ayodhya. Any breach of peace would be detrimental for the future. However, the differences over the timing of the *kar seva* were sorted out at the sant conclave at Haridwar on 23 and 24 June 1990 and a decision to begin *kar seva* from the Devosthani Ekadashi (30 October) was taken.

Haridwar Conclave

The VHP's main strategy had been to keep the sants in the forefront of the agitation. But at the Haridwar convention the observers noted that the Shankaracharya Swaroopanand was not falling in line. Suprisingly, not a single prominent sant from Varanasi was present. Likewise, from Prayag (Allahabad), only Shankaracharya Basudevanand, Swami Ram Dutt and Shiv Gopalji participated. Even before the Haridwar conclave both the Central and the State Government had decided to scuttle the VHP's programme. The Centre had given Mulayam Singh Yadav the green signal. The Haridwar conclave decided to implement the plan from 1 August with the observance of the Sant Sankalp Diwas at Vrindavan (Mathura). The VHP had chalked out separate programmes to be carried out at the state and the national levels. There was some unhappiness in VHP circles following some BJP leaders' statements saying that whether or not the government allowed the construction of the Ram temple, the BJP would not withdraw its support to the National Front government. VHP leaders conveyed their feelings to the then RSS chief, Bala Saheb Deoras, who sought an explanation from L.K. Advani. The latter assured the RSS supremo that the BJP would abide by his instructions in the matter.

In the 28 June issue of the RSS Hindi fortnightly *Panchjanya*, L.K. Advani committed his party's full support to the VHP's decision to begin construction of the temple at the disputed site on 30 October 1990. Asserting that his party would participate in any agitation for the purpose, he warned the V.P. Singh government that any attempt to scuttle the VHP plan would snowball into the 'greatest mass movement' the country had ever witnessed.

For the first time, the entire Sangh parivar had thrown its full weight behind the VHP's *kar seva* plan. They had decided to take up the gauntlet thrown down by Mulayam Singh Yadav. It was also for the first time that the RSS men in administration, media and other spheres of life were asked to play a pivotal role during the battle. The State Government had chalked out various steps to be taken to pre-empt the VHP move. One of these was to prevent convergence of VHP activists at Ayodhya. This had been tested twice, first during the Shankaracharya Swaroopanand's *shilanyas* bid and later during Mahendra Singh Tikait's attempt to hold a panchayat at Lucknow.

On 1 August, the VHP sants pledged to devote their *tan*, *man* and *dhan* to construct the temple. In August, Sri Ram Karseva Samitis were constituted by the VHP all over the country. On 13 August 1990 L.K. Advani, while releasing a book on Ayodhya, said that if the Muslims voluntarily withdrew their claim over the shrine and allowed the construction of the temple, he would intercede with the VHP to abandon its plans for Kashi and Mathura. But there were no takers for this proposal. Meanwhile the dharma yatras, hoisting saffron flags, blowing of conch shells and other programmes got a poor response.

Likewise in a sudden and surprise move, the VHP's Ram jyoti yatra set off secretly from Ayodhya on 1 September, eighteen days before schedule, to pre-empt any ban or preventive action. Seven jyotis were lit by the fire created out of sandal and peepul wood. Two jyotis were kept at Ayodhya while five were taken to Kashi, Mathura, Allahabad, Lucknow and Gorakhpur by the Bajrang Dal and VHP leaders.

Originally the Ram jyoti yatras were to begin from Ayodhya on 19 September. The administration was taken by surprise and it felt the Sangh parivar may resort to similar tactics later as well. The VHP leaders decided to send their activists to adjoining districts of Faizabad from where they could sneak through more conveniently. Ironically, while both the government and the VHP decided to call each others' bluff, V.P. Singh was issuing statements expressing hopes for an amicable settlement. A series of meetings were held by the then minister of state, Subodh Kant Sahay, but they did not appear to bear fruit.

The issue was also discussed at the National Integration Council (NIC) in Madras on 22 September 1990 though this meeting was boycotted by the BJP. Queering the pitch further, L.K. Advani began his 10,000 km rath yatra from Somnath to Ayodhya on 25 September to participate in the *kar seva* on 30 October 1990. Mulayam Singh Yadav planned anti-communal rallies in different towns which attracted massive crowds mainly of backward castes (OBCs), Harijans and Muslims. Rallies were also organized by the Janata Dal, Bahujan Samaj Party and the Left parties. Mulayam Singh Yadav spoke against a confrontation but reiterated that he would deal strictly with any attempt to incite communal violence. Referring to the proposed *kar seva*, he boasted of foolproof security arrangements. Addressing a massive rally in Faizabad on 16 September, he said that a diabolical plan was afoot to create trouble during the *parikrama* fair at Ayodhya on 30 October, unmindful of the thousands of pilgrims at stake. Even as the Janata Dal and Left parties were organizing 'anti-communal' rallies, efforts were afoot to create a communal divide. To create panic and feelings of insecurity, miscreants set off bombs during the Dussehra and Durga Puja festivals. Rumour mills were working overtime. About 60 km from Ayodhya, communal violence flared up in which eighty innocent persons including women and children were massacred in Colenganj town of Gonda district. Hundreds of houses were set on fire in a dozen villages. Later it became clear that a disinformation campaign had incited passions.

On the night of 30 September 1990 when a Durga Puja procession was carried out in Colenganj town, the chariot was stoned and bombed. This was in retaliation to slogans shouted by some in the procession when it reached the Yatim Khana locality inhabited by the members of the minority community. The resultant violence left seven persons dead. Of these, one belonged to the majority community. But the rumour went that over 500 Hindus were killed by Muslims. The rumour also had it that when trouble started, women and children accompanying the procession were called into Muslim houses on the pretext of extending protection, where they were butchered. Many villagers from nearby areas had also gone to see the Durga Puja procession but when the violence erupted some of them could not return owing to the curfew. This gave further credence to the rumours. The villagers went berserk and about 4,000 Hindus from the area gathered and raided the Muslim localities of Pandey Choura and killed nine persons. As a result of these baseless rumours, a similar cycle of death and destruction was repeated in other villages. Of the eighty persons killed, only one was Hindu. The riots created a communal divide at a time when preparations for the *kar seva* were afoot. On 7 October, the former Prime Minister Rajiv Gandhi visited riot-affected areas and spent seven hours there listening to the pathetic tales of victims and survivors. Rajiv Gandhi was of the view that the anti-communal rallies being organized by the Janata Dal and Left parties were also contributing to the worsening of the situation.

On 20 October, in Faizabad, about 10,000 women from different states participated in a communal harmony march to Ayodhya organized by the National Federation of Indian Women. This was the biggest ever march of women held in Faizabad. They had reached Faizabad a day earlier for the scheduled date of the march but in the evening, the District Magistrate banned the meet. This caused serious resentment and the women leaders decided to defy the ban. They also threatened to gherao the District Magistrate. Late at night, after consulting the State Government, he communicated to the organizers to allow the peace march to Ayodhya, skipping Faizabad town. Significantly, Ayodhya was not considered a sensitive area, for nothing untoward had happened there over the disputed shrine during the last forty years after the idol was installed in December 1949. Thus a confrontation was averted. In the morning such slogans like '*Mandir masjid nahin girenge; Hindu Muslim nahin larenge; Hindustan ke char sipahi, Hindu Muslim Sikh Isai; Na Hinduraj na Khalistan, jug jug jiye Hindustan*' rent the air as the women marched from Faizabad to Ayodhya.

Acquisition of Land

In a last-minute bid to avert a showdown the Union Government held discussions with leaders of the Muslim community and the VHP in New Delhi and decided to acquire the disputed structure and the land around it on 19 October 1990 and an Ordinance to this effect was issued by the President of India. The possession of the acquired land was undertaken by the Divisional Commissioner Madhukar Gupta on behalf of the Central Government the next day. However, this opened a Pandora's box since it was opposed by both sides. Consequently, on 23 October 1990 the Ordinance was withdrawn. There are many versions as to what prompted the Union Government to acquire the structure and the land. The VHP blamed the Union Government for backing out of the agreements because of Muslim pressure. In addition there was pressure from Mulayam Singh Yadav. The BJP version of the understandings has been detailed in its White Paper reproduced below:

> The Prime Minister V.P. Singh called Shri S. Gurumurthy on 15th October 1990. The two sat in four sessions for four hours, from the evening to well past midnight. Shri Gurumurthy suggested that the government should acquire the entire disputed area, and hand it over to the VHP trust but retain the entire disputed structure with a 30 feet area around it under its title and possession, and refer the issue—whether there was a pre-existing Hindu structure—for judicial opinion to the Supreme Court under Article 143 of

the Constitution. Shri V.P. Singh readily accepted the suggestion. When Shri Gurumurthy asked him whether this could be communicated to the RSS-VHP as the decision and final one of the government, V.P. Singh said that he was saying so as the Prime Minister. He also said that the movement of kar sevaks should be stopped or slowed down. Shri Gurumurthy communicated this to the RSS-VHP and relayed back their acceptance to the Prime Minister.

On 18th October, two sets of meetings took place, and definite steps were taken. The then railway minister, Shri George Fernandes, and the then information minister, Shri P. Upendra, met Shri Ashok Singhal at the RSS headquarters, Keshav Kunj in New Delhi. The ministers said that the government proposed to bring forth an ordinance on the issue. By this the government would hand over to the Sri Ram Janmabhumi Nyas the entire land except the garbha griha—that is, the disputed structure. Shri Ashok Singhal maintained that no agreement could be reached till the government handed over the entire land to the Hindus.

The same day, Shri V.P. Singh invited Shri Govindacharya, Shri Arun Jaitly, the then Additional Solicitor General and a journalist to discuss the Ayodhya issue. They urged that the government acquire the entire disputed area, retain the disputed structure as well as 30 feet land around it, hand over the rest to the Ram Janma Bhumi Nyas, and request the Supreme Court under Article 143 to determine whether there was a pre-existing Hindu structure. After the discussion an additional secretary was called around midnight and asked to initiate steps to implement the proposal.

Accordingly a three point proposal and draft ordinance was prepared at night. At 5 a.m. a committee of officials met at the Cabinet Secretary's residence and finalized the draft. At 10 a.m. the cabinet met at the PM's residence and approved the ordinance and the three point solution. Since the ordinance had to undergo vetting from several angles it was not released immediately.

On Thursday, 18 October 1990, Shri V.P. Singh called Gurumurthy, who was then in Madras, to go over to Delhi and accordingly, he reached Delhi on the morning of 19 October. In the forenoon of Friday, there was a meeting at the Sunder Nagar guest house of the *Indian Express* in which Shri L.K. Advani who was to proceed to Dhanbad to continue his rath yatra, was present. Also present were Shri R.N. Goenka, S. Gurumurthy and some other friends of the newspaper. Shri Advani explicitly said that it was not his intention that the government must fall, but that, if the ordinance proposal went through, and the land around the disputed structure was handed over with or without the VHP nominee as the receiver at the disputed structure, he would support it.

In the afternoon, Shri Gurumurthy spoke to the Prime Minister. By then, a visible change had taken place. He said that not just the disputed structure, but the disputed land also be in the possession of the government and would not be handed over to the Ayodhya movement. When Shri Gurumurthy said that was not the understanding, the Prime Minister asked him to meet at his residence. Shri V.P. Singh told Shri Gurumurthy that L.K. Advani should defer the rath yatra by a day, so that a solution was arrived at. And after that, Shri V.P. Singh said 'he would go along with Shri Advani to Ayodhya for kar sewa'. When this was communicated to Shri Advani, he said that his presence was not required, and if the ordinance proposal as originally understood was given effect to, that would be agreeable to him.

In the evening, there was again a marathon session at

Shri V.P. Singh's residence extending to well beyond 9 p.m. Shri V.P. Singh told Shri Gurumurthy that he should discuss the matter with his colleagues, and that he had briefed Shri George Fernandes, Shri Arun Nehru, Shri Ajit Singh and Dinesh Goswami, all ministers were present throughout the discussion, and besides Shri Gurumurthy, Shri Arun Jaitly and a leading journalist were also present. Shri V.P. Singh was in and out of the meeting, obviously meeting several persons in different rooms at the same time.

The law minister Dinesh Goswami said that because of the multiplicity of the suits and hundreds of issues involved, it was not possible to issue the ordinance; in fact, it was impossible to legislate on the subject because of the pending cases. It was explained to him by Shri Arun Jaitly and Shri Gurumurthy that the hundreds of issues fell under just three heads—one, whether Ram was born at that site; two, whom did the different lands belong to; and three, whether there was a pre-existing Hindu structure. It was explained to him that the first aspect was not capable of judicial or even legislative determination, the second aspect was capable of legislative action under the undisputed power of compulsory acquisition, and the third aspect was capable of judicial opinion or judicial verdict. Arun Nehru said that, if the explanation was correct, the ordinance should be issued. Later, late at night the ordinance and scheme were issued to the press. The three point formula was: (i) The government would acquire the shrine and the adjoining land, (ii) Barrring the shrine and the disputed land the other acquired areas could be made available to the VHP trust 'Ram Janma Bhumi Nyas', (iii) The question about the shrine would be referred to the Supreme Court. There were mixed reactions to the new formula. N.T. Rama Rao,

Tamil Nadu Chief Minister Karunanidhi, Left parties and some others welcomed it.*

The BJP attributed the withdrawal of the Ordinance to a threat from Mulayam Singh Yadav that he would not allow it to be implemented. The BMMCC had also rejected the government's formula saying that it should not bypass the judicial process. The Ordinance suspended all previous court orders including the injunction order of 14 August 1989. Under it the Central Government had also transferred the dispute in the Allahabad High Court to the Supreme Court for expeditious disposal under Article 143. The BMAC had threatened to organize a Bharat bandh on 30 October to demand the withdrawal of the Ordinance saying that it was a direct interference in Muslim personal law. The BMAC also alleged that the National Front government had cheated the Muslim community by doing this.

* I am giving in some detail a description of the pitched battles that raged in Ayodhya in those days in 1990, in order to bring out the well-matched determination on the part of the VHP, as well as Mulayam Singh's state government, in the ensuing confrontation. My intention is simply to demonstrate the contrast between the 1990 State Government's performance and that of Kalyan Singh's government in December 1992. The Central Government sent para-military forces equally promptly on both occasions—which was all it could do. Just to mention one point of contrast, while Mulayam Singh's state administration went to great lengths, even sometimes counter-productive, in preventing crowds from gathering at Ayodhya on the crucial dates, Kalyan Singh's outfit in the same state did nothing of the kind, while the ruling party in the state went to great lengths in inviting, exhorting and collecting larger and larger crowds country-wide, regardless of whether the administration could control the crowds under adverse circumstances—for which it was obviously not prepared, whatever their statements. I do not have to elaborate on the possible motivations behind this contrast. I leave that part to the reader.

Multi-tiered Security Arrangements

Notwithstanding continuing talks for a way to avert a showdown, preparations by the government and VHP went on in Ayodhya. In UP, the government strategy was to seal Ayodhya. This would prevent *kar sevaks* from reaching the temple town. Officials in all districts were to stop *kar sevaks* from passing through their districts. The aim was to prevent the convergence of *kar sevaks* in strength at Ayodhya. The State Government had made arrangements to check the influx of *kar sevaks* at its borders. Apprehending the biggest influx from the BJP-ruled state Madhya Pradesh (MP), over a dozen centres were set up all along the MP borders where forces were deployed heavily. The VHP had apparently set up camps at several places on the MP borders from where the *kar sevaks* were to storm UP. The border, from Jhansi to Mirzapur and Sonbhadra district in UP were considered crucial from the security point of view. It was also feared that the VHP activists from other states would converge there prior to entering the state. Similarly, elaborate arrangements were made at the UP border in Deoria district to stop L.K. Advani's rath yatra. Significantly, given the uninterrupted journey of the rath yatra, the UP Government was not sure that Advani would be detained in Bihar. As such, Mulayam Singh Yadav was determined not to let him enter UP at any cost. Thereafter the entire district was sealed by the administration.

The *kar sevaks* had started trickling into Ayodhya as far back as 17 October. The buses were stopped from passing via Faizabad from 18 October. The first batch of the *kar sevaks* from Andhra and western UP arrived by train at Sohawal and Bilhar Ghat railway stations, about 20 to 25 km from Ayodhya. The arrangements for their lodging and boarding were made in nearby villages. But about 600 *kar sevaks*—530 from Andhra and 85 from Bijnore and Muzaffarnagar district—were rounded up by the police on 20 October near Sohawal railway station.

Advani Arrested

L.K. Advani was on his rath yatra in Bihar. On 23 October the Bihar Government arrested him in the early morning from the circuit house at Samastipur. This was under the National Security Act. He was flown out to Dumka and then taken by road to Masanjore where he was detained. The rath was confiscated by the Bihar police.

The same day, the BJP informed the then President R. Venkataraman in Delhi that it was withdrawing its support to the government following the stopping of the rath yatra. V.P. Singh told the President that he would prove his majority on the floor of the House on 7 November.

Security Tightened

The State Government had put an elaborate security cordon around the disputed shrine. In the lane leading to the shrine, the first iron barrier was put up near the Hanuman temple, while the next was at the Bara Asthan crossing. Likewise, there were at least four barriers ahead, each guarded by the para-military forces. After L.K. Advani's arrest, an undeclared curfew was imposed in the Ram Kot area around the disputed site in Ayodhya on 24 October. Although darshan at the Ram Janmabhumi temple was not banned, since the people were not allowed in the vicinity of the shrine it was seen as a kind of ban. However, pooja, *akhand Ramayan path* and *akhand* kirtan went on uninterrupted. The priests and *Ramayan* reciters were given special passes for this. But after there was too much furore over the restrictions, the undeclared curfew was withdrawn the next day. However, the Ayodhya-Faizabad road was sealed at various places and people going to Ayodhya were allowed to enter only after proper screening.

As the government's security plan was somehow leaked to the

VHP, the Sangh parivar was determined to answer in kind. According to them it was not a mere crowd but the committed cadre that was coming to participate in the *kar seva;* so they were confident that it would not be possible for anyone to stop them from reaching Ayodhya. In fact the movement of the *kar sevaks* was well planned and was being conducted by retired army and civil officials. All the *kar sevaks* were given identity cards bearing a chart of their journey and destination. Some of these were recovered from the *kar sevaks* arrested by the police. A large number of the hardcore activists had penetrated into the district earlier.

On the evening of 26 October, indefinite curfew was clamped in Faizabad and Ayodhya and the para-military forces staged a precautionary flag march. After the imposition of curfew, over 2,000 persons were arrested from various places when they tried to proceed towards the *parikrama* road. The then deputy chief of the RSS, Prof. Rajendra Singh, popularly known as 'Rajju Bhaiya', was arrested at Lucknow's Amausi airport on 26 October and flown to Pantnagar. Vishnu Hari Dalmia, Ghuman Mal Lodha, Swami Chinmayananda, Mahant Avaidyanath and the president of the Kar Seva Samiti, Shankaracharya Basudevanand, were arrested on 27 October.

Rajmata Vijaya Raje Scindia was arrested on 28 October by the UP police while leading about 15,000 *kar sevaks* across the border of MP at Sitapur Ram Ghat in UP.

Atal Bihari Vajpayee was arrested by the UP police on the night of 29 October at the Amausi airport. But Singhal, Dixit, Vinay Katiyar, Uma Bharti and other leaders went underground to escape the pre-emptive arrest after the government geared up its security measures. Singhal and Dixit managed to reach Faizabad.

Meanwhile, about 10,000 *kar sevaks* had sneaked into the temple town even as thousands of others were trying to enter from all sides on the night of 29-30 October. The biggest pressure of *kar sevaks* was from across the Saryu bridge, which was blocked by concertina wire. After diverting trains, the *kar sevaks* would pull the chain and alight from the trains at a convenient stop and cover long distances on foot by country roads to reach the temple town.

Even as a large number of *kar sevaks* were mounting pressure to enter the town, those who had already sneaked in were trying to reach the shrine in batches. However, three such attempts were foiled by the para-military forces at Hanuman Garhi. At around 8.30 a.m. on 30 October another group tried to approach the shrine but were beaten back by the forces. Later, they returned on the Hanuman Garhi crossing of the national highway. Here, police officials and the magistrate told them that they were under arrest. Transport was not available and they stopped to help their counterparts and so the number of *kar sevaks* swelled. Some *kar sevaks* forced their way into the Hanuman Garhi lane. There the CRPF foiled their attempt despite some brickbatting from rooftops. Meanwhile, some *kar sevaks* from Andhra led by their MLA also arrived. Faced with a determined police, the MLA suggested they were ready to court arrest peacefully. The police agreed. Two buses reached there from the Sringarhat side and the *kar sevaks* boarded them. But when it was time to move, a sadhu who could drive suddenly pushed the driver off the bus and drove towards the shrine, leaving the forces stunned. Breaking the iron barriers, the speeding bus moved ahead, but was stopped a few hundred metres before the shrine. This proved a morale booster for the *kar sevaks*.

Half an hour later, a 500-strong crowd of *kar sevaks* emerged from the Digambar Akhara lane opposite the Hanuman Garhi. When they attempted to approach the disputed spot, the CRPF held them back. The crowd pelted the CRPF, injuring an inspector. Seeing him bleeding profusely, the infuriated forces asked the District Magistrate, who was present, for permission to use force, including firing. Finding the District Magistrate reluctant, the entire force stepped aside, refusing to control the mob. But as the crowd pressure mounted, the magistrate asked the CRPF to use force. Meanwhile, the crowd of *kar sevaks* swelled considerably and tried to proceed peacefully. But the CRPF held them off. The crowd again became restive whereupon the District Magistrate announced that he would bring in S.C. Dixit and Swami Vamdev at the spot and added that the crowd should abide by what they said. The crowd agreed, but some managed to wind their way towards the Hanuman Garhi side.

This breakaway group was stopped by para-military forces at Hanuman Garhi and in the process the CRPF resorted to a mild lathi charge. Ashok Singhal was informed and this proved to be provocation for the *kar sevaks* accompanying him. Though only seventy in number, they advanced towards the shrine.

They first bluffed and pushed the police personnel guarding the barrier between Hanuman Garhi and Bara Asthan Tiraha. As the group proceeded further, 2,000-3,000 *kar sevaks*, who were hiding in the temples in the Ram Janmabhumi lane, joined them. The crowd tried to force entry into the shrine but the police opened fire. Five persons were killed. Within minutes, the crowd returned and tried to enter the outer security gate. Meanwhile, S.C. Dixit and Mahant Nritya Gopal Das were brought from the kotwali to placate the *kar sevaks*. Dixit asked permission for himself and the mahant to stand on the high tilla inside the gate in order to calm the crowd. But as the gate was opened for Dixit, a large number of *kar sevaks* forced their way inside and started damaging the disputed structure. Several *kar sevaks* climbed atop the domes and hoisted saffron flags. No magistrate was there. In the meantime, some senior officials including the commissioner reached the spot and the mob came out. But after twenty minutes, another group attempted to enter the shrine from the back, crossing the barbed wire fencing. The police fired on them and one *kar sevak* was killed. Then the SSP Subhash Joshi with a large contingent of para-military forces swooped down on the temple complex and the lane where the *kar sevaks* were staying and had it vacated. The situation was then brought under control.

The death toll in Ayodhya on 30 October was officially stated to be six. The next day the army and the para-military forces staged a flag march and the administration hardened its stand. The *kar sevaks* across the Saryu bridge gathered again and insisted on marching towards the disputed shrine for a darshan of the Ram Lalla idol installed there. Likewise, those already present in the town also tried to reach the shrine, but the large contingent of para-military forces prevented them.

2 November Firing

It was the Kartik Purnima when lakhs of devotees come to the temple town to take a dip in the Saryu. But this time Ayodhya was turned into a battlefield. There were *kar sevaks* and para-military forces at every pilgrimage spot in town. The atmosphere was tense since early in the morning. More *kar sevaks* had sneaked into Ayodhya. Thousands of *kar sevaks* had assembled in the Mani Ram Ki Chawni, the nerve centre of the temple agitation. They were determined to proceed to the shrine.

Indeed, it appeared to be a decisive battle. Even as the VHP was determined to storm the shrine, the administration had made all arrangements to thwart it. Heavy contingents of para-military forces were deployed on all approach roads.

The security men said that they had no alternative but to fire, failing which the *kar sevaks* would have overrun them and destroyed the shrine. Even so, there was a comment on the nature of the random firing. It was said to be aimed at the head and upper portion of the body while according to the established principle, it should normally be aimed at the legs to disperse the crowd. In all, nine persons were stated to be killed.

Nonetheless, the *kar sevaks* remained firmly committed to

their cause and a large number of them stayed on in the town. The exaggerated reports of the casualties and brutality had aroused the emotions of people in the twin cities. Processions were taken out in Faizabad defying the curfew. All help was extended by the local people to the injured *kar sevaks*. A procession gheraoed the residence of the commissioner.

One thing was clear during the agitation. The Sangh parivar had a most powerful propaganda machinery. They left no stone unturned to project Mulayam Singh Yadav as an incarnation of Ravana and Hiranyakashyap. Even though some *kar sevaks* returned home, many stayed on in the town to participate in the next phase of the *kar seva*.

As V.P. Singh was voted out in the Parliament during the trial of strength, Chandra Shekhar became the Prime Minister with the support of the Congress. The Samajwadi Janata Party (SJP) was formed.

Even as the peaceful satyagraha continued, an attempt was made to blow up the disputed shrine on 9 December. The CRPF personnel, however, foiled the bid and arrested one Suresh Chandra bearing dynamite sticks, though his accomplice escaped. After the arrest the accused was found to be from Vrindavan (Mathura). He told the police that he and his associate had surveyed the Ramjanmabhoomi area for six days before putting their plan into action. They reached the Kuber tila in the south of the shrine around 6 p.m. and when the number of the security men posted to guard the shrine decreased after 8 p.m., crossed the pipe barricades and barbed wire fencing and hid themselves behind the bushes near the Sumitra Bhavan. Later, around 10 p.m. when they slowly started moving forward, an alert guard of the CRPF saw and overpowered Suresh. He told the police that he had courted arrest once in Delhi and once in Mathura. In Mathura he had courted arrest on 29 October 1990 in protest against L.K. Advani's arrest. He said that they had the dynamite sticks tied to their waists. In all, four bundles of dynamite were recovered, each about eight to nine inches long and one inch thick.

Talks Initiated

Chandra Shekhar arranged a meeting between the VHP and Babri Masjid leaders on 1 December and 4 December 1990. Chief Ministers Sharad Pawar of Maharashtra, Bhairon Singh Shekhawat of Rajasthan and Mulayam Singh Yadav of UP were also present at the meeting. The meeting decided to ascertain whether the Babri Masjid was constructed after demolishing the temple which existed at the spot. Three decisions were taken at the meeting in this connection: both sides should furnish evidence to the minister of state for Home by 22 December 1990; the minister would then make available photocopies of the evidences to all concerned by 25 December 1990; and after receiving the evidence both parties were to meet in Maharashtra Sadan on 10 January 1991. Even as both the parties were meeting, Chandra Shekhar announced on 22 December 1990 that he would soon meet the Chief Justice to pursue the Rajiv Gandhi formula for settlement of the issue. In a letter to the Prime Minister, Rajiv Gandhi had suggested, among other things, that a commission of inquiry comprising five judges of the apex court be appointed to determine whether the Ram temple at Ayodhya was actually destroyed to build the Babri Masjid, and asked to submit its report in three months.

At the next meeting, two sub-committees—one of historians and archaeologists and the other of legal experts—were constituted. Half the members were nominated by the VHP and half by BMAC. The sub-committee of historians and archaeologists comprised Prof. R.S. Sharma, Prof. Athar Ali, Prof. Suraj Bhan, Prof. D.N. Jha, Javed Habib, Prof. B.P. Singh, Dr S.P. Gupta, Harsh Narain, Prof. K.S. Lal, Prof. Devendra

Swaroop and Dr B.R. Grover. The sub-committee of legal experts comprised Justice (Retd.) D.V. Sehgal, V.K.S. Choudhary representing the VHP side and Zafaryab Jilani, M.A. Siddiqui, S.A. Sayed and Zafar Ali Siddiqui representing the BMAC side. The historians and archaeologists nominated by the VHP submitted documents to support their case. For the archaeological evidence they relied on fourteen pillars of black stone (*kasauti*) contained in the Babri Masjid on which Hindu motifs were carvcd. According to VHP archaeologists, art and historical evidence identifies these pillars as belonging to a Hindu temple structure dating back to the eleventh century AD. They further asserted that the excavation conducted by the Archaeological Survey of India (ASI) under the supervision of Prof. B.B. Lal from 1975 to 1990 had revealed the existence of a series of burnt brick pillar bases at regular intervals in the vicinity of the RJB–BM site. These were found arranged in a directional alignment of the black stone pillars used in the disputed structure.

Besides, two pillars of black stone, similar to ones found in the disputed structure, were found buried upside down by the side of the grave of one Muslim saint, Fazal Abbas alias Musa Ashikan, who has been mentioned in the documents as having motivated the destruction of the temple and the construction of the mosque. Dr S.P. Gupta (of the VHP side) mentioned other evidence to prove that Ayodhya was inhabited at least as far back as the seventh century BC and that there had been continuous habitation upto the third century AD.

The VHP historians' note also discussed the alternative hypothesis that a temple known as Janmasthan to the north of the Babri Masjid structure is itself the original Janmasthan shrine and declared it to be untenable because this according to them, was a new structure not more than 250 years old. The VHP note listed various attempts made by the Hindus to reclaim the shrine. About the pleading that the entire controversy was created by the British as another instance of their divide and rule policy, the

VHP's note in its concluding parts of 7.4 said: 'A simple test whether the anti-mandir hypothesis deserved any consideration at all, is the element for which the evidence should be most easy to find—the British concoction hypothesis. In the plentiful and well-kept archives which the British have left us, it should not be too difficult for genuine historians to find some piece of evidence. But so far, no proof whatsoever has been given either for such an actual course of events or even for similar British tactics at another time and place. If the anti-mandir polemists cannot even come up with that, their whole hypothesis stands exposed as a highly implausible and purely theoretical construction.'

The VHP side also submitted extracts from *Ain-i-Akbari* of Abul Fazal (written in the late sixteenth century) to show that Avadh was associated with the birthplace of Shri Ram Chandra of Treta age. The VHP also quoted two books by foreign scholars, viz. *Ayodhya* by Hans Baker (1984) and *Ram Janmabhumi vs. Babri Masjid* by Koenraad Elst, released by L.K. Advani shortly before his arrest in October 1990. According to the VHP note both the writers have observed that the Babri Masjid was constructed after demolishing the temple.

Commenting on the efforts and procedures of examining the historical and legal points of the case of both parties, the historians and archaeologists nominated by BMAC, at the outset of the introductory notes of their reports submitted in May 1991 said: 'Thus the dispute over the facts of the history were now to be decided by the litigants, with the Government of India as an umpire, and not by any independent forum of historians—a very unhappy procedure. We, therefore, approached the Government of India to include impartial historians in the process of forming judgement on historical facts and let us have access to such evidence, archaeological and textual, as has been presented to it or is in possession of the government organizations, such as the Archaeological Survey of India (ASI). We regret to say that the Government of India's response to this was largely one of silence.

The BMAC declared that it was ready to abide by the findings of a set of independent historians, but the position was not acceptable to the VHP.'

Referring to the VHP historians' report, these historians said in their note that people would be surprised to find that the VHP had been unable to cite any ancient Sanskrit text in support of its claim that there had been an ancient Hindu belief in Ram Janmasthan at Ayodhya. Surely if there were such a strong belief, there would have been numerous Vaishnavite texts exhorting worshippers to visit the spot, the note said.

They further pointed out: 'Within 50 years or so of the construction of the Babri Masjid, Tulsidas composed in 1575-76 his celebrated *Ramchartimanas,* the most fervent exposition of the *Ramayana* story in Hindi. Is it possible to believe that Tulsidas would not have given vent to heart-rending grief had the very birth site of his lord been ravaged, its temple razed to the ground and a mosque erected at that place?'

Referring to the VHP's argument that the Babri Masjid contained fourteen black stone pillars with non-Islamic motifs which must have formed part of the structure of the destroyed temple, these historians noted: 'We have consulted a number of art historians including Devangna Desai, Mr Dhakay, Krishna Deva, N.P. Joshi and R.C. Sharma. The general consensus is that some motifs suggest a date around 9th and 10th century. It is, therefore, evident that the pillars cannot belong to a single structure. The motifs found on the pillars seem to have been similar to the pillar motifs in eastern India.'

Dwelling at length on the VHP's assertion that the black basalt stone pillars used in the mosque and also found in the graveyard were part of one and the same structure, they said: 'The variations in the style and the diameter of these pillars, and more important, the total lack of their stratigraphic association, completely rule out this possibility.' The historians emphasized in their note that it was quite possible that the pillars used in the Babri Masjid were brought from outside to decorate it.

As far as the carving on the pillars was concerned, they did not agree with the VHP's argument that it showed Vaishnav associations. According to them any good Vaishnavite or even historian cannot think of Vaishnavite affiliation without the representation of the 'sankh' (conch shell), the 'chakra' (wheel), 'gada' (mace) and 'padma' (lotus). These are inseparable emblems of Vishnu, they maintained.

Replying to the VHP historians' argument that excavation conducted by the ASI under the supervision of Prof. B.B. Lal from 1975 to 1980 had revealed the existence of a series of burnt brick pillar bases, the BMAC archaeologists noted that the brick pillar structure had already fallen down and gone out of use around the thirteenth century and the site was inhabited by Muslims from other parts of Ayodhya. According to the BMAC historians the legend that the Babri Masjid occupied the site of Ram's birth did not arise until late eighteenth century. 'The full blown legend of the destruction of a temple at the site of Ram's birth and Sita-Ki-Rasoi is as late as the 1850s. Since then what we get is merely the progressive reconstruction of imagined history based on faith,' the note concluded.

The last meeting of the committee was held on 6 February 1991. In fact, it was a time-consuming exercise that only served to buy some time, which the Chandra Shekhar government wanted for its continuance. The VHP, on the other hand, also needed some breathing space. At that time the BJP included the temple issue in its election manifesto and committed itself to constructing the Ram temple at the disputed site in Ayodhya. On 4 April 1991, lakhs of VHP supporters gathered at the Boat Club in Delhi to participate in a Vishal Hindu Sammelan held there. It was said to be the biggest ever rally in Delhi. The Lok Sabha election, which was halfway through, was deferred following Rajiv Gandhi's assassination in May 1991. It was completed in June and the Congress formed the government at the Centre while the

BJP came to power for the first time in UP. From then on, a whole new ball game began in which I happened to be the central figure—victim, villain, call me what you will.

*

It is indeed amazing how, within a year and a half, many people in the country forgot the first attack on the Babri structure in 1990 and what happened at that time. It is even stranger because the Janata Dal government, after receiving the full support of the BJP on the anti-Congress plank in the 1989 Lok Sabha election, lost that support suddenly and got voted out within a few months of its formation, mainly because of the BJP's opposition. The sole reason, as is well known, was the temple issue. In their first flush of anti-Congress bonhomie, they had forgotten that they were approaching the people in the 1989 election on contradictory—or potentially contradictory—promises (or what could easily develop into that contradiction) on this issue. Since there was pressure on both sides for doing things contrary to each other, and they discovered that conciliation was impossible, V.P. Singh's government was—since it had to be—brought down as the inevitable logic of their respective commitments to the electorate. Be that as it may, what led to the crisis were the Ayodhya events of October-November 1990. In particular, I would like to make a pointed reference to the manner in which Mulayam Singh Yadav handled the Ayodhya situation as Chief Minister of UP and how, in the face of their contradictory commitments, the Janata Dal and the BJP had to fall out and become implacable opponents, ending their close friendship forged only on the anti-Congress front, with nothing else of substantive nature in common in their views.

7

Ayodhya 1992: The Building Blocks of Dispute

In December 1990, at the instance of Prime Minister Chandra Shekhar, negotiations were started between the VHP and the BMAC to address the issue. Four meetings were held and papers on each side's respective claim exchanged. At the third meeting it was decided that the papers categorized under the Historical, Archaeological, Revenue-related and Legal headings, would be examined by experts proposed by both parties. These experts met on 24 January 1991. While there was disagreement on many points, the fourth meeting on 6 February 1991 resolved that the government would compare the papers, as presented by both the parties, with the originals, and attest their authenticity. It was further resolved that each party would submit its viewpoints and its experts' analysis of the view of the opposite party. While the VHP submitted its statement of case on 24 February 1991, the BMAC did not make its presentation at that time but did so on 13 May 1991, by which time, with the resignation of the Chandra Shekhar government, the talks had been discontinued.

Meanwhile, we had elections to the Lok Sabha in May 1991, at which the Congress party made the following formulation in its election manifesto. This formulation became the commitment of the Congress party and was expressed as hereunder:

> Ramjanmabhoomi–Babri Masjid: The Congress is

committed to finding a negotiated settlement of this issue, which fully respects the sentiments of both communities involved. If such a settlement cannot be reached, all parties must respect the order and verdict of the court. The Congress is for the construction of the Temple without dismantling the Mosque.

I reiterated the above commitment of the Congress party during the election campaign, in my public address to the people on 15 August 1991 and on many other occasions, in unequivocal terms.

In June 1991, the elections brought a Congress government to power at the Centre, and a Bharatiya Janata Party government in Uttar Pradesh, which declared its commitment to the construction of the temple.

The BJP Government in UP took certain steps like the acquisition of land adjoining the disputed structure and demolition of certain other structures, including temples standing on the acquired land. The focus of the temple construction movement from October 1991 onwards was to start construction of the temple by way of *kar seva* on the land acquired by the Government of UP while leaving the disputed structure intact. However, this was not legally tenable as the acquired land was subject to court orders prohibiting any permanent construction and also because a plan of the proposed temple released by the VHP envisaged the location of the *sanctum sanctorum* of the temple at the very site of the disputed structure.

The Government of India's stand in the matter was that it favoured a negotiated solution of the dispute and if such a negotiated solution was not possible, all concerned should abide by the orders of the court. The Government of India was for the construction of the temple in Ayodhya while leaving the disputed structure intact. Towards this end it maintained constant pressure on the State Government to ensure that the disputed structure remained secure and that no construction activity was taken up in violation of the court orders.

At a meeting of the National Integration Council on 2 November 1991, the Chief Minister of Uttar Pradesh Kalyan Singh affirmed:

> As regards the disputed structure, I want to make it clear that as I assured you the entire responsibility of the protection of that disputed structure is ours, we will be vigilant about the protection of that structure and have strengthened the arrangements for its protection. Nobody will be able to go there now. In the incident that took place, three persons had climbed atop the dome, but now repetition of any such incident will not be permitted there. I want to convey this assurance to you through this Council. On the whole, it is our clear submission regarding the Court that we will abide by the order that has been given by the Court. We are bound by the order of the Court, we do not want to do anything by violating its order.

The Chief Minister gave four specific assurances of which the National Integration Council took note. These were:

i) All efforts would be made to find an amicable resolution to the issue;
ii) Pending a final solution, the Government of Uttar Pradesh would hold itself fully responsible for the protection of the Ramjanmabhoomi–Babri Masjid structure;
iii) Orders of the court in regard to the land acquisition proceedings would be fully implemented; and
iv) Judgment of the High Court in the cases pending before it would not be violated.

While on the one hand it gave the above assurances, the BJP government, on the other hand, started removing various arrangements for the security of the structure from December

1991 onwards. In February 1992, construction of a boundary wall (named Ram Diwar) enclosing a large area around the RJB–BM including the land acquired in October 1991 was started. In March 1992, the Government of UP leased out approximately 42.09 acres of land acquired in the year 1988-89 purportedly for implementation of the Ram Katha Park project of the previous government, to the VHP-sponsored Ram Janmabhumi Nyas. Between March and May 1992, all other structures on the acquired land were demolished including Sankat Mochan Temple, Sumitra Bhavan, Lomas Ashram, Gopal Bhavan and shops and also the major portion of Sakshi Gopal Temple (except for the room containing the deity and an adjoining room, because of the interim order passed by the High Court). In May 1992, along with this demolition, extensive digging and levelling operations were also commenced in the land around the disputed structure.

The earth dug from the area in front of the RJB–BM structure was transported and dumped on the western and southern sides. The RJB–BM structure had a steep slope on the west, a gradient on the north and south, and level ground on the east. As a result of these digging operations, a depression of 12 feet was caused on the eastern side. These levelling and digging operations led to apprehensions in the minds of many people and caused concern about their possible effect on the strength and safety of the RJB–BM structure. Fear was also expressed that the collection of water during the rains in the dug-up ground could seep into the foundations of the structure and weaken it. Similarly, the dumping of earth upto the height of the perimeter wall and fencing around the structure could render these preventive security arrangements ineffective. These aspects were repeatedly brought to the notice of the State Government by the Central Government, but with no effect.

Feeling aggrieved, the petitioners of the pending petition (Mohd. Hashim vs. State of UP) filed another application for restraining the State Government from undertaking/continuing digging and levelling operations. The High Court, however, refused to stay these operations, believing in the assurances given and repeated before it by the State Government towards the security of the structure.

By July 1992, the decks were cleared by the Government of UP for the BJP and VHP to renew their attempt to undertake construction of the proposed temple. The VHP announced its programme to start construction by way of *kar seva* on a part of the acquired land on a large scale. On 9 July 1992, the construction of a concrete platform was commenced by the *kar sevaks*. It was openly declared by the VHP that it was being constructed as a *singh dwar*, i.e. the main gate of the temple. (It was obliquely hinted that the temple would ultimately have a projection on the Central dome of the structure, forming the *garbha griha* of the temple).

An application for stoppage of construction activities was immediately filed before the High Court in the pending petition (WP No. 3540/1991). This time the court passed the following orders on 15 July 1992 prohibiting undertaking or continuing construction activities on the acquired land which was the subject matter of the writ petition:

> In the meantime, the opposite parties are restrained from undertaking or continuing any construction activity on the land in question. If it becomes necessary for the opposite parties to undertake any such activity, they will seek prior permission from the Court.

In the affidavit filed before the High Court (in Writ Petition No. 3540 of 1991) also, the Government of UP asserted that any attempt to use force with a large assembled crowd of sants and sadhus, and minor children and other pilgrims might result in breach of peace, bloodshed and loss of innocent lives.

However, despite the Government of UP repeatedly giving detailed and specific assurances on the security of the structure and on the implementation of the Court's orders, the construction of the platform continued unabated, rather on a bigger scale. The Government of India took up this matter with the Government of UP to ensure that the orders of the court were implemented. The Home Minister of India personally visited Ayodhya on 12 July 1992 to take stock of the situation arising from this construction as also the security arrangements made for the RJB–BM structure. He emphasized the need to augment the security of the disputed structure to the UP Chief Minister and various measures were suggested towards this, including making the close circuit TV operational. It was also observed that the police control room that had been shifted from the original location was working from a temporary location, which was rather small and at a longer distance. The Chief Minister of UP reacted favourably to the Union Home Minister's visit and promised to implement the suggestions made. The NIC meeting on 18 July 1992 devoted its attention to these developments.

Through a Contempt Petition, a prayer was made to the Supreme Court for prohibiting the construction work. The Supreme Court of India also took notice of the construction work in its proceedings on 22 and 23 July and reiterated that the existing orders of the High Court and Supreme Court had the effect of restraining the parties from undertaking any construction on this land and passed an interim order on the same on 23 July 1992. The operative part of the order reads as under:

> So far as the question of imposing a restraint on the continuation of the work is concerned, there are already earlier orders of the Court as well as of the High Court of Allahabad, which interdict any constructions. What we are examining in these proceedings is the very complaint that those earlier orders have been flouted and disobeyed by the respondents. As there are already existing express orders of the Courts interdicting further constructions, there

is, in these proceedings concerned with consideration of the question of consequences of their disobedience, no point in adding to the series of orders already passed, except to say that the orders already made, have that effect.

Thus, despite the fact that the land under acquisition was in the possession of the State Government and there was so much controversy regarding the acquisition and subsequent activities on this land, the situation had step by step been allowed to escalate to a point where construction activity was proceeding despite court orders restraining it, and the State Government said that it was helpless to stop the activity. Ultimately, the Chief Minister had to request that the Home Minister or I should intervene and persuade the sadhus and sants to comply with the orders of the court.

Since the situation had become very critical and the State Government had expressed its inability to do anything and had, in fact, requested me and the Home Minister to intervene, I had a meeting with the religious leaders on 23 July 1992. I drew the attention of the delegation to the serious situation created by the non-compliance with the court orders and said that we would be in a position to begin the process of dialogue only after the construction activity came to a halt. It was only following this meeting that the construction was ceased on 26 July 1992.

In my statement to Parliament on 27 July 1992 (the full text of which is given in Appendix IV), I affirmed that the efforts of the Central Government had been to 'defuse the situation, avoid a confrontationist approach and to bring about a reconciliation of the views of the various concerned parties'. I confirmed that I had been making preliminary soundings for some time past towards an amicable settlement through negotiations. In addition to these, I would revive the efforts in this regard by the previous government that had remained unfinished. In case it became necessary, the litigation pending in various courts on the subject would be consolidated and considered by one judicial authority, whose decision would be binding on all parties.

Thereafter, I reiterated the commitment of the Congress party given in its election manifesto to 'finding a negotiated settlement to this issue which fully respects the sentiments of both the communities involved. If such a settlement cannot be reached, all parties must respect the order and verdict of the court. The Congress is for construction of the temple without dismantling the mosque.'

In the end, I expressed hope for the future and made a passionate appeal in the following terms:

> I hope this will pave the way for arriving at an agreed solution to the problem and bring about an amicable settlement of this long-standing issue. Therefore, I appeal to all political parties and all sections of the people to help in strengthening the traditional values of religious tolerance and in maintaining peace, tranquillity and communal harmony.

As a follow-up measure, a special cell on Ayodhya was set up in the Prime Minister's Office which started its work of collection, authentication and examination of the records relating to the negotiations started by the previous government, and preparation of summaries of cases sought to be established by the two sides. It also set about its task of collecting details of cases pending in the High Court and the Supreme Court relating to the dispute, notwithstanding the difficulty that the Union of India was not a party to most of the proceedings. Special arrangements were made to obtain copies of important documents and orders relating to these cases and arrangements put in place for regular monitoring of the proceedings in the Supreme Court and the High Court.

Simultaneously, I held a large number of meetings with individuals and groups directly concerned with the dispute, as well as journalists, political, religious and social leaders. The discussions I held facilitated a better understanding of the position of the parties concerned and enabled various sections of them to put forward their own insights into the various facets of the problem. No specific proposal or suggestion for a solution was put forward on behalf of the government, whose endeavour was to be accessible and open to any ideas that might contribute to a settlement. These consultations, backed by the examination of the record by the special cell on Ayodhya, helped prepare the ground for the start of the negotiations. On the eve of the resumption of these talks, I wrote to the leaders of all recognized parties requesting their support, the text of which letter is given in Appendix V.

According to my detailed statement in both the Houses of Parliament on 27 July 1992, the process of negotiations for finding an amicable settlement to the RJB–BM issue was recommenced.

Resumption of Negotiations

The negotiations between the BMAC and the VHP resumed with the first meeting on 3 October 1992, which was held under the chairmanship of the Union Home Minister. Both the organizations responded favourably to the invitation. The meetings were attended by the office-bearers and representatives of these organizations as well as by historical and archaeological experts nominated by them.

This meeting picked up the thread of the negotiations where it was left off in February 1991. The statement of the case of the VHP presented on 24 February 1991 and the report of historians presented by the BMAC in May 1991 were exchanged between the two sides and it was decided that they would respond to them. A questionnaire was addressed by the VHP to the BMAC. A resolution was unanimously adopted in this meeting urging the continuation of the negotiations and calling upon the two sides to furnish further evidence and written appraisal of the evidence presented by the other side. The date for the next meeting was fixed and it was agreed that the two sides would maintain peace while the negotiations were on.

In the second meeting on 16 October 1992, the BMAC presented a questionnaire addressed to the VHP. Several decisions aimed at making the negotiations more purposeful were taken in this meeting. The cut-off date of 23 October 1992 was fixed for giving written opinions on the material and the evidence presented upto 16 October to the government. The same cut-off date was made applicable to the submission of fresh evidence. It was agreed that copies of material and evidence furnished by either side by this date would be made available to the other side by 24 October 1992. The final cut-off date of 29 October 1992 was fixed for furnishing of comments on the evidence submitted by 23 October. The date for the next meeting was not fixed, but it was accepted that there would be another meeting, the date for which would be announced by the government.

Two controversies relating to archaeology and history were raised in this meeting. The VHP objected to the historians nominated by the BMAC describing themselves as 'independent'. The VHP historians stuck to their stand that the report given by the nominees of the BMAC in May 1991 could not, therefore, be considered as a statement of the case by the BMAC and hence the VHP was not bound to respond to it. The other controversy related to the excavations conducted by Prof. B.B. Lal at Ayodhya during 1975-80. According to the VHP he had discovered a series of pillar bases in the vicinity of the RJB–BM structure; a finding which, according to the VHP, supported its claim. The BMAC, however, challenged the authenticity of this finding as the historians nominated by it had not been allowed to verify the original record and material relating to this excavation.

The first controversy was settled when the BMAC formally adopted the report of May 1991 by the historians nominated by it and the VHP agreed that it would respond to it.

The second controversy was settled by giving experts of both sides an opportunity to examine the material record as decided in this meeting. The material relating to the excavations conducted by Prof. B.B. Lal including photographs, drawings, pottery, register of antiquities etc. was made available to the experts of both sides in the offices of the ASI on 23 October 1992. The experts of both sides examined the material and gave their comments to the government by 29 October.

Developments between 23 October and 8 November 1992

As decided in the meeting of 16 October, each side furnished its statement of the case and comments on the evidence furnished by the other side to the government by 29 October.

The government, in consultation with the two sides, fixed the date of the next meeting as 8 November 1992. Crucial decisions were expected from this meeting as the work of presentation of evidence and offering comments on it was over.

It was at this point that in a sudden and unexpected move, the Kendriya Marga Darshak Mandal of the VHP met in New Delhi, followed by a Dharm Sansad between 29 and 31 October 1992, and announced the call for resumption of *kar seva* from 6 December 1992. This move was totally inexplicable in view of the smooth movement of the negotiations as detailed in the foregoing paragraph. The only explanation imaginable could be that the intention of this unilateral announcement was to disrupt the course of the negotiation and prevent the expected reference of the dispute to the Supreme Court, thus dragging the matter into confrontation again. Since then, various representatives of the VHP and related organizations reiterated the call for resumption of the *kar seva*, and hectic preparations were immediately commenced for the *kar seva*.

Stone chips, sand and other construction material were already available in the RJB–BM complex at the site of the Sheshavtar Lakshman Temple. Additional construction material was available in other locations in Ayodhya. Two concrete mixers were also available in the RJB–BM complex. An opening approximately 16 feet wide had been made in the boundary wall near the Sheshavtar Lakshman Temple. Reportedly, this was adequate for movement of men and machinery. Wooden logs were erected in a straight line from about 20 feet south of the south-east comer of the iron pipe barricading of the disputed structure up to the western perimeter wall.

Though earlier arrangements were made to accommodate 50,000 *kar sevaks* at a time, it soon appeared that about 100,000 *kar sevaks* would arrive by 4–5 December 1992. A total of 750 tents for accommodating the *kar sevaks* had been pitched mainly in the Ram Katha Kunj, in the immediate vicinity of the RJB–BM complex. The plans were that a large number of *kar sevaks* should be available at very short notice in the RJB–BM complex.

Both the BMAC and VHP delegations attended the meeting on 8 November 1992. The BMAC circulated a letter protesting against the announcement of *kar seva* from 6 December, and said that the negotiations would be meaningless unless this announcement was withdrawn. The VHP was not willing to consider any change in its programme of the resumption of *kar seva*. Because of the rigidity exhibited at this meeting, it was considered advisable not to pursue the decisions expected at this meeting earlier when the atmosphere had been cordial. Such a course would perhaps have made matters even more difficult. So it was considered safer to adjourn the meeting and pursue the matter in separate meetings with both groups, with a view to keeping the process intact even after the setback and to deal with effects of the setback in due course.

A series of meetings were held with representatives of the VHP, BMAC, the leaders of the BJP and the Chief Minister of UP to narrow down the differences. When these failed, attempts were made to get an agreement on a reference to the Supreme Court on the contentious issues. Alternatives of making this reference under Article 138 (2) of the Constitution as well as under Article 143 were put forth by the government. Adjudication of the dispute by the Supreme Court under Articles 139 and 142 of the Constitution was also suggested. There was no agreement even on these suggestions. The Government of UP in particular refused to give its consent under Article 138 (2) for enlargement of the jurisdiction of the Supreme Court. This consent is mandatory as per the Article of the Constitution.

The Central Government, on its part, however, made a determined bid to keep the dialogue going in order to end the impasse. I held a meeting with Kalyan Singh on 18 and then again on 19 November consecutively before departing for Senegal to attend a G-15 meeting. But Kalyan Singh refused to budge from his stand that the only comprehensive solution to the Ayodhya dispute was to hand over the disputed structure to Hindus. The *Times of India*, in its issue dated 20 November reported, 'The Chief Minister told Mr Rao that Muslims could be persuaded to give their consent for constructing the mosque about 15 km to 20 km away from the disputed structure for which the UP Government was prepared to provide land and other help.' It was not difficult to understand the change of intentions that led to this *volte face* at the last moment.

It further reported that 'Mr Singh told Mr Rao that the Muslims had not staked any claim on the 2.77 acres of land. Therefore, there should be no hindrance in allowing the kar seva in the area. The Chief Minister requested the Centre to make an appeal to the Allahabad High Court to deliver its judgment on the acquisition of the 2.77-acre land and said the State Government would make a similar appeal to the Court.'

Immediately thereafter, a meeting of the Cabinet Committee on Political Affairs of the Central Government was convened.

The CCPA discussed various scenarios and options with the specific intent of ensuring that the country was not faced with a delicate law and order situation. Besides, it found little merit in the BJP's stand contrary to the court's order to de-link the 2.77 acres from the main structure and allow the *kar seva* to be resumed at the site from 6 December.

In the cirumstances, I decided to convene a meeting of the NIC at short notice on 23 November itself. I felt that the NIC would provide the necessary forum for wider consultations in keeping with the government's desire to find a negotiated settlement to the vexed issue.

While the entire non-BJP opposition welcomed the decision to call a meeting of the NIC, the BJP decided to boycott it. Its national executive declared that the NIC had discussed the Ayodhya issue over and over again and no purpose would be served by having yet another discussion. The VHP went further to declare that 'the NIC mostly represented anti-Hindu forces'; its president Vishnu Hari Dalmia told newspersons that the government had convened the NIC meeting mainly to appease the Muslims. Dalmia claimed that the UP Chief Minister Kalyan Singh, during his talks with the Prime Minister a day before, had got the impression that the Centre was adopting a tough posture towards the Hindus. Further, in a joint statement, V.H. Dalmia, the VHP general secretary Ashok Singhal, and the joint general secretary Giriraj Kishore called upon the *kar sevaks* to proceed to Ayodhya by whatever means they could find in case the Centre dismissed the UP Government or ordered a crackdown on the VHP leaders. The leaders asked the *kar sevaks* to reach Ayodhya by 6 December, the day the *kar seva* was proposed to be resumed.

Ever since the announcement of the *kar seva,* various leaders of the Sangh parivar including the VHP, the Bajrang Dal and the RSS made statements in support of it by sants and mahants. These included statements by Ashok Singhal, Paramhans Ramchandra, L.K. Advani, V.H. Dalmia, Kalyan Singh, Prof. Rajendra Singh,

Mahant Avaidyanath, Giriraj Kishore, Murli Manohar Joshi, Govindacharya, Sachidananda Sakshi and Mahant Sevadas. Reports of these statements had been appearing every day in the press. Many statements included veiled threats to the disputed structure if the *kar seva* was stopped or the Uttar Pradesh Government was dismissed. There were also statements that stiff resistance would be offered if the *kar seva* was interfered with. Such statements continued even after an assurance was obtained during the contempt proceedings by the Supreme Court from the Government of Uttar Pradesh that no construction activity or movement of construction material or equipment would take place in the acquired land. Many representatives of the Sangh parivar were critical of the Supreme Court's orders.

M.M. Joshi regretted that courts were being involved in deciding an issue of religious faith. He alleged the misuse of the media for distorting facts and confusing public opinion on the Ram temple and hoped that the Allahabad High Court judgment would be received before 6 December 1992. Govindacharya alleged that I—instead of finding a solution to the issue—had passed it on to the Supreme Court and was interested in the minorities' vote. Sachidananda Sakshi warned that if the UP Government was dismissed the Central Government would also fall, the Babri Masjid would be demolished and communal violence may be unleashed for which the Central Government would be responsible. In a press interview, Prof. Rajendra Singh disclosed that the Sangh parivar had prepared for a direct confrontation with the Central Government but the Centre had brought the court in between. While efforts would be made to honour the court's order, in case the UP Government was dismissed many things may be affected. The yatras of M.M. Joshi and L.K. Advani from Mathura and Varanasi respectively had made it clear that the Sangh parivar had not abandoned its claim on the Krishna Janma Bhoomi and the Kashi Viswanath temple. Acharya Giriraj Kishore said that the *kar seva* would be in the form of cleaning and sweeping the complex but claimed that the VHP had not given any assurance in writing to the UP Government. Mahant Sevadas declared that *kar sevaks* were not afraid of paramilitary forces and he had met religious leaders who had informed him that *kar seva* would be done on the foundation terrace.

L.K. Advani undertook a yatra from Varanasi towards Ayodhya while M.M. Joshi took it from Mathura to Ayodhya. Both leaders made statements in regard to the *kar seva*. L.K. Advani addressed meetings at Mughal Sarai and Varanasi. He described the movement for construction of the Ram temple as a national movement for recapturing the national identity. Crediting the BJP for receiving a massive mandate through enhanced representation in Parliament and in four state governments, he claimed that while the dignity of the Constitution, judiciary and rule of law was always respected by the BJP, the aspirations and the mandate of the people were supreme. The misuse of the judiciary and the suppression of the faith and belief of the people would not be tolerated, he said. He clarified that *kar seva* was not just recitation of bhajans and kirtans but contribution of physical labour, which may be clearing, sweeping and digging holes. He remarked that he was not bothered about the possible dismissal of the UP Government. M.M. Joshi charged that I had complicated the RJB–BM problem and accused me of instigating the Muslims and encouraging the BMAC to oppose the VHP and trying to create schisms among the sants and mahants.

Emphasizing the defiant mood of the BJP, the *Times of India* claimed on 23 November that, 'The senior party leader, Mr Atal Bihari Vajpayee, said the least the Centre could do was to move an application in the Allahabad High Court, seeking an expeditious judgment on the case involving the acquisition of 2.77 acres by the State Government. He said all party MPs and MLAs would participate in the kar seva scheduled to start from 6 December, but ministers in the four BJP-ruled states could do so only after resigning from their offices. The only thing to be seen is whether the kar seva begins peacefully or violently. After all, violation of law has always been a form of protest and struggle for a cause.'

At the same time, L.K. Advani warned the Centre that a confrontation with the UP Government would be politically profitable for the BJP, but would not be in the interest of the country. It might be 'disastrous' for the Congress government at the Centre, he was reported as saying.

The VHP leaders also talked in the same vein. The *Times of India*, dated 23 November, reported thus:

> The Vishwa Hindu Parishad (VHP) today said there were indications that the Centre may dismiss the Uttar Pradesh Government any time from November 25 to 27. The joint general secretary of the VHP, Acharya Giriraj Kishore, told newspersons here that the Centre had sent four companies of CRPF to UP. This had been done without the approval of the State Government. Of these four companies, two had been stationed in Faizabad and two in Lucknow; another 40 companies had been kept as standby in Delhi.
>
> The VHP leader said that, according to information received from UP, about 500 buses of the Delhi Transport Corporation (DTC) had been sent to the state for carrying the Central forces, whenever necessary, to Ayodhya.
>
> He claimed that the Centre was having consultations even with the Governor of Punjab on the possibility of stopping kar sevaks from reaching Ayodhya. According to him, rubber bullets and water jets had been kept ready by the Central forces for use on kar sevaks in Ayodhya. The Rapid Action Force (RAF) had also been alerted.
>
> The VHP leader said the Centre was trying to create instability and if, under such circumstances, the law and order situation in the state got out of control, then the responsibility for this would be that of the Centre.

> Asked about the number of kar sevaks that had so far reached the temple town, the VHP leader said that 10 lakh people had signed the pledge to reach Ayodhya. Refusing to give the number that had already reached Ayodhya, he said on any given day the number of kar sevaks at the construction site would be anything between 60,000 to one lakh.

In Patna, Vijaya Raje Scindia also declared that the Centre would not be given more time to settle the Ramjanmabhoomi–Babri Masjid dispute and *kar seva* at the shrine would begin on 6 December 'at all costs'.

Amidst the boycott of the BJP and VHP, the NIC held its meeting as per schedule on 23 November 1992. A four-line resolution was moved by the CPM leader Harkishan Singh Surjeet, and was adopted by thumping of desks. The resolution stated: 'The NIC meeting after considering all aspects of the Babri Masjid–Ram Janambhoomi dispute and the report of the Government extends its whole-hearted support and cooperation in whatever steps the Prime Minister considers essential in upholding the Constitution and the rule of law and in implementing the Court orders.'

Two former Prime Ministers, Chandra Shekhar and V.P. Singh, were among the main speakers. 'It is time the NIC takes a tough stand because reason has not prevailed. The attitude of the BJP is likely to create a serious law and order situation and any action of the government to uphold the rule of law and the Constitution will be supported by the NIC,' Chandra Shekhar said.

V.P. Singh said, 'We are back to the situation witnessed in July and there is no point in hoping that the BJP-VHP combine would relent at this stage.' This was a challenge to the courts, the Executive and the Parliament, he said. It was the government's responsibility to ensure that court orders were respected and the disputed structure protected. The Government should become a party to the dispute, seek legal advice and requisition the property in Ayodhya, he thought. 'We will stand by any action taken by the government, even dismissal of the UP Government if necessary, to uphold the dignity of the judiciary,' V.P. Singh said, while urging the government to come out with its decision.

Both Houses of the UP Legislature also witnessed noisy scenes following protests and walk-out over the Ayodhya issue by the opposition members. The *Times of India* reported on 25 November: 'Amidst noisy scenes the Chief Minister told the house that he had not attended the NIC meeting because he did not see its utility. He further declared that it was a futile exercise to call the NIC meeting to resolve an issue like Ayodhya, which had not been solved for the last fifty years. Terming the NIC as a "political forum against the BJP", he further added that its meeting was called only to isolate the BJP. "We are committed to build the Ram Temple, as we have been given mandate for this by the people," Sri Kalyan Singh declared.'

Build-up for *kar seva* on 6 December

As pointed out earlier, when large-scale digging, levelling of land and demolition work was done on the land acquired by the Government of UP in early 1992, contempt petitions were filed against the State Government, Chief Minister Kalyan Singh and the Vishwa Hindu Parishad in the Supreme Court. Fresh applications were moved in these petitions when construction of the concrete platform was started on 9 July 1992.

Faced with the 21 October 1992 declaration of the VHP to resume *kar seva* with effect from 6 December 1992, a fresh application in the contempt petition was moved before the Supreme Court on 2 November 1992 expressing grave apprehensions in view of the announcement of *kar seva* from 6 December and praying for passing 'a very strenuous order' restraining the respondents and other functionaries of VHP, BJP and other organizations and the so-called *kar sevaks*, sants, sadhus etc. from committing further contempt of the earlier orders of the Court, to enforce a complete halt to the proposed *kar seva*. The counsel for the petitioners further pleaded for immediate direction to the UP Government to stop lakhs of people from coming to Ayodhya for the proposed *kar seva*. The application also sought directions from the Court to the Central Government to take possession of the site as Receiver or otherwise use para-military or military forces to contain a very serious situation.

In its submissions to the Court through its counsel on the said application on 20 November, the UP Government said that it did not favour immediate coercive action as there were 'ongoing parleys amongst the various groups for settlement.' The *Times of India*, in its issue dated 21 November 1992, reported that:

> Mr Venugopal replied that the negotiations were on between the State Government, the Central Government and others on the proposed kar seva. He read out excerpts from the affidavit which was filed by the UP tourism secretary, Mr Alok Sinha. Meanwhile, Mr O.P. Sharma insisted on a mandamus to the authorities concerned against any other construction on the acquired land and against the proposed December 6 kar seva.
>
> Mr Justice Venkatachaliah also remarked that the UP Government did not seem to be inclined to obey the Court's orders. 'The State Government is lukewarm on implementing the order against any construction near the disputed structure,' remarked the judge. This evoked a sharp comment by Mr Govind Mukhoty, counsel for Mr Acchan Rizvi who has sought contempt action against the Government. 'In fact the State Government is hand in glove with the VHP and others,' the Counsel added. Mr Mukhoty too sought a direction from the Court to injunct the State

Government against permitting congregation of about 10 lakh people for kar seva.

However, Mr Venkatachaliah pointed out that the State Government should itself stop such congregation and assembly of people to start construction. He reminded the State Government's counsel that the court had passed several directives against any construction activities on the acquired land.

In its order passed after hearing the parties at the close of the day on 23 November 1992, the Court took note of the submissions of the parties thus:

Shri Venugopal submitted that the State Government is second to none in its anxiety to ensure the enforcement of the orders of this Court. He stated that as there are on-going parleys amongst the various groups for settlement, any contemplation of immediate coercive action on the part of the Government might, according to him, be counter-productive. The State Government would be able to spell out its programme of action to ensure obedience by about the end of this month when it will be able to know or reasonably anticipate the possible outcome of the parleys . . .

Shri Govind Mukhoty and Shri Sharma, learned senior counsels appearing for the petitioner-complainants expressed serious concern over the developing situation and sought to recollect what happened in the month of July, 1992, where, according to them, adjournments were taken advantage of to present the petitioners with a 'fait accompli'. We appreciate the concern expressed by the learned counsel. At the same time, we request all the learned counsel to serve to shed an adversarial approach in the matter and assist the Court in a way which will not disturb social equilibrium.

On consideration of the stand taken by the parties, the Court further directed that 'we think it is necessary for the Union Government to indicate its stand in the matter so that we may have its assistance in making such orders as would ensure enforcement of the earlier orders of this Court. We, therefore, direct the Attorney General/Solicitor General to be present in Court at 2 p.m. on Monday, the 23rd November, 1992.'

Perhaps on the basis of the observations made during the Court proceedings of the day, the *Times of India* on 21 November reported that 'The Supreme Court today issued a notice to the Solicitor General of India to appear on Monday and inform about the Central Government's stand on whether it can be appointed the Receiver to the 2.77 acre acquired land near the disputed structures at Ayodhya. This direction was passed on the submission by Mr O.P. Sharma, counsel for a contempt petitioner, who wanted an immediate direction to the UP Government to stop lakhs of people who may be participating in the proposed kar seva on December 6.'

On resuming the hearing on 23 November the Supreme Court asked the UP Government to clear its stand by 25 November on the proposed *kar seva* to be resumed from 6 December and to inform it about the steps proposed to be taken for implementing the directives against any construction on the acquired land near the disputed structure in Ayodhya.

The Court passed the order after the Solicitor General of India, Dipankar Gupta, stated that although maintenance of law and order was primarily the State Government's duty, the Central Government would give all possible help in view of the situation. While giving this assurance, he referred to statements published in newspapers indicating that *kar sevaks* would start pouring into Ayodhya from 27 November to participate in the proposed *kar seva* from 6 December.

Reporting the Court proceedings in detail, the *Times of India* pointed out that the apex court had in the past issued directives to the UP Chief Minister, Kalyan Singh, and the state administration not to allow any construction on the acquired land and prevent *kar sevaks* from doing so. The paper reminded that despite these, *kar seva* did take place in July and *kar sevaks* constructed a concrete platform, the *singh dwar* of the multi-crore worth temple proposed to be constructed by the VHP, the Bajrang Dal and other like-minded organizations.

Even as the judges were still considering whether Kalyan Singh and the State Government were liable for contempt of court for allowing the *kar seva* and construction, O.P. Sharma, a counsel for the petitioners—Acchan Rizvi and Mohd. Aslam—sought fresh directives saying that about 10 lakh people were expected to reach Ayodhya to participate in the event. He recalled the repeated instances of the defiance of the Court's directives by the State Government.

Govind Mukhoty, another counsel for the petitioners who were litigating for hauling up the Chief Minister and others for committing contempt of court, strongly objected to any adjournment sought by the State Government's counsel, K.K. Venugopal. The counsel said the State Government had been taking advantage of the adjournments to 'present the petitioners with a fait accompli'.

While expressing the Court's concern on the developing situation at Ayodhya, Justice M.N. Venkatachaliah and Justice G.N. Ray asked K.K. Venugopal to state categorically whether the State Government would comply with its orders. The counsel said he would seek instructions from the authorities concerned and inform the Court on 25 November.

However, Venugopal urged the Court to pass an order asking the Allahabad High Court Bench, which had reserved its verdict on the legality of the acquisition of the 2.77 acres of land, to deliver the verdict soon. At least the High Court should pass a decretal order, K.K. Venugopal said. He reiterated that the proposed congregation at Ayodhya would not be affected if the

High Court either affirmed legality of the acquisition or declared it illegal. The land, the counsel said, belonged to the Ram Janmabhoomi Shilanyas Trust, which was set up to ensure completion of the temple.

K.K. Venugopal further added that it was regrettable that despite the apex court's request to the High Court to dispose of the matter expeditiously, the High Court had treated it like any other issue. If the High Court's judgment had come by now, 'there would not have been any political crisis', the counsel added. The judges reminded him that the Court was concerned about the legal issues involved in the matter, and not political ones.

The Solicitor General clarified that the Centre did not want the incidents of July at Ayodhya to recur. The Central Government was of the firm view that no congregation should take place on the acquired land, nor should any construction work start there, he declared. He also requested the Court that the machinery and material required for construction should not be allowed to reach the disputed structures at Ayodhya. 'The situation on the ground is escalating day by day,' he informed the Court and urged an urgent order to avert an ugly situation.

While disapproving disobedience of its orders by the State Government, the judges observed that 'whatever might be the might of the political parties, we are not worth our salt if this kind of thing is allowed to happen.'

'The time of reckoning has now come,' Justice Venkatachaliah told K.K. Venugopal. 'Don't you think this kind of defiance by the political parties weakens the democratic structure? We have had enough of it,' the judge warned the State Government.

Referring to the instances of defiance by the State Government, Justice Venkatachaliah remarked, 'We are not on the political side of the issue. The political parties can do what they want. We are only concerned with your state (UP) in taking steps to comply with our orders.'

Saying that it was a national problem, K.K. Venugopal claimed that this 'controversy' should not have been in existence at all. He said the petitioners had no *locus standi* to seek the Court's order against the congregation or construction of the temple.

Justice Venkatachaliah again told him that judicial procedure could not 'buckle under any kind of pressure'. But the counsel said the Court should not have issued the order on 15 July. 'The country should not be thrown into a ferment on a non-issue, such as acquisition of land by the State Government,' he declared and disclosed that the State Government had filed a petition seeking a review of the Court's earlier directives.

Justice Venkatachaliah, however, maintained that the Court was not concerned whether the temple should be constructed at Ayodhya or not, but it was concerned about the majesty of the institution. He said nobody had approached the Court to solve the problem.

Replying to the Court's query about the stand of the Central Government, Dipankar Gupta said the government could sit with the UP Government in the next few days to work out what kind of help it needed.

Affirming faith in the Supreme Court, Dipankar Gupta said the Central Government was of the view that the orders passed by the apex court must be honoured by all. He denied that intensive negotiations were going on with the UP Government or with any other organization. The talks between the Babri Masjid Action Committee and the Vishwa Hindu Parishad had already failed, he added.

The widespread concern over a possible confrontation once the threatened resumption of *kar seva* at Ayodhya took place was brought into focus on the opening day of Parliament held on 24 November. In the Lok Sabha, the BJP reaffirmed its demand for de-linking the problem of the disputed structure from construction work at the 2.77-acre plot adjacent to the shrine acquired by the UP Government, even as leaders of the CPM,

CPI, Janata Dal and Samajwadi Janata Party urged the main Opposition party to reconsider its stand.

Chandra Shekhar (SJP), former Prime Minister, sought a categorical assurance that the BJP would abide by the judicial verdict in respect of the shrine and agree not to do anything about the structure until then so that the problem could be settled peacefully. He warned that the country would have to pay a heavy price if the issue was further complicated. To this, L.K. Advani said, 'The structure would be protected.'

The Supreme Court resumed hearing on the contempt petition after the expiry of the two days' time given to the State Government on 25 November. The Attorney General of India, Milon Banerji, objected to the adjournment granted to the state. He pointed out that the situation in Ayodhya had reached a 'boiling point' and added that the State Government should be asked to defer *kar seva* in view of the ongoing adjudication by the court. Referring to the intelligence reports, Milon Banerji submitted that there had been a 'tremendous build-up' in Ayodhya and warned that even one day of adjournment could prove costly. The Attorney General declared that the Central Government was keen to offer all possible assistance to the Kalyan Singh government, adding that the Central Government did not want to interfere with the State administration, but would not hesitate to perform its Constitutional duty to implement the Court orders. He further pointed out that though the Special Secretary of UP (Home) Shekhar Aggarwal had filed an affidavit affirming that the State Government was duty-bound to obey the Court orders, the State Government had at the same time stated that use of force to prevent *kar seva* will not be appropriate.

After holding an elaborate hearing, the Court passed a detailed order which in effect took note of the pleading of all the parties, as under:

In response, Shri Venugopal has filed an affidavit by the Special Secretary to the Home Department of the Uttar Pradesh Government, in which, inter alia, it is stated:

'The State Government has been giving grave and anxious consideration to the situation arising from the call given for resumption of kar seva on the acquired land. The State Government agrees that the duty of preventing the violation of orders of the Court lies on it and is its reponsibility.'

Then adverting to certain delicate and sensitive issues, as the state perceives them, involved in the handling of the situation and to the possibility that any decision to exert force, might result in a very grave situation and the braving of disastrous consequences which might become irreversible, the affidavit proceeds to say:

'The State of UP would therefore be seeking direct negotiations with the leaders of the VHP and the leaders of the Dharm Sansad for the purpose. So that the solution for achieving the religious aspirations should be achieved without violating the orders of the Court. If this were to be done, the State Government will need at least a week to report to the Court the outcome of its negotiations with the leaders mentioned earlier.'

It appears to us that if no assurance of an effective implementation of the Court's orders is forthcoming from the State Government, it will be our Constitutional duty not merely to expect but to exact obedience in an appropriate manner. This step, we believe, would become necessary to preserve the meaning and integrity of the Constitutional institutions and their inter-relationships, essential to the preservation of the chosen way of life of the Indian people under the Constitution.

Shri Venugopal shared our concern and expressed the hope—he was not in a position to hold out any more than that at this stage—that given a week's time, the Government would negotiate with the religious groups to avoid a collision course and persuade them to take a rational view of the situation.

Learned Attorney General who was present at our request, and the learned counsel appearing for the petitioners in the contempt petitions, say that the situation is already almost out of control and that any further delay might make the situation irreversible in practical terms from the point of view of management of the situation.

The Central Government is, of course, at liberty to make its own assessment of the matter and take such action on its own as may appear to it proper and permissible.

We do notice from the submissions of Shri Venugopal that the situation is not without its emotive surcharges; but it is at these trying times the capacity for statesmanship of those who bear the burden of Government is put to test. They should display statesmanship and deal with matters in such a way that would not result in the destruction of Constitutional institutions and in the upsetting of social equilibrium. However, we make it clear to Shri Venugopal that if the State Government is not in a position to come forward with a convincing stand that will reassure the Court that no violation of its orders will be permitted, we might have to consider the prayers in IA No. 5 for the appointment of a Receiver or directions to the Central Government to ensure obedience to the Court orders. We do hope that the State of Uttar Pradesh will not compel the Court to take that course, leaving it no other option.

The Court then passed the following order:

In view of the serious situation pointed out by the learned Attorney General, it may not be proper to adjourn the matter for seven days as sought by the State Government.

It will be reasonable to adjourn the matter till Friday 2.00 p.m. on the assurance of Shri Venugopal that the honesty of purpose on the part of the State Government to pursue the negotiations with the religious groups carries with it an implicit assurance that, in the meanwhile, the ground realities would not be altered to the detriment of the Court orders. Shri Venugopal said the State Government would seek to persuade the religious groups to defer kar seva till after the pronouncement of the High Court or at least for a reasonable time in future. If any constructive response is forthcoming from the State Government, we might, in order to strengthen the hands of the State Government in its handling of the religious groups, consider making appropriate request to the High Court in the matter of a need for most expeditious decision on the matter.

The same day, 26 November, addressing a Congress parliamentary party meeting, I informed that the temple dispute had reached a 'crucial state' with the VHP already having given orders to *kar sevaks* to gather in large numbers in Ayodhya on 27 and 28 November and the Supreme Court about to intervene in the matter. I pointed out that not much time was left before the *kar seva*. The deliberate intention of the State Government appeared to be to delay the Court intervention and thus sabotage the move for a peaceful resolution of the dispute, I told the gathering.

The next day, 27 November, the *Times of India* published an interview with the UP Chief Minister Kalyan Singh, accusing the Centre of 'complicating the Ayodhya tangle by deploying para-military forces in UP without the State Government's concurrence.'

'I fail to understand the urgency for sending these forces in such a large number when there is no need for it. The law and order situation is perfectly under control. This has only vitiated the atmosphere,' he added.

'The Centre's move is indicative of its confrontationist attitude. The confrontation is not only against UP and the State Government but against the federal structure of the Constitution, democratic institutions and the people of the country,' declared Kalyan Singh.

Asked whether his government was likely to be dismissed, he said, 'Not at all.' Any such move would be suicidal for the Centre, he added.

Defending his stand, he said there was no reason why his government should be dismissed. 'It is a democratically elected government discharging its duties under the Constitution and making an all-out effort for the welfare of the people. The law and order situation is normal and there is no cause for concern on any front, which goes to the discredit of the government.' Sending para-military forces had only made the people panicky, he said. The Centre had also put the Army on alert and issued instructions for immediate deployment of seventy-five companies of the CRPF from Punjab, Assam and Delhi, besides keeping the BSF ready for movement at short notice. The Rapid Action Force (RAF) had also been kept ready at its base office in Meerut. Fifteen top officials of the Central forces held a meeting a few days ago to chalk out their strategy, Kalyan Singh disclosed. He also confirmed that the Centre had hired more than 300 DTC buses to transport the Central security personnel.

Reiterating that the disputed structure would be protected, the Chief Minister said security had been beefed up in Ayodhya. He said his government, though committed to honour the Court order, would not use force to stop the *kar seva*, scheduled to begin on 6 December. It would only lead to a severe law and order problem throughout the country, he reasoned. The issue was extremely volatile and its solution was possible only through cooperation, not confrontation, he added.

Taking a dig at the High Court, Kalyan Singh declared that the State Government's efforts had already brought the dispute near to a solution. But the delay in disposal of the case by the

Allahabad High Court had resulted in an impasse, he claimed.

Though the Supreme Court had on the last date fixed 27 November as the next date for hearing, on 26 November a request for a restraint order was again made by the petitioners before the Supreme Court. The petitioners' counsel, Govind Mukhoty and O.P. Sharma, referred to the morning *Times of India* carrying a front-page interview with the VHP leader, P.N. Singh. It said the VHP had started sending *kar sevaks* to Ayodhya and indicated that the *kar seva* programme may be preponed. Another news item published in the *Hindustan Times* quoting the vice president of the BJP, Krishan Lal Sharma, was also produced for the judges' perusal. K.L. Sharma was reported to have said that *kar seva* would not be stopped at any cost.

K.K. Venugopal, counsel for Chief Minister Kalyan Singh, said he would be filing a detailed affidavit the following day about the prevailing situation in Ayodhya. The State Government would also indicate the steps it proposed to take to implement the orders. Expressing their dissatisfaction over the State Government's reply, the petitioners' counsel reiterated that the Central Government should be appointed Receiver of the acquired land and the disputed structure at Ayodhya. However, Justice Venkatachaliah, who headed the three-judge bench, ruled out any directive now but said the Court would wait for the State Government's affidavit expected the next day.

On the next date of the continued hearing, i.e. 27 November, the Government of Uttar Pradesh took the stand that it was negotiating with various parties. Its affidavit dated 27 November 1992, *inter alia*, stated the following:

> The process of negotiations with various parties has been initiated by the State Government. The response has been positive. The State Government is now confident that as long as the Writ Petitions regarding acquisition are pending and the interim orders of High Court are in force, no

construction, permanent or temporary, will take place, though to allay the religious aspirations of the Ram Bhakts, kar seva other than by way of construction, as stated, may take place.

This stand of the State Government that there should be no violation of the Court orders while performing *kar seva* was supported by Swami Chinmayananda, BJP MP and functionary of the VHP in a letter annexed to the affidavit of the State Government.

The UP Government opposed the offer of Central assistance for maintaining law and order in Ayodhya and also asserted that, 'The assistance of force offered by the Central Government is not necessary in the present circumstances. The UP Government has an enviable record of maintaining law and order and communal harmony in the State.'

The State Government also pleaded in the affidavit that it was committed to protect the 'Ramjanmabhoomi structure', and affirmed that there was no need to entrust any other authority with the task of implementing the Court's order. It also sought to play upon the concern of the Court by adding that, 'If any other authority is so entrusted, it will amount to abandonment of the course of negotiation or persuasion and is likely to lead to avoidable use of force.'

Justice Venkatachaliah at this juncture observed that the congregation of lakhs in Ayodhya without any occasion or festival 'creates apprehension in our mind'. He pointed out that even in July, under the 'guise' of *kar seva* a lot of construction activity took place near the disputed structure. If lakhs of people congregated and started construction, it would be difficult to stop them, he said.

The State Government also gave the undertaking to the Court that 'It will ensure that no construction machinery or construction material will move into the acquired land and no construction activity will take place or be carried out as long as the interim order of the High Court is in force in the writ petition pending before it relating to the land acquisition.'

In its order dated 28 November 1992, the Supreme Court took note of the above undertaking and the further assurance of the State Government that 'in the name of kar seva no construction activity, either temporary or permanent, would take place or be allowed to take place on the acquired land' and that 'the kar seva would be a symbolic occasion for carrying on certain religious activities to assuage the feelings of the devotees and will not be exploited for any constructional activity, symbolic or otherwise.' The Court further noted that 'the State Government has come forward with an emphatic assurance and undertaking that the orders of the High Court will be obeyed and implemented and that no constructional activity will be carried on or permitted to be carried on by whatsoever agency on the acquired land.'

In order to ensure compliance of its orders and to monitor the implementation of the undertaking given by the BJP government, the Supreme Court was further pleased to appoint an Observer, out of the members of the Higher Judiciary of the state of UP; Tej Shankar, the then District Judge of Moradabad, was posted at Ayodhya itself and was directed to keep a constant watch over the developments in the acquired land and to keep on reporting these developments, especially any untoward development or anything indicating the possibility of violation of Court orders, directly to the Supreme Court without any delay.

In an attempt to clear the prevailing confusion amongst a section of the BJP and VHP leadership about the nature of *kar seva* commencing in Ayodhya on 6 December, the Supreme Court on 29 November urged the State Government's counsel K.K. Venugopal to advise the authorities concerned to publish and clarify that *kar seva* would not mean any construction activity.

The Court reassembled to consider the situation as scheduled on 30 November. It considered the telephonic report of the Court Observer. Then, referring to its earlier order dated 28 November providing for giving publicity to the nature of *kar seva* permitted to be made on 6 December, the Court further directed that, 'It may be appropriate and beneficial for the ensurement of the implementation of the undertaking given by the State Government that due publicity be given to the fact that the proposed kar seva from the 6th December, 1992 should not involve any construction activity or moving of any building material into the acquired land. Such publicity might inform all those concerned about the limitations of the purpose of gathering, if any, at the place. We direct both the Central Government and the State Government to issue appropriate publicity through such media as might seem appropriate including the Doordarshan and the All India Radio. This shall be done immediately.'

The *Times of India* dated 1 December reported on the review of arrangements made by the State Government at Ayodhya. On the general situation prevailing at Ayodhya, the newspaper commented that:

> There are not many takers for the State Government's assurance in the Supreme Court that only a symbolic kar seva will take place. However, a final decision in this connection will be taken at the meeting of sants and the Temple Renovation Committee scheduled for 4 December at Ayodhya. The Convenor of the Committee, Swami Vamdev, the president of the Ram Janmabhumi Nyas, Mahant Ramchandra Paramhans, and the main pillar of the VHP in Ayodhya, Mahant Nritya Gopal Das, said here today in separate statements that Rajmata Vijaya Raje Scindia should not have given any assurance which was contrary to the decision of the Kendriya Marg Darshak Mandai, duly endorsed by the Dharm Sansad at Delhi.

Perturbed by the reports emanating from Ayodhya, the BMAC asked for controlling access to the Babri Masjid. The PTI report published on 2 December stated that, 'The Babri Masjid Movement Coordination Committee (BMMCC) today said the disputed area in Ayodhya be cordoned off to control access of *kar sevaks* to the disputed site as the Supreme Court order for symbolic kar seva might be misinterpreted and misused by the RSS-VHP-BJP combine.'

Further elaborating on the point, Syed Sahabuddin, Convenor, BMMCC, asserted that, 'Since the Supreme Court order does not place any restrictions on *kar sevaks'* access to the acquired land in dispute, this gives rise to the possibility that authorities may, at a critical time, plead their inability to stop any act which goes beyond the symbolic *kar seva* or to use force for that purpose.'

He further added that, 'Even though the temple cannot be constructed overnight, any further construction would be a violation of the *status quo* orders of the Allahabad High Court in the title suit.'

Syed Sahabuddin suggested that the Supreme Court ought to be approached to ask the VHP and the Bajrang Dal to file an affidavit that their volunteers would not go beyond the terms of the symbolic *kar seva.*

*

The safety of the disputed RJB–BM structure had been a matter of serious concern for the Central Government all along. On several occasions, the Home Ministry had written to the State Government emphasizing the need to ensure the security and structural safety of the structure. The State Government had on various platforms committed itself to protect the structure. The Chief Minister gave an assurance to this effect in the meeting of the National Integration Council held on 2 November 1991. The State Government in affidavits submitted to the courts had also reiterated this.

However, on the other hand, various steps taken by the State Government seemed to have diluted the security arrangements in the RJB–BM complex. Several security measures which had been in existence were progressively dismantled—for example, road barricades, iron pipe barricading, physical checking before entry into the complex, shifting of the police control room to a new location, and so on. A boundary wall was constructed enclosing a more or less rectangular piece of land around the structure including the acquired land. The State Government had said that this was a security wall suggested by a team of Central security experts; however, the wall did not have any of the security features that the team had suggested.

These developments and the free entry of visitors into the walled area along with the construction activity and the presence of various kinds of construction material, tools and equipment increased the security risk for the disputed structure. The Home Ministry requested the State Government to comprehensively review the security plan for the RJB–BM complex in view of the change in topography and threat perceptions. It was also suggested that representatives of Central organizations might be included in the team to review the arrangements. The State Government did not accept the suggestion for a review; it pointed out that many of the specific suggestions regarding the security measures had already been implemented while some other specific suggestions were not considered necessary. The State Government reiterated its responsibility for maintaining law and order, and protecting the structure.

In his letters dated 25 November and 2 December 1992, the Chief Minister reiterated the State Government's clear commitment to the protection of the structure and said that the security arrangements had been further strengthened in view of the proposed *kar seva*. He also indicated that fifteen additional companies of the Provincial Armed Constabulary (PAC) had been deployed and there was no requirement for Central forces. Nevertheless, the Central Government remained concerned about the security of the structure. In his letter dated 1 December 1992 the Home Minister again drew the attention of the Chief Minister, UP, to these matters; the Home Minister pointed out that he was not sure whether the measures taken by the State Government would be adequate in the context of the proposed *kar seva* and it was not clear whether any contingency plan had been drawn up in case *kar sevaks* undertook construction activity in violation of Court orders or turned violent if such activity was stopped.

The matter of the security of the structure also came up during the proceedings in the Supreme Court. The deficiencies in the existing security arrangements which were pointed out by the Central Government were taken note of by the Court and it was suggested that these may be brought to the notice of the State Government, whose counsel was asked by the Court to give constructive consideration to these suggestions. The suggestions were immediately communicated to the state counsel in the Court itself. In his letter dated 2 December 1992, the Home Minister expressed his hope that the State Government would give its urgent and serious consideration to these suggestions.

The law and order implications of the RJB–BM dispute had always been serious. It remained one of the most persistent factors in keeping communal tension alive and in giving rise to communal riots in many parts of the country. In 1989, during the period of *shila poojans/maha yagnas* preceding the *shilanyas* function, the communal atmosphere was highly charged in various parts of the country, especially in Bihar, Rajasthan, Gujarat, Madhya Pradesh, Uttar Pradesh and Karnataka. Seventy-nine communal incidents related to this dispute were reported from ten states resulting in the death of 505 persons and injuries to 768 others. Similar communal heat was generated during the rath yatra of the BJP in 1990, which led to a virtual communal frenzy after the arrest of L.K. Advani. During this period, 312 communal incidents took place in which 483 persons were killed and 2,066 were injured. According to reports, 210 mosques and thirty-five temples were damaged or desecrated. (See Appendix I for details)

The same kind of outbreak of communal violence did not occur during 1991–92. However, the communal atmosphere continued to be vitiated. In Malegaon, Maharashtra and in and around Thiruvananthapuram in Kerala, outbreaks of communal violence took place in July 1992; in Malegaon, two persons were killed and thirty-four injured, and in Thiruvananthapuram, five persons were killed and several more were injured. In April 1992, following the bomb explosion in a mosque in Faizabad, communal riots broke out in various places in Kerala resulting in two deaths and injuries to forty-four persons and considerable loss of public property. Based on past experience and the continuing undercurrent of communal tension on account of the RJB–BM dispute, serious apprehensions existed about the outbreak of fresh violence in various parts of the country, particularly if any untoward incident took place in Ayodhya during the proposed *kar seva*.

Before the Supreme Court, the Government of UP had given assurances to secure the safety of the structure as well as the implementation of Court orders. It gave an undertaking that the *kar seva* would be symbolic in nature and would not involve any construction activity in violation of court orders. After some initial hesitation, this undertaking of the Government of UP was accepted by all organizations involved in the temple construction movement and thus, by 5 December it was felt that the *kar seva* to be started the next day would be confined to certain religious ceremonies and symbolic manual labour and would not involve any construction work.

The safety of the disputed structure itself was never the chief issue during 1991 and 1992 and the commitment of the State Government on this count was always clear and unequivocal. In fact, some of the leaders had claimed from time to time that the disputed structure was functioning as a temple. As a measure of abundant caution, however, the Central Government had stationed 195 companies of Central Para Military Forces (CPMFs) near Ayodhya in November 1992 so that these could be made available at short notice if and when required by the State Government or for any other contingent purpose. The Chief Minister of Uttar Pradesh protested against this stationing of forces.

On 24 November, the Home Minister conveyed the decision of the Government of India to station CPMFs to tackle any situation arising out of the proposed *kar seva*. The Chief Minister of UP *vide* his letter dated 25 November to the Home Minister and his letter dated 26 November to the Prime Minister registered his strong protest about the deployment of CPMFs and asserted that the disputed structure was fully safe. (See Appendix X)

In his letter to the Prime Minister on 26 November, while challenging the Constitutional validity of the Central Government's action of stationing its forces unilaterally, Kalyan Singh alleged that the Central Government was deliberately deserting the path of negotiation and amicable and peaceful solution and wanted to take the path of confrontation. The Chief Minister candidly warned that the problem could not be solved by use of force and even if it was prevented for the time being, the same would recur. The Chief Minister also criticized the stand of the Central Government taken before the Supreme Court and asserted that if the Central Government agreed, the solution of the developing situation could be found through negotiations.

Again, on 30 November, Kalyan Singh wrote another letter strongly protesting against the continued despatch of CPMF to Ayodhya and Faizabad by the Central Government unilaterally. (See Appendix X) This time he quoted various provisions of the Centre–State relations in the Constitution of India and alleged that the action of the Central Government was violative of the Constitutional scheme.

Kalyan Singh also made a fervent appeal to his counterparts in the other states of the country to oppose the Centre's decision to send para-military forces to Ayodhya without the concurrence of his government. Expressing concern over it, he said the Centre's decision was a threat to the future of democracy and could lead to wide repercussions.

The reply of Union Home Minister S.B. Chavan dated 1 December is revealing. He pointed out that:

> The security concern acquires an urgent dimension in view of the imminent kar seva from 6 December 1992. It is reported that about 25,000 kar sevaks have already arrived at Ayodhya and that the organizers are expecting that within the next few days the number could increase to as much as 100,000. Many of the representatives of the organizations are reported to be making statements designed to incite the kar sevaks. Some statements have reiterated that the kar seva will be held even in defiance of court orders. Some veiled threats have been held out to the disputed structure especially if the kar seva is interfered with. There are disturbing reports of specially trained squads being arranged during the kar seva for purposes inimical to the security of the structure.
>
> Against the above background, the security aspect needs even greater attention. We are not sure whether the measures being taken by the State Government would be adequate for the occasion. In particular, it is not clear to us if any contingency plan has been drawn up in case the kar sevaks undertake construction activity in violation of the Court orders, or if they turn violent if such activity is stopped.
>
> You have been assuring us about the State Government's commitment to the security of the structure. However, on the other hand, many of the security measures which were earlier in existence have been dismantled in spite of our requests that this should not be done. You have indicated that 15 more companies of PAC have been deployed in Ayodhya. In our view, this force will not be adequate, if in the environment of religious frenzy, violence breaks out at

> Ayodhya. On the other hand, the deployed forces can be unnecessarily exposed to danger if they are not in sufficient number to meet the situation. We have, on earlier occasions, offered to make available Central forces to the State Government and have now even stationed them at nearby locations so that these can be made available at short notice when required by the State Government. I would request you to kindly seriously consider this offer.

S.B. Chavan then took the opportunity to refer to the proceedings in the Supreme Court and the urgent need to consider the Centre's suggestions relating to the security of the structure thus:

> The matter relating to the security of the RJB–BM structure also came up during the proceedings in the Supreme Court today. The deficiencies in the existing arrangements from the security point of view which were pointed out by the Central Government were also taken note of by the Hon'ble Court and, in fact, it was suggested that these may be brought to the notice of the State Government. The State Government's counsel was asked by the Hon'ble Court to give constructive consideration to these suggestions. In deference to the Court's observations, these suggestions were immediately communicated to the State Government's counsel in the Court itself. The Court proceedings thus vindicate the Centre's continuous concern about the security of the RJB-BM structure. I hope the State Government will give its urgent and serious consideration to our suggestions with a view to avoiding serious repercussions for the law and order situation not only in Uttar Pradesh but also in the country.

*

The two-judge bench of the Supreme Court, comprising Chief Justice M.N. Venkatachaliah and Justice G.N. Ray, resumed its hearing on the contempt petitions on 1 December. As the hearing began, the Attorney General, Milon Banerji, said the Central Government was deeply concerned about the protection of the disputed structure. He indicated that efforts had been made to create communal disharmony. The situation had reached the 'flash point', Milon Banerji said, and warned that the fallout of such a situation would be hideous and unimaginable.

He also drew the Court's attention to the two letters sent by the Chief Minister, Kalyan Singh, pointing out that the State Government had objected to the deployment of para-military forces by the Centre in Ayodhya. Such a stand, he said, was against the principles governing the federal structure of the Constitutional set-up. The BJP government had failed earlier in complying with the Court's directives, said Milon Banerji, while referring to certain ugly incidents which had taken place in Ayodhya five months ago.

As the petitioners' counsel, O.P. Sharma, Govind Mukhoty and R.K. Garg sought to quote newspaper reports indicating that the BJP and its allies were determined to start construction of the Ram temple at Ayodhya from 6 December, K.K. Venugopal said that every attempt had been made to prejudice the Court saying that the petitioners were submitting only those newspapers which had favourable reports for them. K.K. Venugopal submitted that the entire argument had been made to seek publicity. He said the Central Government also wanted to derive political mileage.

However, Justice Venkatachaliah declined to take note of the newspaper reports observing that it was difficult to know the real situation. The judge said that the Court's Observer was expected to report on the developments in Ayodhya. If necessary, the court would pass appropriate directions on the Observer's report, he added.

In the meantime, the Attorney General handed over an

envelope containing the Intelligence Bureau (IB) report to the judges. They perused it and later suggested that the State Government should be consulted to provide maximum security around the disputed structure. Although the contents of the IB report were kept secret, it was learnt that only one PAC company had been deployed to maintain law and order during the *kar seva.*

After hearing the counsels for the contempt petitioners and the UP Government, the Court directed that the State and the Central Governments should jointly issue statements clarifying the Court's directives that no construction would take place when *kar seva* commenced from 6 December. 'Such statements should be broadcast on AIR and telecast on Doordarshan immediately,' the judges ordered and said that these should also be published in all the newspapers.

Declining to direct the Central Government to withdraw paramilitary forces from Ayodhya, the judges said that neither of the Court's orders had prevented any Constitutionally elected government from performing its duty in accordance with the law. The Court further indicated that it could still appoint a Receiver to ensure that no construction activity took place in violation of its repeated directives.

In accordance with the directions of the Court, and with a view to discourage the gathering of a large number of *kar sevaks* in Ayodhya, the Central Government gave wide publicity to the assurances given by the State Government and the fact that during the *kar seva* there could be no construction activity as per orders of the Supreme Court, through the electronic media and the printed media.

Meanwhile, Tej Shankar, the Observer appointed by the Supreme Court, informed the Supreme Court on 2 December about the developments at Ayodhya. He informed the Court about the VHP's intention to resume *kar seva* from the spot where it was stopped in July.

Kalyan Singh claimed that the State Government had provided 'all the required facilities' to the specially appointed Court Observer for Ayodhya, Tej Shankar, and that after carrying out an extensive survey of the disputed structure, the *shilanyas* site and the 2.77 acre acquired land, he had not noticed any infringement of the Supreme Court directive. He also denied the reports that he would perform *kar seva* on 6 December and asserted that his government was committed to uphold the sancity of the Constitution and the dignity of the rule of law during the *kar seva*.

The Ayodhya issue dominated the entire proceedings in both Houses of Parliament on 2 December which were repeatedly disrupted over the reported remarks of BJP leaders, L.K. Advani and M.M. Joshi.

Atal Bihari Vajpayee, who spoke amid repeated interruptions, sought to convey that it was quite wrong on the part of the Janata Dal, Left Front and even some Congress members to 'jump to conclusions on the basis of newspaper reports' that court orders would be violated during the *kar seva*. He drew the attention of the members to L.K. Advani's remarks that the final decision about *kar seva* and other programmes for 6 December would be taken at a meeting of the party executive in the capital on 4 December. He also drew attention to a statement by Vinay Katiyar, BJP MP from Ayodhya, saying that there would be no violation of the Court's injunctions.

A.B. Vajpayee said the situation was not as serious or alarming as made out by press. But the real problem was that some members in the House were deeply interested that the tension created by the Ayodhya issue should be made an excuse by the Centre to dismiss the BJP government in UP.

Vajpayee said his party was interested in building a temple and not getting into a confrontation with the Centre over the issue. However, if the Centre was bent upon a confrontation, the BJP was ready to accept the challenge.

The *Times of India* on 3 December reported a statement of L.K. Advani's that the UP Government would not use force; it reported him as saying, 'The UP Government will not use any force against the *kar sevaks* in any circumstances. *Kar seva* will start from 6 December as per schedule. The question does not arise of stopping the *kar seva* or doing it on a symbolic basis.'

L.K. Advani told reporters that *kar seva* was not confined to bhajan and kirtan but also referred to physical labour, *shram dan* by the *kar sevaks* for constructing the Ram temple. The construction of the temple could not be undertaken by *kar sevaks* alone and the services of engineers and skilled labourers would be utilized, he said.

The BJP leader blamed the Union Government for inflammatory and irresponsible speeches against the Hindus and warned the Centre to desist from these.

He also accused the Centre of taking an unnecessary confrontationist stand against the UP Government by sending paramilitary forces without the State Government's consent. The flag march by the Central forces in Ayodhya, at the instance of the Centre, was a clear signal of a confrontation with the State Government, in his opinion.

Replying to a question, Advani said that the construction of the Ram temple would not affect Indian's international relations, as feared by some 'pseudo-secularists'.

Tension was escalating in Ayodhya as 6 December drew nearer and there was total confusion on the question of 'symbolic *kar seva* without any construction activity' to be resumed on that day, further confounded by varying statements and views expressed by the BJP leaders, especially L.K. Advani and M.M. Joshi and the VHP-RSS-Bajrang Dal combine.

Amidst apprehensions expressed by various sections of the Rajya Sabha in its debate of 3 December about the possibility of a confrontation during the proposed *kar seva* in Ayodhya, the BJP claimed that the crisis could still be averted if the court could be persuaded to deliver its judgment over the status of the disputed 2.77 acres of land before 6 December.

Participating in the four-and-half-hour-long debate on the Ayodhya issue, the members belonging to all parties, except the BJP, maintained that the situation was explosive and urgent measures were needed to diffuse it well in time. Several members criticized the government for its 'inaction' and wondered why it had not come out with any definite action plan even after the meeting of the National Integration Council in which it was empowered to do whatever it deemed necessary. The BJP was the target of attack from all sections of the House.

While the BJP raised strong objections to the sending of Central forces to UP, most parties, including some sections of the Congress party, felt that the Centre should assume direct responsibility for maintaining law and order in Ayodhya and protect the disputed Ram Janmabhoomi–Babri Masjid shrine. The matter could not be left in the hands of the BJP government of the state, they thought.

The BJP leadership also came in for sharp criticism for their statements indicative of their intentions to start construction activity at the disputed site despite the Supreme Court's directive against it. The yatras being undertaken by the party leaders, L.K. Advani and M.M. Joshi, were viewed as acts which might provoke violence in UP and elsewhere in the country.

The suggestion for urging the Court to give an early judgment on the status on the 2.77 acres of land adjoining the disputed shrine came from the BJP member, Dr J.K. Jain, towards the end of the debate. He said while the controversy over the shrine was too complicated to be resolved immediately, the case involving the 2.77 acres of land could be settled if the Parliament, the government and all concerned parties appealed to the Court to deliver the verdict before the deadline for launching the *kar seva*. The hearing of the case was already over, he pointed out.

The debate on the issue was started following the statement made by the minister of state for Home, M.M. Jacob, recalling the events which had led to the existing situation in Ayodhya. A similar statement was made in the Lok Sabha by the Home Minister, S.B. Chavan. The members spoke at length over the issue by way of seeking clarifications on the minister's statement.

The senior BJP leader and the leader of the Opposition in the Rajya Sabha, Sikander Bakht, contested the legality of sending Central forces to UP without the consent of the State Government. He said Article 257, which earlier gave the Centre the right to send forces anywhere in the country, had been subsequently amended to make consultation with the State Government obligatory. The presence of these forces was causing tension in the area, he said.

Speaking on behalf of the ruling party, M.C. Bhandare, Madan Bhatia, N.K.P. Salve and several others praised the Union Government for its mature handling of the situation. It was not too late for the BJP and other concerned parties to resolve to obey the Court orders, they maintained. They took the BJP to task for trying to confuse the public by taking one stand before the Court and a completely different one outside. They accused the BJP of trying to incite communal passions for the sake of votes.

The Congress members also suggested that a single-point reference be made to the Supreme Court to decide whether the disputed shrine was a mosque or a temple. One member suggested that a special session of Parliament be held on 5 December to review the decision taken by the Dharm Sansad on 4 December about the shape of the proposed *kar seva*.

The Union Home Minister, S.B. Chavan, in his reply dated 3 December 1992 to UP Chief Minister Kalyan Singh's letters, sought to impress upon the UP Chief Minister the difference between 'stationing' and 'deployment' of para-military forces. (See Appendix XI) He reminded him that following the Centre's assurance to the Supreme Court on 23 November that it was prepared to render all necessary assistance to the State Government for enforcing the directions of the apex court, the Centre ordered para-military forces to move to suitable locations in UP on 24 November. He further pointed out that the State Government was informed the same day about the forces being 'stationed' so as to be available at short notice if and when required by the State Government for 'deployment' in connection with the security of the structure.

The Supreme Court, hearing the Ayodhya cases on 3 December, dismissed the writ petition filed by a lawyer, R.K. Garg, for a mandamus to the Allahabad High Court, Lucknow Bench, to deliver its verdict before the *kar seva* started in Ayodhya on 6 December, as to whether the UP Government's order to acquire the 2.77-acre land near the disputed structure was legal or not.

When R.K. Garg said that undue delay in the pronouncement of the verdict was aggravating the situation in Ayodhya, the Court noted that it had already observed that the High Court could keep in mind the petitioner's aspiration for an early verdict on the issue.

Meanwhile, counsel O.P. Sharma sought the immediate appointment of the Central Government Receiver for the 2.77-acre land in Ayodhya as the situation there was becoming serious. He referred to a newspaper report that the UP Chief Minister, Kalyan Singh, was seriously contemplating resignation on 5 December to leave the Centre high and dry.

Quoting the newspaper report, O.P. Sharma, counsel for Mohd. Aslam seeking contempt action against Kalyan Singh and the State Government, said that if the State Cabinet resigned, the Central Government would have little time to take alternative measures during the *kar seva*. Besides, the BJP government would be relieved of the Court's orders, the counsel argued. The three-judge bench headed by Justice M.N. Venkatachaliah hearing the matter, however, declined to immediately appoint the Central Government Receiver of the acquired land on the basis of newspaper reports. The judges observed that they would take such a decision only on the basis of the report from the Observer,

Tej Shankar, lest the 'silent crowd' became restive in Ayodhya.

In Lucknow, in the meantime, the Lucknow Bench of the Allahabad High Court, through its notification issued by the Additional Registrar dated 3 December, declared that it reserved judgment on the validity of the acqusition of the 2.77 acres of land in Ayodhya.

Replying to a marathon debate lasting six hours on the general situation in Ayodhya in the Lok Sabha on 3 December itself, the Union Home Minister, S.B. Chavan, appealed to all sections of the House to persuade their friends 'not to do anything which will create problems in the country'. Stating that every effort had been made to avoid a confrontation and 'we are still at it', the Home Minister said he did not want to comment or reveal the Centre's plans in case of certain eventualities as it would not be proper for him to do so. Referring to the misgivings in the minds of the non-BJP Opposition about the true intent of the Kalyan Singh government in Uttar Pradesh, S.B. Chavan said these leaders were speaking on the assumption that something was going to happen.

He, however, recalled the categorical assurance given by the State Government that it would protect the Ram Janmabhoomi–Babri Masjid structure and prevent violation of the Court orders. Besides, the National Integration Council had 'expressed its implicit faith in the Prime Minister and the Government, so please don't ask me to reveal the plans in case of certain eventualities. I can't disclose my cards to you. We will deal with it as the situation develops,' he observed.

The Home Minister said that the Centre was well within its powers to send para-military forces to any part of the country. He pointed out that the Centre could easily resort to Article 355 of the Constitution pertaining to the 'duty of the Union to protect States against external aggression and internal disturbances'. He pointed out that the Centre had not done so in keeping with the spirit of the interpretation of the words 'internal disturbance' by the Sarkaria Commission on Centre–State relations.

Referring to the allegation that the Centre was shielding itself behind the judiciary and trying to pressurize it on the Ayodhya issue. S.B. Chavan asserted that, 'We never interfere in the working of the judiciary. The judiciary is independent and please do not malign it by making such uncharitable remarks.'

It is significant that throughout the discussion in both Houses of Parliament, the BJP came in for severe criticism from almost all sections for its stand on the Ayodhya issue. The BJP, on the other hand, tried to justify its stand saying that the UP Government had not committed any crime by trying to fulfil the mandate given by the people to construct a Ram temple at Ayodhya.

Atal Bihari Vajpayee's defence of the major Opposition party repeatedly drew flak from the Congress and other parties. He began his speech by saying that the Ayodhya problem was intertwined with the belief of the people and felt that no decision should be taken in haste.

He spoke of a credibility gap with the government and stressed that 'secularism' was a foreign word and that nobody was bothered about the sentiments of the majority community.

Meanwhile, the BJP vice president announced on 3 December that the *kar seva* starting on 6 December at Ayodhya would be without construction activity. The *Times of India* reported in its 4 December issue that:

> The BJP today said that would not like to precipitate matters and the kar seva to be resumed at Ayodhya on Sunday would not amount to construction activity.
>
> The BJP leader reiterated that the disputed structure was absolutely safe under the UP Government and the Centre should therefore immediately withdraw the para-military forces as such show of strength could be provocative.
>
> He asserted that the Supreme Court was not prepared to appoint the Government of India as a Receiver, until and

unless there was violation of court orders. And even the Supreme Court's Observer in Ayodhya had reported that there was so far no violation.

On 4 December, the Union Home Minister made another statement in the Rajya Sabha that the Centre was keen to avoid confrontation on the Ayodhya issue and was trying to persuade all the concerned parties to agree to a single-point reference of the dispute to the Supreme Court.

Enumerating the various provisions of the Constitution on the basis of which the reference could be made, S.B. Chavan declared that the government had 'not closed its options' and that discussions on the issue were still continuing. The Supreme Court could be approached but there had to be an understanding among the various parties first, he felt. He further said that if consensus could be reached, they may yet succeed in defusing the situation, adding that the government had to 'exhaust all avenues for an amicable solution'.

Elaborating the various options open to the Centre, the Home Minister further explained that the dispute could be referred to the Supreme Court under Articles 143, 138(2) or 139, provided there was an understanding between the concerned parties and that they agreed to abide by the Court's verdict.

S.B. Chavan said Article 138 (2) would extend the jurisdiction of the Supreme Court to the dispute for its expeditious solution but it required the consent of the State Government, which Kalyan Singh had failed to give.

After some initial hesitation, the undertaing of the Government of UP was declared to have been accepted by all organizations involved in the temple construction movement and thus, by 5 December, it was generally felt that the *kar seva* to be started the next day would be confined to certain religious ceremonies and symbolic manual labour and would not involve any construction work.

On 5 December 1992, the Kendriya Marg Darshak Mandai also announced its decision to do only symbolic *kar seva* next day in terms of the Supreme Court directives.

The *Times of India* on 6 December reported that: 'Setting aside all fears that kar sevaks might turn violent, the Chief Minister, Mr Kalyan Singh, today emphatically asserted that his government was committed to implementing the court order in letter and spirit when symbolic kar seva begins tomorrow on the 2.77 acres acquired land in Ayodhya.'

The Chief Minister, however, maintained that the vexed issue could be solved peacefully if Muslim religious leaders voluntarily transferred the disputed structure to the Hindus. In lieu of this agreement, the Muslims could also be given land for construction of a huge mosque 10 km away from Ayodhya and the Hindus could perform *kar seva* for its construction, he said.

The Chief Minister also said: 'I am fully convinced that all *kar sevaks* are disciplined and law-abiding people and there would be no untoward situation during *kar seva* tomorrow.' He asserted that the State Government was in full control of the situation and there was no cause for worry on any front. He, however, feared that the movement of Central security forces might cause some unnecessary panic among the people.

Reiterating his party's stand on the issue, the Chief Minister said that his government was committed to constructing the Ram temple as the BJP had come to power on the people's mandate for temple construction. 'In any case, we cannot backtrack from our electoral promise. But it does not mean that we will violate the court order,' he said. The Chief Minister further claimed that all necessary measures had been taken to protect the disputed structure and to deal with any situation. One of the new measures taken was the deployment of an additional thirteen companies of the Provincial Armed Constabulary and installation of metal detectors at various entry points, he added.

However, not much assured, the Union Home Minister wrote

another warning letter to Kalyan Singh just a day before the commencement of the proposed *kar seva*, pointing out inadequacies in security arrangements and the need to strengthen them immediately. (See Appendix XI) He pointed out that:

> There are reports that the kar sevaks are in a restive and even belligerent mood and that many of them are resorting to extensive purchase of Trishuls which can even be used for offensive purposes. It is also learnt that some of them are hostile to the Central forces. It is further learnt that with the massive influx of kar sevaks, the number of devotees visiting the shrine has gone up considerably.
>
> As I had written to you earlier, the security arrangements made by the State Government may not be adequate for the occasion, especially if any violence breaks out. It has been reported that the control at entry points between the outer and inner cordons is lax, because of which large batches of visitors are exerting heavy pressure to enter the disputed structure. Further, it is reported that massive crowds are gathering freely and unchecked in the Sankeertan area. The crowd pressure, it is reported, resulted in damage to wooden barricades on 4 December 1992, and that there was the danger of people rushing to the shrine which could be stopped only by intervention of the police. Needless to say that the barricading needs to be strengthened considerably. Some other shortcomings in the security arrangements have been brought to the notice of the State Government through a fax message No. 80011/1/92-Ay.II dated 4 December 1992.
>
> In view of the prevailing situation and the fact that the site of the proposed kar seva and other activities will be in the immediate vicinity of the disputed structure, it is necessary to upgrade the security arrangements substantially. I would suggest that the State Government

> should examine this matter very carefully and take immediate measures to strengthen the security arrangements. The shortcomings mentioned in this message need to be addressed on top priority. The buildings overlooking the RJB–BM structure also need to be secured to prevent the possibility of any attempt being made from those buildings to damage the disputed structure. The possibility of some mischievous elements using explosives to damage the RJB–BM structure cannot be ruled out. I am glad that the State Government has accepted our offer to place at its disposal the services of Bomb Detection and Disposal Squad and Sniffer Dog Squad available with Central police forces. Necessary instructions in this regard have already been issued.

It was not the position of the State Government that they would not use the CPMFs even if it became necessary to do so. In fact, the services of the bomb detection squads and sniffer dog squads were actually utilized by the State Government after the Central Government brought to its notice the possibility of threat by explosives. The presumption thus appeared to be that the State Government would use the Central forces if the need arose.

8

Ayodhya: 6 December 1992

From time to time, the Central Government had brought its anxiety regarding the developments relating to the RJB–BM issue to the notice of the State Government. In this regard the Home Minister had, apart from writing to the Chief Minister, UP, on several occasions, held meetings with him, and also visited Ayodhya for an on-the-spot assessment of the situation. At the official level also, the Central Government's concern was conveyed time and again to the State Government. An official-level team was sent to study the situation at Ayodhya. Its report was sent to the State Government with the request to take suitable action. However, the response from the State Government had not been very forthcoming or open, and had not generated any confidence in regard to its intentions. There were instances of inconsistency in the stand taken by the State Government and of divergence between its statements and actions, such as the following:

1) Only a few days prior to the notification for acquisition of land in October 1991, the Chief Minister had informed the Union Minister that there was no proposal on behalf of the State Government to acquire land in the RJB–BM complex. However, shortly thereafter, the notifications for acquisition were issued.
2) Initially, the State Government took the stand that the land was acquired for the purpose specified in the notification

viz. 'development of tourism and providing amenities to pilgrims at Ayodhya'. In a report that had been sent to the Governor, UP by the State Government in October 1991, it had been indicated that the land would be used for providing amenities such as shade and resting place, medical facilities, water, beautification etc. However, details of the development plan were not furnished to the Home Ministry despite specific requests in this regard. On the other hand, in affidavits filed later on behalf of the State Government before the courts, the purpose of the land acquisition was given wider connotation to include 'renovation and reconstruction of the temple'. For example, it was stated that 'a part of the land of Shri Ram Janma Bhoomi will be left vacant for the renovation of the Temple of Bhagwan Shri Ram Virajman' and 'the foremost thing to be done for achieving the objective . . . is the renovation and reconstruction of the temple of Bhagwan Shri Ram Lala Virajman . . . and in doing so the area of Shri Ram Janma Bhoomi and some more land adjacent thereto would have to be kept in reserve for the renovation and reconstruction of the temple of Bhagwan Shri Ram Virajman there, and its appurtenances. All this development work is to be completed, according to the decision of the government, from public funds in accordance with the plans approved by the government.'

3) While no plans for the development work in the acquired land were supplied to the Home Ministry, extensive demolitions and digging and levelling work were undertaken.
4) In an affidavit dated 29 July 1992 before the Supreme Court, it was stated that the platform was being used for seating of pilgrims during religious discourses or ceremonies. However, certain photographs filed by the petitioners before the Court showed that the pilgrims were seated under the *shamiyanas* erected on the acquired land at a distance from the platform. Also, it was not clear how the platform could have been

used for the above stated purpose when the construction activity had been going on till 26 July 1992 with the use of so much machinery and equipment.

Statements often appeared in the press on behalf of the Chief Minister or ministers of UP that the State Government was committed to the construction of the temple and that it had a popular mandate in this regard. The series of developments that took place after October 1991, the highlights of which are given below, also indicate a definite pattern of movement towards the above objective:

(1) Acquisition of land in October 1991 and demolition of certain structures,
(2) Demolition of further structures from March 1992 onwards,
(3) Construction of 'Ram Diwar' which was started in February 1992,
(4) Removal of several security measures and allowing free access into the acquired area,
(5) Extensive demolitions and digging and levelling operations from March 1992 onwards,
(6) Construction of the platform in July 1992,
(7) Construction of a new access road connecting the RJB–BM site to the main road, and
(8) Handing over of 42 acres of land to the RJB Nyas in March 1992.

In official pronouncements, the State Government had been taking care to make the correct noises. For example, in the statements before the NIC and in the affidavits submitted before the courts, the Chief Minister/State Government had given assurances that the disputed structure would be protected and the orders of the court would be implemented and not violated.

However, when seen in the light of the actual course of events and the conflicting statements from other representatives of the VHP and Sangh parivar, these assurances seemed designed more to avoid giving cause to the Central Government or the courts for action against the State Government.

The Central Government was in no way opposed to the construction of the Ram temple. I had stated in my Independence Day speech in 1992 that the Centre was in favour of constructing the Ram temple but without demolishing or damaging the Babri Masjid. In the President's address to Parliament in July 1991 as well as in the Congress election manifesto, it had been stated that an amicable solution through negotiations should be found to the RJB–BM dispute. In the event that this was not possible, the court verdict should be respected.

The rapidly unfolding developments mentioned above, when viewed in the light of the past record of the State Government, gave rise to the following apprehensions:

1) That the State Government may allow the resumption of the *kar seva* for construction activity despite the fact that the Courts had expressed themselves against any construction activity on the acquired land, and the land in respect of which the High Court had ordered that status quo be maintained.
2) The resumption of the *kar seva* would have serious repercussions on the law and order situation in various parts of the country, including Uttar Pradesh. The atmosphere of communal frenzy in which the *kar seva* would take place raised the apprehension of a threat to the security of the RJB–BM structure; any attack on the structure would in all probability lead to outbreak of serious communal violence in many places.

In the months prior to December 1992, strenuous efforts were made to find an amicable solution to the RJB–BM issue and avert the impending crisis. Apart from the continuing meetings with representatives of VHP and BMAC, meetings and consultations were held at my level as well as at other levels with leaders of political parties, religious groups, etc. Leaders of many political parties had expressed anxiety over the course of events and called upon the Central Government to prevent the resumption of the *kar seva.*

Suggestions were also received from some quarters, including L.K. Advani, leader of the Opposition in the Lok Sabha, that *kar seva* should be permitted to be started on the land acquired by the government or at least on the land which was not in dispute. The Home Minister S.B. Chavan had clarified that, to be able to consider such a suggestion seriously, it was necessary that the plan for construction be submitted by the State Government which should clearly indicate that the construction would not extend to any disputed land or structure or would not subsume the disputed structure in any way. There was no response to such a suggestion from any quarter. Thus, even the suggestion for de-linking the resumption of *kar seva* from the other larger issues was sought to be made with a view to creating a situation of *fait accompli* in which the State Government could again express helplessness for non-implementation of the court orders.

A meeting of the National Integration Council was convened on 23 November 1992. The Council, after considering all aspects of the Babri Masjid–Ramjanmabhoomi dispute and the report of the government, resolved to extend its wholehearted support and cooperation in whatever step I considered essential in upholding the Constitution and the rule of law, and in implementing the Supreme Court's orders.

In the contempt proceedings before the Supreme Court on 20 November 1992, the Court directed that the Union Government should indicate its stand on the matter so that the Court may have its assistance in making such an order as would ensure enforcement of earlier orders of the Court. Accordingly, on 23 November 1992, the Attorney General made the following submissions before the Court:

(1) The statement made by the State Government in its affidavit, to the effect that negotiations were going on, no longer held good because as on date such negotiations had broken down and there were no pending negotiations in which the Central Government was involved.
(2) Attention was drawn to the effect that in July 1992 the situation had developed to such an extent that ultimately the State Government pleaded its inability to tackle it. It was, therefore, submitted that the same situation should not be allowed to recur. Therefore, what was necessary was that preventive steps should be taken straightaway without any further delay.
(3) These steps should aim at preventing a large body of persons congregating at the site and also preventing building material and building equipment to be collected and brought to the site.
(4) It was emphasized that the Central Government was most anxious to see that the rule of law was preserved and Court orders were obeyed.
(5) The Central Government was also prepared to assist the State Government in any way that the State Government wanted if they felt that their own resources were not adequate.
(6) The Central Government was prepared to abide by and implement any direction which the Supreme Court may give.

Hearings on the contempt petition had been going on since 23 November 1992. From time to time, the Attorney General had been reiterating the above concerns and submissions of the Central Government. The proceedings progressed to a point where the Supreme Court asked the State Government to spell out clearly the steps it proposed to take to prevent construction activity on the acquired land in violation of the Court orders. As a result, the State Government filed affidavits reiterating its responsibility to prevent violation of the Court orders and indicated that a positive response had been received in the negotiations which it was having with various parties regarding the proposed *kar seva*. The State Government assured that it would ensure that no construction machinery or construction material would move into the acquired land and no construction activity would take place or be carried out as long as the High Court's interim orders were in force in the writ petitions pending before it relating to the land acquisition. The State Government further submitted that the *kar seva* would be a symbolic occasion for carrying out certain religious activities and would not be allowed to be exploited for any constructional activity, symbolic or otherwise.

The Supreme Court in its order of 28 November 1992 took note of the emphatic assurance and undertaking given by the State Government and abstained from granting the prayer sought in the interim application for the appointment of a Receiver, keeping the application pending. The Court decided to appoint a judicial officer as an Observer for a period of two weeks in the first instance to observe and monitor the situation and submit a report to it whenever, in his opinion, developments tending to be detrimental to the effecting of the Court's order took place. It was also decided to request the Chief Justice of Allahabad High Court to spare the services of a District Judge in the State judicial service for this purpose.

In regard to the request of the State Government for an expeditious decision by the Lucknow Bench of the Allahabad High Court in the writ petitions relating to land acquisition, the Supreme Court agreed to request the High Court to consider the expectations of the parties and the requirements of justice and bestow on it such thought as it might consider proper.

In accordance with the direction of the Supreme Court, the

matter was heard again on 30 November 1992. The Court took note of a communication from the Observer that there appeared to be some problem of accommodation and other facilities to the Observer to enable him to effect his commission. The State Government's counsel assured that the State Government would provide all the facilities so as to enable the Observer to discharge his duties. On behalf of the Central Government, it was pointed out before the Court that any assistance required by the Observer would be made available.

On 1 December 1992, the Supreme Court received a brief report from the Observer indicating that he had not noticed any activity on the acquired land which would constitute a breach of the Court's order. However, the Court passed an order directing both the State Government and the Central Government to issue appropriate publicity indicating that the *kar seva* would not involve any construction activity or movement of any building material into the acquired land so that the *kar sevaks* may be properly informed of the limitation in this regard. On 3 December 1992, the Court received a further report from the Observer indicating *inter alia* that no construction of any nature, either temporary or permanent, was being carried out, although the number of *kar sevaks* was increasing and several tents had been fixed for their residence near the acquired land and speeches were being given saying that the *kar seva* would be done from the place where it was stopped.

On 23–24 November 1992, the Government of Uttar Pradesh moved an application before the Lucknow Bench of the Allahabad High Court praying to decide the land acquisition cases pertaining to the land around the disputed Ramjanmabhoomi–Babri Masjid structure at the earliest or to suitably modify the interim orders dated 25 October 1991 and 15 July 1992 so as to enable the State Government to proceed with the purpose for which the land had been acquired and make suitable arrangements. Though, by an order dated 24 November 1992, the court rejected the application, it is important to note these two submissions made by the Government of Uttar Pradesh in the application. These clearly show the intention of the State Government and the pretext it had tried to keep handy in order to keep its options open, just in case.

Meanwhile, the Government of India received a categorical letter from the Governor of UP dated 1 December on the subject. After giving the background of the dispute and stating that 'the general law and order situation in the State, specially on the communal front is satisfactory', the Governor went on to say as under:

> There are reports that a large number of *kar sevaks* are reaching Ayodhya, but they are peaceful. The State Government has given a categorical assurance to the Hon'ble Supreme Court, who has accepted the Government's assurance. The State Government has also fully assured the full protection to the disputed structure and adequate arrangements have been made to protect the disputed structure.
>
> In my opinion at present the time is not ripe for taking any drastic step like the dismissal of the UP Government or the dissolution of the State Assembly or the imposition of President's Rule in the State. If it is done, it may have far-reaching consequences. It may also lead to large-scale violence not only in this state but also in other parts of the country. The possibility of the damage to the disputed structure itself may not be ruled out. Therefore in my opinion we should be very cautious on this issue and should weigh the various alternatives and pros and cons of any decision to be taken on this issue. Any decision in haste should be avoided.

And who was this Governor? The Governor was Satyanarayan Reddy, handpicked and appointed when V.P. Singh was the Prime

Minister. They had been in the same political party before the appointment. Reddy was himself not like-minded with the BJP and could not therefore be branded as pro-BJP. Although the political leanings, if any, of a Governor have strictly no bearings on his actions, this relevant fact is being brought on record here to allay any lurking suspicions.

The gravamen of this report clearly was that the Governor gave a good chit to the State Government on the law and order issue, protection to the disputed structure and likely peaceful conduct of the *kar seva* at Ayodhya. Having so assured the President—and evidently in the light of this factual situation—the Governor went on to give the warning in the latter part of the paragraph, implying that in view of the conditions he described, any action by the President under Article 356 would be uncalled for and therefore counter-productive—inclusive of posing a threat to the Babri structure. A sterner warning from a Governor to the President of India could hardly be imagined.

In pursuance of the submissions made before the Supreme Court, the Government of India initiated action on 24 November 1992 to move Central Para Military Forces to suitable locations in Uttar Pradesh so as to enable these to be made available at short notice to the Government of Uttar Pradesh for its assistance in ensuring compliance with the orders of the Court. The Government of Uttar Pradesh was informed of this fact on 24 November 1992 itself.

The movement of CPMFs had progressed as per the contingency plan prepared earlier for this purpose. One hundred and ninety-one companies of CPMFs (CRPF—112 companies, CISF—54 companies, RAF—25 companies) collected at different points were moved towards Faizabad/Ayodhya on 24 and 25 November 1992. From there they were sent to suitable camping sites in Faizabad and surrounding areas, including locations like Jagdishpur, Mankapur and Rae Bareli. Approximately 500 vehicles had also been sent to Faizabad/Ayodhya to transport these troops to their camping locations and for further movement for deployment purposes. Arrangements had also been made for necessary infrastructural and support facilities. The forces started arriving in Faizabad/Ayodhya on the morning of 25 November.

In the letters written by the Chief Minister, UP on 25 November 1992, 30 November 1992 and 2 December 1992, he had strongly protested against the stationing of CPMFs in various places in UP, describing the move as unnecessary, unconstitutional and unilateral. He argued that this move was against the basic principles of the Constitution, an attack on the federal structure, and against democratic traditions. He stated that the Central Government did not have the authority to move Central forces without the request of the State Government, and demanded withdrawal of these forces. Since then, the Home Minister had replied to the Chief Minister pointing out that, so far, these forces had only been stationed at suitable locations in UP so as to be available at short notice if and when required by the State Government for deployment in connection with the security of the RJB–BM structure and the maintenance of law and order. In this letter, the Home Minister indicated the distinction between 'stationing' and 'deployment' of forces.

As stated earlier, since the Supreme Court's order of 28 November 1992, several important leaders of the BJP, VHP and Bajrang Dal had distanced themselves from the stand taken by the UP Government that the *kar seva* would be only of a symbolic nature without involving any construction activity. A number of public pronouncements, press conferences and statements which appeared in the newspapers brought this out fully. A very disturbing element of the whole scenario was the building up of communal tension. Statements were made by leaders of VHP and Bajrang Dal that if the *kar seva* was resisted in any manner, nearly 3,000 mosques that had been constructed by destruction of temples in the country would be razed to the ground along with the Babri Masjid.

Despite the emphatic assurance given to the Supreme Court by the State Government that the *kar seva* would be symbolic and there would be no construction activity on the acquired land, no effort on the scale required seemed to have been made by the State Government to give wide publicity to this changed concept of *kar seva,* although the Supreme Court had made suggestions to this effect in its observations of 28 November 1992. As a result, the flow of *kar sevaks* continued to Ayodhya and the number swelled to over 2 lakhs by 5 December 1992.

In the meantime, the KMDM which was scheduled to meet and decide on the mode of *kar seva* on 4 December, postponed the same and met only on 5 December. After the meeting the impression given out was that the *kar seva* would be observed without violating the Court orders.

Considering the influx of *kar sevaks* into Ayodhya and the laxity of control being exercised on their entry into the complex, the Union Home Minister again wrote to the Chief Minister of Uttar Pradesh pointing out the need to further strengthen the security arrangements for the disputed structure. The bomb detection and disposal squad as well as the dog squad available with the Central Para Military Forces were also ordered to be placed at the disposal of the State Government.

*

Initial reports from Ayodhya in the beginning of the day on 6 December indicated an air of normalcy. About 70,000 persons had assembled in the Ram Katha Kunj for a public meeting with some 500 sadhus and sants gathered on the foundation terrace for performing pooja. Everything seemed to be going according to the plan announced by the organizers for doing a symbolic *kar seva* and observing other formalities of *kar seva* not involving violation of the Court orders. As the crowd was being addressed by leaders of the BJP, VHP, RSS and Bajrang Dal, roughly 150 persons in a sudden move broke through the cordon on the terrace, regrouped and started pelting stones at the police personnel. All this happened a few minutes before noon and within a very little time, around a thousand persons broke into the RJB–BM structure. Around 12.20 p.m. about eighty persons had managed to climb onto the RJB–BM structure and started damaging the domes. At this time, the crowd inside the complex was around 25,000 with larger numbers milling around outside. By 2.40 p.m. the crowd had increased to about 75,000.

The UP police moved away as the *kar sevaks* scaled barricades and clambered on to the domes of the mosque where saffron flags were hoisted. Then began a frenzied demolition with shovels, iron rods and pickaxes.

While this was going on, the local authorities and the police appeared to be standing as mute spectators. This dismal picture of inaction and dereliction of duty was because of orders from the Chief Minister of UP not to use force. Even the small contingent of CRPF was rendered inactive and powerless by express directions given to them by the local magistrate and higher State Government authorities.

The chronology of the happenings of 6 December 1992 between 9.30 a.m. and 7.30 p.m. reveals that the Central Government had maintained constant contact with the UP Government and the officers of the CPMFs at Ayodhya and constant pressure was kept on the State Government to make use of the CPMFs for the protection of the structure. The State Government at no point of time said that it would not make use of these forces. On the other hand, it adopted a dilly-dallying policy. On more than one occasion during the day the forces were actually requisitioned but their movement was prevented/ delayed by not making available the magistrate, without whom the movement was not possible under law.

At 1.45 p.m., the Director General (DG), Indo-Tibetan Border Police (ITBP) informed the Ministry of Home Affairs (MHA) that considerable damage to the structure had taken place but the UP police was not taking any action.

At 1.50 p.m., DG, ITBP informed MHA that three battalions had moved out of camp along with a magistrate and circle officer at 1.25 p.m. and the remaining battalions were waiting for the magistrates to arrive. He also intimated that the district administration had asked for fifty companies and had been requested to send magistrates wherever CPMFs were stationed so that forces could converge and be used by the local administration.

At 2.00 p.m. the Home Minister spoke to the Chief Minister, UP to inquire about the action taken for the protection of the structure.

At 2.20 p.m., DG, ITBP informed MHA that the three battalions which had moved from camp had met with resistance and obstructions. En route there were a lot of road blocks and people stopped vehicles. The convoy reached Saket Degree College with great difficulty, where the force was again stopped and the road was blocked. Minor pelting of stones also took place. The magistrate then asked them in writing to return. DG, ITBP further informed that the three battalions had returned accordingly. The Commissioner who had been contacted informed that the Chief Minister, UP had ordered that there should be no firing under any circumstances.

At 2.25 p.m., the Home Secretary spoke to the Deputy General of Police (DGP), UP informing him of sending back of the force by the local administration and requested him to issue necessary instructions for use of force. DGP, UP informed him that the Chief Minister's instructions were that firing should not be resorted to but other kinds of force could be used. The Home Secretary asked DGP, UP that the State Government should issue necessary instructions immediately. The DGP promised to attend to this matter at once.

At 2.30 p.m., the Home Secretary spoke to the Chief Secretary, UP and requested him similarly. He then spoke to the Defence

Secretary to keep helicopters ready if any force would have to be moved by air immediately. He was also requested to keep one or two transport planes ready for movement of additional troops if necessary.

Between 3.30 and 4.30 p.m., the Home Secretary was informed that communal incidents had started occurring in Ayodhya, and spoke to the DGP, UP and told him that the situation was fast deteriorating; not only had Central forces been unable to move but there was serious apprehension of communal riots. DGP, UP informed that the situation could not be controlled without resorting to firing and orders of the Chief Minister were being obtained.

By 4.30 p.m., the entire structure was demolished. Idols which were taken out during the demolition process were placed back where the central dome of the erstwhile disputed structure stood at 6.45 p.m. Lakhs of *kar sevaks* continued to mob the entire area and the entire city of Ayodhya. By 7.30 p.m., they started work on the construction of a temporary structure for the idols.

In view of the developments of the late afternoon of 6 December, a meeting of the Union Cabinet was called at 6.00 p.m. The Cabinet resolved to recommend the issue of proclamation under Article 356 of the Constitution with the President assuming to himself all the functions of the Government of Uttar Pradesh and dissolving the UP Vidhan Sabha. This recommendation was taken personally by the Home Minister to Rashtrapati Bhavan and the proclamation was issued by 9.10 that very night. In order to assist the Governor, two senior officers were posted as his advisors. Accordingly, the Kalyan Singh government was dismissed, the UP Assembly dissolved, and President's Rule was proclaimed in the state.

The BJP took 'moral responsibility' for the day's developments in a statement issued by the party's vice president S.S. Bhandari. L.K. Advani and M.M. Joshi were among the prominent BJP leaders present in Ayodhya at the time of the demolition of the

Babri Masjid. As the *kar sevaks* chipped away at the structure, BJP-VHP-RSS leaders had pleaded in vain with them to stop.

Immediately after the demolition, riots spread through the by-lanes of Ayodhya just behind the fallen structure. Houses of a particular community were singled out and set on fire. It was said that some of the victims' families had retaliated by firing at the *kar sevaks*. The administration clamped an indefinite curfew on the twin cities of Faizabad and Ayodhya. In Ayodhya, the police nervously patrolled the by-lanes. *Kar sevaks* were in a defiant mood as they went about setting houses on fire. The VHP-RSS-BJP leaders repeatedly urged *kar sevaks* not to leave the RJB–BM area, but nobody listened.

As an immediate aftermath of the 6 December happenings in Ayodhya, the communal situation became tense and explosive throughout the country. The army was put on alert in seven states including Andhra Pradesh, Assam, Bihar, Gujarat, Himachal Pradesh, Madhya Pradesh and Rajasthan, and curfew was clamped in Allahadad, Kanpur, Lucknow and Varanasi. Security was beefed up in several places across the country.

The immediate Muslim reaction to the incident is reflected in the statement of Shahi Imam of Delhi's Jama Masjid, Syed Abdulla Bhukhari. Blaming the Central Government, he declared that the Muslims felt betrayed. Displaying his anger, the Imam added that the Centre should have dismissed the UP Government long ago. He claimed that he had warned the government that it would be tragic if the structure at Ayodhya was damaged; but the Centre had failed in its duty to protect the rights of the Muslims.

In view of the situation in the RJB–BM complex and the presence of over 200,000 *kar sevaks* in an aggressive and militant mood, the decision about the timing of the entry of the Central forces was left to the forces themselves. Action was also initiated for evacuation of *kar sevaks* from Ayodhya. As a result, by the evening of 7 December, nearly 70,000 persons had left Ayodhya. The officers commanding the security forces decided to move the force during the night of 7 December and the morning of 8 December so as to use minimum force. Action was taken accordingly, and the RJB–BM area was quickly secured. This was managed without having to resort to firing.

According to later reports, the State Government had requested for fifteen companies of para-military forces and the same was made available to them. The Union Home Secretary and DGP of UP brought to their notice that the Central Para Military Forces were unable to move to Ayodhya because of the above-mentioned stand of the local administration. As stated above, there was no action on this and, thereafter, the crowds carried out the demolition of the structure without let or hindrance.

As already stated, the Central forces were all ready to move from Faizabad since the morning of 6 December, but in spite of repeated requests from the commander of the force as well as from the Union Home Secretary in Delhi, a magistrate, as required by law, to accompany the force in its effort to reach the disputed structure (a distance of about 8 km) with a view to protecting it, was neither refused, nor actually made available by the State Government. After the storming of the structure by the crowd had actually commenced and there was no trace of the state police on the spot and the crowd had been left in full run of the place—only then, a magistrate at last reached Faizabad—at 1.15 p.m. to be exact. The force started at once towards the Babri structure, but on the plea of crowd resistance the magistrate gave them written orders to return to Faizabad, as described above.

It will thus be seen that on 6 December, until the very last moments, the Central Government kept pressurizing the UP state authorities to make use of the Central forces available with them to save the Babri structure. Even at the very last moment when the force had actually moved halfway towards the structure, at 2.20 p.m.—by which time the demolition was going on, but could have been stopped even then—the deliberate act of the magistrate in not allowing the Central force to proceed further and thus officially aborting the very last possibly successful attempt to save the structure, became transparently visible, and will always be cited as a wanton and *mala fide* step to stop the saving of the structure.

Until late in the evening of 6 December, the Supreme Court was reviewing the happenings at Ayodhya. When the final news of the demolition reached the Court, they expressed their extreme annoyance and distress at the unfortunate turn of events. The State Government had deliberately misled the Supreme Court over the past few days and when the ultimate vandalism took place, the Court called the senior counsel of the State Government and called for an explanation. To this, the counsel replied, 'I was misled by the party and my head hangs in shame.'

*

The incident found its vibrations in Parliament as well. Almost the entire non-BJP Opposition joined hands to stall the proceedings of the Lok Sabha on 7 December, in protest against the dastardly act and alleged default of the Central Government in preventing the tragedy. Some even charged me and my government of connivance and collusion with the Hindu fundamentalists in the demolition of the structure.

The full-fledged statement about the happenings at Ayodhya and the Central Government's future strategy after the demolition of the structure to salvage the situation and to find a permanent solution to the RJB–BM dispute came before Parliament from the Union Home Minister, S.B. Chavan, on 18 December 1992. The Home Minister apprised Parliament about the post-demolition action taken by the Central Government as under:

> The Central Government has taken several actions swiftly and firmly. These include:
>
> (1) The strongest action possible under the law has been initiated against those who incited people all over

the country and brought crowds to Ayodhya and persuaded them to commit the heinous act. Cases under relevant provisions of law have been registered and some arrests have also been carried out. This includes leaders of various organizations and political parties involved in the events of 6 December 1992.

(2) The investigation of offences connected with the demolition of the RJB–BM structure and related incidents has been entrusted to the CBI; orders in this behalf were issued on 14 December 1992.

(3) Notification has been issued on 16 December 1992, for setting up of a Commission of Inquiry consisting of Justice Manmohan Singh Liberhan, a sitting judge of the High Court of Punjab and Haryana, to inquire into the matters relating to the events at Ayodhya on 6 December 1992.

(4) Government has declared Rashtriya Swayamsevak Sangh, Jamaat-e-Islami Hind, Vishwa Hindu Parishad, Islamik Sewak Sangh and Bajrang Dal as unlawful associations under the Unlawful Activities (Prevention) Act, 1967. The powers to take action under the various provisions of the Act have also been delegated to the State Governments. Reports about the implementation of the orders have started flowing in.

(5) The Central Government has been deeply concerned about the assault on mediapersons at Ayodhya on 6 December. The Commission of Inquiry which has been set up will look into this matter fully. The State Government has been asked to entrust the investigation of these cases to a separate cell headed by senior police officer of the rank of Inspector General of Police. The Government has also decided that mediapersons whose equipment was damaged in Ayodhya would

> be allowed to import replacements and clear the same free of customs duty.

With reference to my statement in Parliament on 7 December (See Appendix XII), S.B. Chavan added that, 'As already announced, the government will see to it that the demolished structure is rebuilt. Government has decided that appropriate steps will be taken regarding the construction of a Ram temple.'

The Home Minister concluded his statement conveying the Central Government's pledge to the minorities thus: 'To the minorities in India who live in every corner of this sacred land, we have only one message to give. The government will not and shall not default on its basic commitment to protect and preserve their rights, their lives and liberty. We will walk every extra step that is needed in fulfilling this commitment which has been given to them not only by the Constitution of this country, but also by our great leaders—Gandhiji, Pandit Jawaharlal Nehruji, Lal Bahadur Shastriji, Smt. Indira Gandhi and Shri Rajiv Gandhi. Let no one mistake our resolve or determination under any circumstances.'

The debate that ensued in Parliament needs special mention; interestingly, the debate on Ayodhya started on the motion moved by the leader of the BJP in Parliament, Atal Bihari Vajpayee, that, 'this House expresses its want of confidence in the Council of Ministers.' I pointed out this irony while replying to the debate on 21 December and lamented that:

> It is rather strange, Mr Speaker, Sir, that this discussion should come in the form of a no-confidence motion. The Bharatiya Janata Party has no confidence in the Government of India. Why? Because the Government of India reposed confidence in the State Government of the Bharatiya Janata Party. Maybe, this is good justice meted out to the Government of India. I have to own that. I have

to admit that. But how do we run the country? How do Centre–State relations run? On the basis of suspicion? On the basis of mistrust? How do we run the governments of the states which are so inextricably linked with the Centre, that they have to be running a three-legged race all the time? One of them cannot run in advance, leaving the other behind . . .

But is it possible, is it conceivable for the Central Government of any federation to even imagine that one of the units, a State Government, would keep giving affidavit after affidavit after affidavit, giving solemn assurances, and finally violate those assurances in a manner that until the last moment it cannot be detected? That is why my first reaction was that for all appearances it was pre-planned . . .

Sir, I have been arraigned, I have been criticized for believing. That is the only sin I seem to have committed. I agree, I plead guilty of believing a State Government. I have no explanation on that. But the point is that I believed it not only as the Central Government; I found that there was nothing else but to believe the assurance of the State Government. Was there any other way when the Supreme Court believes it? The Supreme Court in hearing after hearing placed more reliance on the State Government; asked the State Government to come back with more affidavits; asked me at some point of time to keep out because they would like to try the State Government. They had full faith in the State Government. I am not a party. The Central Government is not a party before the Supreme Court not in the High Court for that matter. But I was called for a particular purpose. We said: 'We are prepared to help the Supreme Court in whatever manner the Supreme Court wants us.' That was all the role we played. And ultimately on the 6th itself, the Supreme Court had been

> shocked, what they said is revealing. I do not remember any State Government in a federal set-up having behaved this way. So, those who told me and tell me now, 'Did we not tell you?' Yes, they have been proved right. But I was proved right in July. So, it is not a question of who is proved right. What happens to Article 356? It lies shattered. I would like Constitutional experts to go into it. Where is it that a situation has arisen whereby the governance of the state cannot be carried on according to the provisions of the Constitution? What is the precise point?
>
> (See Appendix XIII for the full text of the speech)

All this however related to act an of retribution to what had already happened in the past. The question that loomed large was how to remedy the wrong done and to secure the rights of the minorities, and at the same time, find an amicable and mutually acceptable solution to the problem. The strategy evolved by the Central Government was twofold: (1) to acquire the disputed property and freeze the situation there till a solution acceptable to both Hindus and Muslims was found and (2) to refer the core question of the dispute for adjudication by the Supreme Court through a Presidential reference under Article 143 of the Constitution of India.

The two decisions were further elaborated on 27 December as follows:

> The Government has decided to acquire all areas in dispute in the suits pending in the Allahabad High Court. It has also been decided to acquire the suitable adjacent areas. The acquired area excluding the area on which the disputed structure stood would be made available to two Trusts which would be set up for construction of a Ram temple and a mosque respectively and for planned development of the area.

> The Government of India has also decided to request the President to seek the opinion of the Supreme Court on the question whether there was a Hindu temple existing on the site where the disputed structure stood. The Government has also decided to abide by the opinion of the Supreme Court and to take appropriate steps to enforce the Court's opinion. Notwithstanding the acquisiton of the disputed area, the Government would ensure that the position existing prior to the promulgation of the Ordinance is maintained until such time as the Supreme Court gives its opinion in the matter. Thereafter, the rights of the parties shall be determined in the light of the Court's opinion.

In pursuance of these decisions an ordinance named 'Acquisition of Certain Area at Ayodhya Ordinance' was issued on 7 January 1993, for acquisition of 67.703 acres of land in the Ramjanmabhoomi–Babri Masjid complex. A reference to the Supreme Court under Article 143 of the Constitution was also made on the same day.

These two actions of the Central Government, however, became the target of further attack by some Muslim as well as political leaders. Both the Land Acquisition Ordinance/Act as well as the Presidential Reference were challenged by the opponents of such measures before the Supreme Court and a special five-member bench of the Court heard them for almost a year and decided the matter vide its judgment and order dated 24 December 1994. The Supreme Court while upholding the validity of acquisition of disputed land and the adjoining land by the Central Government, refused to answer the reference for the reasons given in the judgment.

On behalf of the Central Government, it was urged that in the existing situation and in view of the widespread communal flare-up throughout the country on account of the events at Ayodhya on 6 December 1992, the most appropriate course, in the opinion of the Central Government, was to make this acquisition along with the Special Reference to decide the question which would facilitate a negotiated solution of the problem, and if it failed, to enable the Central Government to take any other appropriate action to resolve the controversy and restore harmony in the country. It was made clear that acquisition of the disputed area was not meant to deprive the community found entitled to it of the same, or to retain any part of the excess area which was not necessary for a proper resolution of the dispute or to effectuate the purpose of the acquisition. It was submitted that an assurance of communal harmony throughout the country was a prime need for Constitutional purposes and avoidance of escalation of the dispute in the wake of the incident at Ayodhya on 6 December 1992 was an essential step in that direction, which undoubtedly was to promote the creed of secularism instead of impairing it.

In this context the Supreme Court held that 'the demolition of Babri Masjid in brazen defiance of the order of this Court is indeed a challenge to the majesty of law and the Constitution. This act of defiance is indeed a defiance of the Constitution and also the powers of the Constitutional authorities of the Centre and the State. The demolition is an unprecedented attack on the secular foundation of democracy, the authority and dignity of this Court. The Court thus stands betrayed as never before.' The Court went on to hold that, 'Having regard to the developments in this case which, prima facie, indicate that in spite of repeated undertakings made to the Court by no less an authority than a Constitutional Government of a State and its officers, they have committed or permitted to be committed acts of a very serious magnitude that it is necessary to issue *suo moto* notice calling upon Shri Kalyan Singh, the Chief Minister of the State of Uttar Pradesh and its officers who had filed affidavits in this Court or otherwise said to be associated with the events, to show cause why proceedings for contempt of Court should not be initiated against them.'

Further, going into the contempt aspect in detail, the Supreme Court held that 'we find that the undertaking given by Shri Kalyan

Singh was both in his personal capacity and on behalf of his government. There has been a flagrant breach of that undertaking. There has been wilful disobedience of the order.'

While concluding the verdict, the Supreme Court held, 'It is unhappy that a leader of a political party and their Chief Minister has to be convicted of the offence of contempt of Court, but since it has to be done to uphold the majesty of law, we convict him of the offence of the contempt of Court. Since the contempt raises a larger issue, which is the foundation of the secular foundation of our nation, we sentence him to a token imprisonment of one day. We also sentence him to pay a fine of Rs 2,000.'

(See Appendix XVI for the full text of the Supreme Court judgment)

*

From the above chronology of events and explanations given, it should be clear that there was no lapse whatever on the part of the Central Government and that if the State Government had at least made use of the Central force in time and meaningfully, the Babri structure could certainly have been saved on 6 December 1992. The UP Government and the BJP, the party of the State Government, would have to be held completely responsible for this wanton vandalism perpetrated on the secular credentials of the nation on that unfortunate day.

However, from millions of people has come the inevitable and irresistible question: Why did the President of India not impose President's Rule under Article 356 of the Constitution of India and save the structure in time? The Central Government certainly owes a full explanation to the people. It has been given several times, but it would be proper to consolidate the reply to the question in all its relevant aspects, to stand witness to history and throw light on the future.

This is taken up in the next chapter.

Why Was Article 356 Not Invoked?

I cannot count how many people, both friends and opponents, have hurled at me the question, 'Why did you not impose President's Rule in Uttar Pradesh in order to save the Babri Masjid from vandalism on 6 December 1992?' Indeed, this question must be examined, and if it had been gone into during the relevant days, it must be clarified what the conclusion was and how the President of India arrived at it.

In the first place, it requires no great persuasion to be convinced that when a Constitutional provision is sought to be brought into operation, the prior conditions which the Constitution lays down for that operation have to be meticulously fulfilled. Subjective impulses, hunches, prejudices and desires, howsoever intense and widespread, need to be subordinated to the exact provision of the Constitution. Likewise, in this particular matter, this approach should be taken as imperative to any proposal to promulgate Article 356.

The text of Article 356 is as follows:

> Art. 356: Provisions in case of failure of Constitutional machinery in States.
> (1) If the President, on receipt of a report from the Governor of a State or otherwise, is satisfied that a situation has arisen in which the government of the State cannot be carried on in accordance with the provisions of this

Constitution, the President may, by Proclamation—

(a) assume to himself all or any of the functions of the Government of the State or all or any of the powers vested in or exercisable by the Governor or in any body or authority in the State other than the Legislature of the State;

(b) declare that the powers of the Legislature of the State shall be exercisable by or under the authority of Parliament;

(c) make such incidental or consequential provisions as appear to the President to be necessary or desirable for giving effect to the objects of the Proclamation, including suspending in whole or in part the operation of any provisions of this Constitution relating to any body or authority in the State;

Provided that nothing in this clause shall authorize the President to assume to himself any of the powers vested in or exercisable by a High Court, or to suspend in whole or in part the operation of any provision of the Constitution relating to High Courts.

The remaining sub-clauses of the Article consist of procedural details, which need not be quoted in detail here.

As is clear from the text, the prior condition is that a given situation, as described in this Article, *has arisen* (i.e. already).

I would like to lay emphasis on this condition, because in actual operation the fact of a particular situation having (already) arisen is definite and specific. The obvious implication is that it should be possible to ascertain the exact stage at which that situation *has arisen*. Only on determining that exact stage is it possible to order imposition of President's Rule—not before, not otherwise. Only at that stage does the cause of action for invoking Article 356 become available. In this interpretation of the Article, the natural question would be: with regard to Ayodhya, when exactly did the situation arise in which Article 356 could legitimately have been brought into operation? Going through the chronology of events as they happened, every thinking person has to ask himself this question and answer it, if the imposition of President's Rule is meant to be in accordance with the relevant provision of the Constitution.

Again, it is important to note the situation that the Constitution envisages for invoking Article 356 is described in the words, 'the situation in which the government of the State cannot be carried on in accordance with the provisions of the Constitution.' Scanning the events described in the foregoing paragraphs, the particular event with which the situation described in the last sentence *has arisen*, needs to be identified. It is my humble but emphatic submission that it was not possible to identify the stage, event or moment that could fit in the above description (i.e. when it could be said that the government of the state could not be carried out according to the provisions of the Constitution). * The exact scenario was as follows:

1. The large congregation of *kar sevaks*;
2. The ambiguous attitude of the State Government whose responsibility it was to protect the structure;
3. The tense atmosphere all around the structure;
4. Provocative speeches and statements;
5. Rath yatras;
6. The BJP State Government's claim that it had the people's 'mandate' to construct the Ram temple.

Neither any of the above factors, nor their combination, could

---

* This is neither an afterthought nor an argument for argument's sake. It was a most genuine factual difficulty to which I drew the pointed attention of the Lok Sabha in my intervention during the debate on the subject just a day after the demolition of the Babri structure.

be characterized as 'a situation in which the government of the State cannot be carried on in accordance with the provisions of the Constitution.'

In all such cases, the Governor's report is generally the basis of the Central Government's decision, since the Governor is in charge of the state. The Governor's recommendation regarding invoking Article 356, which has high credibility in this matter, is generally accepted, although it is not obligatory on the President to do so. Sometimes it may happen that even without the Governor sending a report, the material available with the Government of India could furnish the basis for a decision, one way or the other. However, calling for a report from the Governor and considering it in all seriousness is the normal practice and all these years the imposition of President's Rule has been more or less in accordance with this practice. In any event, it is obvious that the Governor's opinion, when received, is of considerable value. Now, the specific recommendation of the Governor may be either positive or negative; or it may be to wait and see. In the case of a positive recommendation, he makes out a clear case, and says that Article 356 be invoked. In a negative case, he brings out all the pitfalls, all the dangers, all the greater problems that would arise by imposing President's Rule and recommends *against* such imposition. In such a case the reasons that he may adduce deserve to be taken as particularly weighty, since what the Governor says here is, in effect, that the remedy of Article 356 is really worse than the malady—in other words, worse than the situation in the state before the imposition of President's Rule.

The relevant extract from the letter of the Governor of Uttar Pradesh is as under:

> There are reports that a large number of kar sevaks are reaching Ayodhya, but they are peaceful. The State Government has given a categorical assurance to the Hon'ble Supreme Court, who has accepted the

> Government's assurance. The State Government has also fully assured the full protection to the disputed structure and adequate arrangements have been made to protect the disputed structure.
>
> In my opinion at present the time is not ripe for taking any drastic step like the dismissal of the UP Government or the dissolution of the State Assembly or the imposition of President's Rule in the State. If it is done, it may have far-reaching consequences. It may also lead to large-scale violence not only in this State but also in other parts of the country. The possibility of the damage to the disputed structure itself may not be ruled out. Therefore in my opinion we should be very cautious on this issue and should weigh the various alternatives and pros and cons of any decision to be taken on this issue. Any decision in haste should be avoided . . .

One thing is clear, that today's hindsight was not available to anyone in the Government of India on those dates. Hindsight is often a dangerous guide. Its main characteristic is to mislead and confuse. It makes one feel how easy the matter in question had been, the way it happened—looking back—and how it should have been dealt with. The formidable snag is that no one at that crucial time knew *how it was going to happen.*

There is another important aspect to consider. Of late there has been a clear qualitative shift in the Supreme Court's approach to Article 356. Once upon a time, in the initial stages, the imposition of President's Rule was held to be a matter of the President's 'subjective satisfaction' and therefore not open to scrutiny by the Court. Whether by the persistent complaints of repeated 'misuse' of Article 356 by the Executive over a long period, or/and other circumstances, it is no longer possible to assert today that the President's action under this provision is immune from judicial scrutiny. While not minimizing the fact of 'misuse' of the provision, it has to be admitted that the changed attitude of the Supreme Court has introduced an in-built inhibition on the part of the Executive. This is an undeniable fact, which necessarily enters the decision-making process as a fairly important preliminary consideration.*

One has to reconstruct, as closely as possible, the situation of those days when the Government of India received the Governor's letter extracted above. Only then can one judge whether in those circumstances the decision not to impose President's Rule was, after all, correct and justified. This is the crux of the matter. Obviously, some parameters had contributed to the Government of India's assessment of the situation of those days, viz.

i) First, the general atmosphere as was gathered by the government from its own sources, agencies both at the Central and State levels;
ii) The general expectation of the common people as was assessed from the media, the public, the man in the street, the general life in the towns and villages where tension of any kind was immediately felt;
iii) The attitudes which the Ayodhya matter had evoked in the courts, including the Supreme Court, in any related matter that came up before that Court for any decision or order during those days;
iv) The trend of thinking in national bodies in which the matter came to be discussed specifically and opinions were expressed by members thereof—like the National Integration Council and similar bodies, if any;

---

* To illustrate this, it may be recalled that after the demolition when the four BJP state governments were dismissed, the Madhya Pradesh High Court actually set aside the imposition of President's Rule and ordered the revival of the dismissed State Assembly and government. This order was overruled by the Supreme Court.

v) Detailed consideration of the logistics and practical factors, both time-wise and strategy-wise; and finally,
vi) The gut feeling of the government, in the light of all the above factors close to the crucial date.

These were the important inputs available to the government in assessing any developing situation. It could not be rumour, imagination, prejudice or hearsay. The National Integration Council, for instance, had the leaders of all the political parties in the country represented on it—plus some respected personalities. This council was fully aware of the gravity of the situation in Ayodhya at the crucial time, on the crucial days. It went into this matter threadbare when it met on 2 November and again on 23 November 1992. From the discussions and the opinions that emerged, I found a definite view, by and large, that President's Rule should not be imposed in UP. If this trend of opinion emerged, by and large, the Government of India had to consider it in all seriousness. Here is a case where not only did there exist no reason for not complying with the NIC's general opinion, but something contra-indicative in the form of the Governor's clear warning of the possible destruction of the Babri structure in case of imposing President's Rule was also in the hands of the President and the Prime Minister. It was not possible to disregard the above-mentioned two factors facilely—on the possible ground of a subjective mistrust in the BJP government in UP. Any such attitude would have been promptly dubbed as political prejudice and condemned all round.

Coming to logistics, everyone knows that the Central Government did not have even a toe-hold anywhere in UP at the time. In the absence of such a hold, the Centre could not have found it feasible to take an extremely crucial step like the imposition of President's Rule in the teeth of determined resistance by an entrenched State Government. It was at this juncture that a party who was represented in the case before the Supreme Court made a request to the Supreme Court, *inter alia*, that the Central

Government be made the Receiver of the property at Ayodhya (the Babri structure and some area around it). That would have been a useful step and would have given the Central Government the hold which it so badly needed under the circumstances. It would have given security to the structure, and time to the Centre to decide on other more effective options. On the other hand, taking over the entire state under Article 356 at one go was fraught with several risks, foreseen and unforeseen. The Government of India had already given a general consent to cooperate in whatever manner it was called upon to do so. But the State Government opposed the request and reiterated that it was fully conscious of its duty as a duly elected government, to protect the structure and therefore appointment of a Receiver was unnecessary. On the basis of these emphatic assurances, the Supreme Court, by its order of 28 November, did not decide to appoint a Receiver and kept the matter pending. Instead, the Court appointed a judicial officer as its Observer.

So, the Central Government had two options:

a) To take the risk of the destruction of that structure by taking action clearly against the Governor's advice and other contra-indicative factors as described above; or,
b) To keep persuading the State Government to make use of the 20,000 Central forces stationed in Faizabad, for saving the structure. It is important to note here that the State Government did not *refuse* to use the Central forces, but in fact did not allow the forces to operate either. Indeed at some point they also asked for some companies of Central forces, which were promptly made available. This naturally gave an impression of their sincerity in the matter and allayed doubts. A request was made to the State Government to give a magistrate to accompany the Central forces, because without a magistrate the forces could not move. Again, the State Government did not refuse to provide the magistrate, but kept dilly-dallying

and did not send the magistrate on some pretext or the other until it was very late. They gave the magistrate at long last and the forces started to go towards the structure. But just then hooligans stopped them, while the local police looked on. Then the magistrate gave them a written order to go back from midway, from near the Saket College, and not to proceed towards the structure. Under these conditions, the forces had no option but to return to the barracks. The Central Government had no power at all around the structure, none of their authorities near the structure and their 20,000 uniformed forces had been completely immobilized and confined to Faizabad. This was the actual situation in Ayodhya on that fateful day.

c) All these facts explain what made up the Government of India's mind on those two or three days, after continuously monitoring the situation from hour to hour and taking the overall circumstances into account. It was utterly inadvisable to have risked the destruction of the structure in the very process of trying to save it. In addition to losing the structure, there was the further risk of a large number of persons in the crowd being killed in the process. The Government of India simply did not consider it wise to invite these horrendous developments by ignoring the Governor's warning.

d) The State Government was obviously opposed to imposing President's Rule and was trying to thwart it. Therefore, the logistics of the actual process of imposing President's Rule at once became crucial—perhaps for the first time since the Constitution came into force.

e) The procedure for promulgating Article 356 obviously cannot be carried out as a lightning military manoeuvre. The following is the procedure:

   i) A Cabinet note recommending promulgation of Article 356 to the President of India is circulated;
   ii) Cabinet is convened;

iii) Cabinet takes the decision suggested in the Cabinet note;
iv) The recommendation is submitted to the President of India;
v) The President decides as per the recommendation; and
vi) A Proclamation issues.

While considering these steps, it had to be borne in mind that a large and belligerent crowd was already gathered at the site, courtesy the State Government. The disputed structure was a helpless hostage in their hands. Any piece of information about the intended President's Rule was bound to furnish the provocation and lead to what the Governor had warned about. What they really needed was not even provocation, only a pretext that could pass off as a provocation. Nor was it possible to complete all the above procedural steps in complete and impenetrable secrecy in the Central Government. Although no State Government likes to be dismissed and to give way to President's Rule, such an extraordinary situation of Centre-State confrontation over the imposition of President's Rule had never arisen since Independence.

Further, the time taken for these steps, and for the Government of India to actually get into the field had also to be accounted for in this case for the first time. *That time could not be minutes*; it had to be some hours, at the very least. The action consisted of physically taking over the state administration at all levels, particularly at the cutting-edge levels necessarily in this case—from the DCs, the SPs, officers right down to sub-inspectors, replacing several persons handpicked and posted there by the State Government. The time factor for this was undeniably crucial. But anything could have happened within those hours when technically and legally the state was under the Central Government, but the actual possession of that particular place, including the structure, was not yet with the Central Government authorities. This meant that anyone could do anything and the State Government could say with impunity that they were not responsible, since their rule had ended.

What kind of situation would that be? Under those circumstances no one could, with any reasonable certainty, say that the structure could have been saved without the consequences mentioned above. And any amount of havoc could have been wrought in that highly volatile situation. Anyone can easily see that earlier in 1990, Mulayam Singh Yadav could control a similar situation because he was in charge, he was the Chief Minister, he put his handpicked men there, and he did everything to ensure full and proper protection. That was how he could save the structure—and still some deaths took place and also some damage to the structure, not to speak of the subsequent political fallout, which is well known.

I would like to further elaborate some questions regarding the operational aspects of Article 356, to which I have made reference in the foregoing paragraphs. In the first place, this provision has gathered a lot of controversy over the decades and has proved to be largely unpopular. The Sarkaria Commission, as well as many other authorities and expert bodies, have frequently commented unfavourably on it. As a result, governments have become wary of imposing it, except in the case of unavoidable necessity. As a result, the question often asked is: 'Why was Article 356 imposed?' and not: 'Why was it not?'

Next, the question of its phraseology and its exact purport. It contains two expressions that present operational difficulty, viz.

i) 'a situation has arisen'; and
ii) 'Government of the State cannot be carried on in accordance with the provisions of this Constitution.'

Regarding i) I have already explained its operational complications in the foregoing paragraphs. The result of my analysis is that Article 356 could be brought into operation only when a given situation *has* arisen, and not when that situation has not yet arisen and is therefore intended to be prevented. Thus it cannot be invoked *in anticipation of that situation.*

As regards ii) it is not a categorically defined situation that one is dealing with. It is with reference to the fact that the state government cannot be carried on in a given manner, on which the invoking of Article 356 is predicated. The President of India is expected to apply this litmus test in each case. In recent years, when the courts have begun not only to comment, but even to set aside the President's decision in this behalf and restore dissolved Assemblies and dismissed governments, the Government of India faces a delicate task. Where such a reversal of the President's action under Article 356 takes place, the continuance of the Central Government becomes obviously untenable. As a result, the tendency is likely to be not to impose President's Rule, even when it is necessary. Whether this tendency (which means a total swing to non-use instead of alleged misuse) is desirable, needs to be seriously examined.

Coming to the Ayodhya issue, what exactly do the words, 'the Government of the State cannot be carried on in accordance with the provisions of this Constitution' mean, when applied to this context? There were two allegations against the State Government of UP viz.

a) Doing or permitting construction in violation of court orders;
b) Failure to protect Babri structure.

The first allegation stands disposed of because the *kar seva*, as such, was eventually peaceful and did not violate any court order, whatever the threats or fulminations of the leaders had been. So, on this score, invoking Article 356 could have no justification.

The second allegation was entirely justified, but there was no order, as such, of any court regarding the protection of the Babri structure. The charge is of violating the State Government's own duty and repeated commitments and promises to the court. This called for action for contempt of court, which the Supreme Court actually took. On this account also, it would be difficult to justify the promulgation of Article 356 until the specific moment at which it became justified and due. That moment could only be the moment of demolition. Thus even if we stretch the meaning of the words 'the government of the State cannot be carried on etc.' to the utmost, they would become applicable only when the State failed in its Constitutional duty to protect the structure and, as a result, the demolition took place—*not before*. And as a matter of fact, Article 356 was clamped just on the heels of that moment. Thus, both in not imposing President's Rule earlier, and in imposing it at the moment it became due, the Central Government's action was entirely justified and correct. It is clear that on a correct construction of Article 356, it is not possible to invoke the provision to serve a preventive purpose in time. This is not a happy situation and calls for a re-look at the language of Article 356, if it is to be provided with any legally valid 'teeth' to serve a preventive purpose.*

*

I shall now come back to the circumstances that obtained in Ayodhya during the few days before 6 December 1992. A stream of affidavits flowed almost daily from the UP State Government to the Supreme Court. Over the decades, a general psychological atmosphere had been built up against the use of Article 356 (including even a vociferous demand for its repeal) and it was alleged that it was being used by the Congress government at the

---

* A comparison of the wording used in Article 356 and Article 359 brings this out clearly. Under Article 359, the promulgation of emergency is made possible whenever the country is 'threatened', thus giving the President much more freedom and scope to act preventively, after anticipating a given danger. This is not the case in Article 356.

Centre to get rid of the state governments of other parties. In this very matter, the Supreme Court's refusal even to make the Central Government a Receiver for the limited and specific purpose of giving adequate protection to the disputed structure at Ayodhya is also a meaningful pointer; it only translates into a 'hands off the state' directive to the Centre. Finally, as explained in the foregoing paragraphs, there were formidable logistic handicaps and absolute paucity of time (plus control) faced by the Central Government to act with safety. This combination of factors was the rationale that led to the decision not to impose President's Rule. Any prudent President or Prime Minister would not have gone ahead and clamped Article 356 under those circumstances.

10

Ayodhya: What Happened and Why

Constitutional pundits, administrators and others understand that in some crucial situations, time is of the essence in taking a decision. It is not simply a matter of emotions, although everyone is overwhelmed by emotions. The 500-year-old structure at Ayodhya had been there as a part of history, and its historical heritage cannot simply be allowed to be vandalized and go without safety. But who has gone into these questions? The essence of the efforts of some of our leaders was to wield the one stick that they had got to beat me with. I understood this. I told many people that those responsible for the vandalism had got not only the Babri Masjid demolished, but along with the Babri Masjid it was me whom they were trying to demolish. If the Central Government cannot trust the main Opposition party, how can democracy function at all? That party, along with others, was being consulted for almost everything—whether their cooperation was available or not—from day one, following the consensus method.

The religious leaders until that time did not respond to anyone except Advaniji and Atalji, the BJP leaders. When I first spoke to them, it was Advaniji who said to me, 'We have no control over them, you deal with the religious leaders yourself.' I called them and argued for more than an hour and a half with them and ultimately I bought four months' time for negotiations, which was mentioned in my statement in Parliament. It was hailed as a success, where there had been no success for years. After a while, however, the VHP realized that the negotiations were becoming far too successful for their comfort. So, at the end of three months, they started the agitational approach. In the negotiations, I had said that nothing less than four months would suffice, and I was not merely haggling with them. It was a question of getting things done and making a settlement possible. On the other hand, psychologically, they thought they were caught in this friendly and positive situation and wanted to get out of it. So, at the end of three months, they went back on their original stand. I told them several times, I told them through friends, I told them through others, I also called them and told them myself that bargaining was not my intention, the intention was to see that the negotiations were successful.

This kind of rigidity was not the right way of dealing with such a delicate matter. However, the VHP and the RSS had decided to wreck the negotiations and the BJP, of course, connived all the way. This was exactly what happened. The case was being argued actually in the Supreme Court; every hour, every two hours I was reporting to Parliament as to what was happening there. The situation was so tense. Where was the need for such tensions in religious matters? In fact, instead of four months they should have been ready to give me five months, or six. To whom were they giving these four or five months? To the Prime Minister of India, in order to disentangle the most difficult question impinging on the nation's existence. Was it not worthwhile giving another month or at least sticking to the original four months? They were behaving as if I was a supplicant; there was that kind of arrogance, arrogance unbecoming of saints. It was very clear that they did not want a settlement. It was clear that they wanted some confrontation in the name of *kar seva*, so they were making all these pretences. However, they met with nothing but reasonableness from my side which was quite disarming to them since they could not provoke a public controversy to blame the government. That is why they just made an announcement, without any explanation or rationale whatsoever. And stuck to it doggedly and went ahead.

In view of the fact that things were getting out of hand in Ayodhya, should the Central Government have stepped in and taken over control of the RJB-BM site before the *kar seva* on 6 December 1992? What could have happened in case of such intervention needs to be considered on both sides. On one side was the disastrous prospect of lakhs and lakhs of people falling on the Babri structure and demolishing it. On the other side was the likelihood of the same demolition if we ignored the Governor's warning and went ahead forcibly, in a situation wherein even the Central forces reaching the structure had been thwarted officially by the local administration. It was truly a no-win situation. So, to avoid the same danger coming from one side or the other, the only course possible at that moment was to somehow persuade the local administration to secure access by the Central forces to the disputed structure so as to ensure its safety. There was absolutely no reason for the carnage, for the destruction of houses of minorities in several other states; yet all these things happened, unfortunately. Now, this point needs to be very clearly understood, that by rousing communal passions the BJP aggravated the situation further, even after the Babri demolition. Clearly, therefore, the BJP is responsible for what happened. It is said that the Central Government was responsible for not stopping it. The question is, could it have been stopped? Under what circumstances could it have been stopped? How could it have been stopped?

We had to go meticulously by what is borne out by the acts of the governments, by the acts of the organs of the Constitution and the attitudes of those who were holding official positions. In the first instance, what was the trend of the Supreme Court? One may argue that the Supreme Court was acting independently and the Government of India need not have been influenced by the Supreme Court in taking executive decisions. But is this possible?

Every day the Government of India, in some way, was interacting with the State Government of UP and the bench of the Supreme Court. Things were constantly discussed, instructions were issued from day to day, affidavits were being submitted solemnly almost every day by the State Government. Now, was it possible for anyone to say that in spite of all the affidavits, all the affirmations, all the promises, the Government of India should have acted on the assumption that all the affidavits were false? That the affidavits were going to be violated? Thus it was a complication of the Constitution, not a complication of logistics. It was not the absence of the force in Ayodhya that was crucial, but the absence of the consent of the State Government to use the force, because it could not be used without the permission, express permission, of the State Government. This was the position.

The Central Government could therefore do nothing beyond pleading with the State Government, to make use of the Central forces available just at a distance of eight or nine kilometres. They never did so. When asked for magistrates to accompany the forces, they never said that they would not give the magistrate, but in fact never gave the magistrate until it was too late and even after the magistrate was given, after going a distance of about five kilometres, the District Collector or whatever his designation was, actually gave orders in writing to the contingent to withdraw from that spot and not to proceed towards the Babri structure, on the plea that he was under orders from the State Government not to use force. This was, on the face of it, a facetious plea because 'show of force' need not necessarily mean firing and loss of life. Thus at the exact moment when the force could have scared the crowd and found its way to the Babri structure, with a fair chance of protecting it, it was turned back—deliberately—by an official order of the concerned functionary of the State Government. Here were two governments, creatures of the same Constitution, come into confrontation. So the Central force had to act according to the Constitution, there was no other way.

Although brave words have been said after the event and many people now look like sages who knew everything beforehand, I must say that all this is a pose, because having been the authors of the crisis and enacted the whole drama of destruction, those responsible wanted to have some specific role assigned to themselves in history, something even wrongly to be proud of. That is why BJP leaders bragged about the Babri demolition as a great achievement for quite some time. Not one of my colleagues who suggested the imposition of President's Rule came up with reasons based on objective conditions there, nor had they any ghost of an idea of how President's Rule could be imposed in those specific conditions obtaining in UP, on 6 December, as distinguished from the introduction of President's Rule elsewhere in normal times. The officers told me again and again that whatever was being done for queering the pitch was for political reasons and not based on what obtained on the field. They said they had studied the field and were quite clear that the *kar seva* would be peaceful. This was the situation.

In the initial stages the Ayodhya matter had been shaping up so well that the sanyasis themselves who had never talked to any Congressmen earlier, talked to me for months and months and gave me time for negotiation, at least in the beginning. At that stage, it appeared, *prima facie*, that they only wanted the Ram temple to be built. Then why did they go back on their promise? It was clear that there was a change of mind on their part or, what is more likely, on the part of the political forces that controlled them. These forces deliberately wanted to get out of the friendly situation which the sanyasis were getting into with me and which, if left to itself, would have made the mandir issue *wholly apolitical*. This subtle aspect of the Ramjanmabhoomi matter is very important and brings home the undeniable fact that while Hindu masses were swayed by their devotion to Ram and their intense desire for the temple, the political forces behind the issue could not care less for the temple; they only wanted to retain a long-term vote-rich communal issue for as long as they could. Indeed, in its majority communal orientation, they saw it as a permanent, evergreen issue. It may be noted that it was not just one temple that was being agitated for; the number was three and for good measure, in the unlikely event of all the three temple issues being settled amicably, there was a never-ending store of more than three thousand controversial temples lined up all over the country!

The very fact that the Ayodhya issue had a regular knack of becoming very active a few months before every election could not possibly have been—in fact it was *not*—an unintended coincidence. However, so long as socio-economic and political issues piloted by leaders of great ability, perspicacity and popularity remained entrenched in the electoral process, the efforts to exploit the religious faith of the common people for electoral purposes did not show any promise of a big response from the people. The performance of Jan Sangh-BJP in successive elections (until 1984) had been small and did not pose any real ideological challenge. And the limit was reached when in the 1984 Lok Sabha election the BJP was reduced to exactly 2 seats. In fact that was even lower than what it normally got at the earlier elections. But by 1989 the BJP not only jumped from 2 to 88, it also created a situation where almost every party—notably the Congress—was forced to include a reference to the Ram temple in its 1991 Lok Sabha election manifesto. It is also significant that between 1984 and 1989 some decisive steps were taken by the Congress Government in UP, which demonstrated that the concern with the temple issue had become very real with the Congress under Rajiv Gandhi.

After 1989, the BJP did not stop or look back. So the question naturally arises: what was—or could have been—the extraordinary ocean of service that the BJP continued to drown the people in (unmatched anywhere in the world presumably at any time in the history of democracy) so that its Lok Sabha tally soared from

2 (in 1984) to 88 (in 1989) to 119 (in 1991) to 161 (in 1996) and to 181 (in 1998) in an almost geometric progression? Nor could this galloping ascent be attributed to the voters suddenly getting enamoured of any of the BJP's other declared policies such as uniform civil code, abrogation of Article 370 et al. It is crystal clear that there was a strong emotional religious dimension constantly assisting the BJP and motivating the people in a manner that was not available to other parties that entered the electoral fray with their normal secular manifestos, with normal secular promises.

The situation inevitably throws up some very intricate Constitutional and ideological questions. Are the BJP, the Muslim League, the Hindu Mahasabha etc. on the one hand and the other parties such as the Congress, Janata Dal, the Communist parties etc. on the other, participating in the elections under the same Constitution? Is it a level playing field that they have had in the elections, say, of the 1980s and 1990s? It is not my intention to go into these questions in this book, since I am confining my comments specifically to the Ayodhya issue. Yet I thought it proper to flag these pertinent questions very briefly, since they are bound to affect future elections, for the simple reason that religious faith in India, if allowed to be used as an electoral issue, is much too tempting a short cut to votes. It will be impossible to set things right after allowing this trend to continue for a long time, bringing in signal successes again and again on the basis of a grossly unfair and impermissible advantage to one party, which flies in the face of our Constitution. Never mind who wins and who loses in a given election. Having taken full advantage of religion in some elections, the BJP may lose in later ones for other reasons; that is always possible and may even happen with equally surprising unexpectedness. Nonetheless, the legitimacy of religious sentiment as an accepted and practised means in a secular electoral process would still remain intact. And before we realize what is happening, our cherished Constitutional pillar of secularism will become and remain little more than an empty shell. It is time to pause and think whom history will hold responsible for this complacency and its disastrous consequences.

To the BJP also goes the dubious credit of not only hijacking the political process right into the religious ambit, but to some extent dragging other parties along with itself on the same path, if only to counter the BJP attack. The net result, however, has been that the admissibility as well as the respectability of the communal card have both been accepted, at least by necessary implication, on both sides, obviously for opposite reasons. And once the admissibility of the issue was accepted, everyone was stopped to some extent from disowning it. The result has been that the importance of the Ayodhya issue, as a *politically* (and electorally) potential one, was willy nilly acknowledged, judging from the actions taken by succeeding governments.

I tried to explain all these things to my colleagues, but on their side also political and vote-earning considerations definitely prevailed and they had already made up their minds that one person was to be made historically responsible for the tragedy, in case the issue ended up in tragedy. If there had been success (as there definitely seemed to be, in the initial months) they would of course have readily shared the credit or appropriated it to themselves. So they were playing either for success, or an alibi through a scapegoat in case of failure! It was a perfect strategy. They could loudly proclaim later that the Muslim vote did not come to the Congress after the demolition of the Babri Masjid solely because of me. It remains to be seen whether the future will vindicate me in this regard; if it does, I shall, of course, feel happy.

Appendix I

Major communal riots relating to Ramjanmabhoomi–Babri Masjid issue during 1989 and 1990

S.No.	*Date*	*State*	*Place*	*Number of persons*	
				killed	*injured*
1989					
1.	29 September	Madhya Pradesh	Mhow	-	53
2.	29–30 September	Madhya Pradesh	Khargone	5	54
3.	6 October	Rajasthan	Jaipur City, Shastri Nagar	1	15
4.	17 October	Bihar	Jharia Town, Dhanbad District	1	16
5.	10 October	Rajasthan	Ladnum, Nagaur District	1	16
6.	22–24 October	Gujarat	Godhra, Panchmahal District	4	9
7.	24 October onwards	Bihar	Bhagalpur	432	191
8.	25 October	Bihar	Mungher	29	11
9.	6 November	Bihar	Sasaram, Rohtas District	6	49
10.	9 November	Karnataka	Arsikere, Hasan District	-	14
11.	10 November	Karnataka	Shimoga	1	5
12.	11 November	Uttar Pradesh	Varanasi	9	49

S.No.	*Date*	*State*	*Place*	*Number of persons killed*	*injured*
1990					
13.	24–29 October	Rajasthan	Jaipur City	50	218
14.	26–28 October	Bihar	Ranchi	4	16
15.	22 October–17 November	Andhra Pradesh	Hyderabad City	40	202
16.	23 October–2 November	Gujarat	Ahmedabad City	31	82
17.	30 October–7 November	Madhya Pradesh	Indore	17	189
18.	30 October–20 November	Gujarat	Baroda	10	72
19.	30 October	Uttar Pradesh	Bijnore	51	23
20.	30–31 October	Uttar Pradesh	Muzaffarnagar City	15	32
21.	28 October	Bihar	Ranchi City	1	5
22.	30 October	Karnataka	Chetali, Coorg District	2	2
23.	1–4 November	Karnataka	Sakleshwar, Hasan District	3	7
24.	2–3 November	Uttar Pradesh	Hapur Town, Ghaziabad District	27	28
25.	2–3 November	Gujarat	Morvi, Panchmahal District	8	-

Appendix II

Resolution adopted by the National Integration Council at its meeting held on 2 November 1991 in New Delhi

The National Integration Council views with deep concern the deterioration in the communal situation in the country during the last two years, which have witnessed increasing communal tension and serious incidents of violence leading to heavy loss of life and property. Along with the continuing activities of terrorists and militants in certain parts of the country, communal animosity can seriously undermine the national unity. The Council reaffirms the resolve of the people to resolutely meet any challenge to the country's unity and integrity and its secular democratic polity.

The Council noted that one of the factors which has added immensely to the build-up of communal tension is the Ram Janma Bhoomi–Babri Masjid dispute. The Council expressed its concern at the recent happenings in Ayodhya and hoped that such situations will not recur.

The Ram Janma Bhoomi–Babri Masjid dispute has continued to evade a satisfactory solution. The Council appeals to all concerned parties and organizations to work towards an amicable, negotiated solution of the dispute in a spirit of cooperation and mutual understanding.

The Council noted the following assurances given by the Chief Minister of Uttar Pradesh:

(i) All efforts will be made to find an amicable resolution of the issue;
(ii) Pending a final solution, the Government of Uttar Pradesh will hold itself fully responsible for the protection of the Ram Janma Bhoomi–Babri Masjid structure; and
(iii) Orders of the Court in regard to the land acquisition proceedings will be fully implemented; and
(iv) Judgement of the Allahabad High Court in the cases pending before it will not be violated.

The Council welcomed the invitation given to it by the Chief Minister of Uttar Pradesh to visit Ayodhya on any suitable date.

The National Integration Council calls upon all concerned, including the political parties, religious leaders, the media and other organizations, to act with restraint and in a manner that will promote harmony and goodwill between all communities. Everyone must make efforts to desist from vords or deeds that are likely to inflame communal passions or give encouragement to disruptive forces. Indian society is traditionally marked by a spirit of tolerance and respect for each other's faith. This spirit should continue to guide our thoughts and actions. The Council appeals to all people to maintain peace and tranquillity and create an atmosphere conducive to the satisfactory settlement of the Ram Janma Bhoomi–Babri Masjid dispute.

Appendix III

Extract from the report of delegation of the members of the National Integration Council and Members of Parliament to Ayodhya, 27 April 1992

From the facts stated earlier, the following issues arise for the consideration of the Delegation:

(i) Whether the admitted acts of the UP Government are in conformity with the assurances given by the Chief Minister of Uttar Pradesh at the meeting of the National Integration Council, held on 2nd November 1991.

(ii) Whether the orders passed in the suits regarding maintenance of status quo from time to time continue to be in force in spite of the orders by the High Court in the writ petitions on 26-10-91. If the orders in the above suits continue to be in force even after the land acquisition, whether the above said acts of UP Government are in consonance with the letter and spirit of the orders passed by the High Court in the suits pending before it, on 3-2-1986, 14-8-1989, 7-11-1989 and 5-2-1992.

(iii) Whether the admitted acts of UP Government of demolition of all buildings, structures except two rooms of Sakshi Gopal Temple, levelling of land construction of boundary wall are in consonance with letter and spirit of the order passed by the

High Court on 25-10-1991 and 26-10-1991 in the writ petition challenging the land acquisition proceedings.

(iv) Whether the acts of the UP Government are in consonance with the letter and spirit of the orders passed by the Supreme Court on 15-11-1991 in the writ petition challenging the land acquisition by the UP Government.

Conclusions

The Ram Janma Bhoomi–Babri Masjid issue is not only the subject matter of litigation, but has aroused passions and sentiments throughout the nation. This issue has assumed such a magnitude where people of different communities have expressed strong opinions, involvement and concern. It is, therefore, not proper to take a purely technical view on such a sensitive matter which has a bearing on the unity and integrity of the nation and maintenance of harmony among people. It is in this background that we proceed to give our views in an objective manner:

(i) The committee had carefully gone through the records and also given due consideration to the views of the Government of Uttar Pradesh as submitted to us. The map made available to us by the State Government shows that plot Nos. 582, 584 to 591 and 378, which are the subject matter of suits, have also been included in the land notified by the UP Government in acquisition proceedings.

(ii) A perusal of the interim orders, passed by the High Court from time to time, on 3-2-1986, 14-8-1989, 7-11-1989 and 5-2-1992, shows that the parties to the suit have been specifically directed not to change the nature of the properties as then existed and to maintain status-quo. The Court has also further clarified in its order dated 7-11-1987, what they meant by 'status quo'. It is pertinent to note that the High Court has passed its order on 5-2-1992 following the clarifications sought on its earlier order in writ petition challenging the land acquisition on 25-10-1991 and 26-10-1991. Therefore, the Delegation is of the view that the latest order passed by the High Court in February, 1992 continues to have force inspite of the order passed by it in the land acquisition proceedings. Hence the Committee is of the opinion that the admitted acts of the UP Government in demolishing the existing structures and levelling the land are not in consonance with the letter and spirit of the orders passed by the High Court in the pending suits referred to above.

(iii) If one carefully reads the interim order of the High Court, passed on 25-10-1991 and 26-10-1991 and the Supreme Court's order, passed on 15-11-1991, it is clear that the UP Government was permitted only to take possession of the land and to make such arrangements for the purpose for which the land was proposed to be acquired and to erect only temporary structures. But in spite of the urgency pleaded by the UP Government the High Court did not specifically permit it to demolish the structures or level the land, or build a pucca compound wall. The orders passed by the High Court in the land acquisition suit are also not final, but only interim, and are subject to further orders and final decision of the court. Therefore, the question arises whether 'status quo' can be restored if the Court ultimately quashed the notification for acquisition. One can draw legitimate inference that the acts of UP Government in regard to the notified land are likely to render the final decision of the Court infractuous. Therefore, the Delegation is of the view that the acts of the UP Government are not in consonance with the orders passed by the High Court and the Supreme Court in the land acquisition matter.

(iv) It is the view of the UP Government that after taking possession of the land u/s 17(1) of the Land Acquisition Act, it has every right to demolish all the structures, and, therefore, has not violated any orders of the Court. The Delegation does not agree with this view for the reasons stated above.

(v) So far as the wall built by the Ayodhya Development Authority is concerned, the UP Government is of the view that the boundary wall does not pass through any of the suit properties and it has been built on a different land, as mentioned in their note.

However, we have received a representation, during our visit, that the boundary wall passes through some suit plots and divides the suit property. In order to get a clear view, the Delegation sought the relevant land revenue records and details of the co-relation between the suit plots and the land acquired and also of the land on which the boundary wall has been built. These records have not been made available to the Delegation. As such, the Delegation is not in a position to give its opinion. It is for the Union Government to hold a further enquiry on this, if necessary, to find out the exact position of the boundary wall.

(vi) The Delegation would like to recall the assurances given by the Chief Minister of UP, Shri Kalyan Singh, to the National Integration Council on 2nd November, 1991. The Delegation having gone into this question deeply regrets to note that the Government of Uttar Pradesh has failed to fulfil the solemn assurance given to the Council by the Chief Minister. This, in our opinion, has led to a heightened sense of insecurity among a section of the population and aggravated the climate of disharmony and tension endangering our secular framework and National Unity.

Recommendations

1. The Union Government should take due note of the findings of the Delegation on the situation at Ayodhya.
2. The Union Government may advise the State Government not to proceed with any further in changing the nature of the suit property until final orders of the Court.
3. The Union Government should request the High Court of

Allahabad to expedite the pending proceedings and hear both the cases on a day to day basis.

4. The Union Government should simultaneously take effective steps for a negotiated settlement of the dispute in the light of the consensus reached at the National Integration Council meeting of 2-11-1991.
5. The Union Government may convene a meeting of the National Integration Council to review the latest situation.
6. The Union Government may place this report before both the Houses of Parliament for information and discussion.

New Delhi,
April 27, 1992

S. R. Bommai
Leader of Delegation
of the Members of
Standing Committee of
National Integration Council
and Parliament

Appendix IV

Prime Minister's statement in Lok Sabha on 27 July 1992

The Ramjanmabhoomi–Babri Masjid dispute has been agitating the minds of all those who believe in the values of secularism and governance based upon Constitutional principles. During the last few weeks, the developments at the Ramjanmabhoomi–Babri Masjid complex have been unfolding rapidly. The order of the Lucknow Bench of the Allahabad High Court dated 15 July was a watershed in the series of recent developments. The High Court, in its interim order, restrained the parties from undertaking or continuing any construction activity on the 2.77 acres of land, which had been notified by the Government of Uttar Pradesh for acquisition. The Court also directed that if it were necessary to do any construction on the land, prior permission from the Court would have to be obtained.

While the Government of Uttar Pradesh repeatedly assured the Government of India as also the National Integration Council that they would undertake to have the orders of the High Court implemented, the construction activity at the Ramjanmabhoomi–Babri Masjid complex continued.

The non-implementation of the High Court orders created misgivings among the people. This matter came up for consideration before the Supreme Court in a writ petition. During the hearing of the petition on 22 July 1992, the Supreme Court called for suspension of construction work of any kind on the acquired land.

In a further affidavit filed by the Government of Uttar Pradesh in the Supreme Court on 23 July 1992, the State Government unconditionally undertook to obey the orders passed by the Supreme Court and by the Allahabad High Court. It was further mentioned in the affidavit that the suggestions made by the Supreme Court at the time of the hearing on 22 July 1992 had given a new dimension to the negotiations which had been going on between the State Government and the religious leaders. The Government of Uttar Pradesh assured the Supreme Court that the State Government was using all means at its command to ensure that an agreement was reached by all parties concerned so that the orders of the Court were effectively implemented. The affidavit, inter alia, referred to the invitation given by me to the leaders of the religious groups to meet me for discussion on 23 July 1992.

In the light of the submissions made by the Government of Uttar Pradesh, the Supreme Court adjourned the hearing of the petition to Monday, 27 July 1992. The Supreme Court said, inter alia, that exploring a solution to this problem is in the larger national interest.

I am sure all the right-thinking people will share the concern of the Central Government to find an amicable solution to the problem. The Central Government believes that all avenues of amicable settlement must be sincerely explored in the first instance. Our effort, therefore, has been to defuse the situation, avoid a confrontationist approach, and to bring about a reconciliation of the views of various concerned parties. While doing so, we have been acutely conscious of the importance of upholding the dignity of the judiciary and respect for the rule of law. It was on this basis that we had repeatedly urged the Government of Uttar Pradesh and all other concerned parties to abide by the directions of the Court, both in letter and spirit, and not to do anything which would undermine the basic principles of the Constitution.

As was stated in the Congress manifesto, we are committed to finding a negotiated settlement of this issue, which fully respects the sentiments of both communities involved. If such a settlement cannot be reached, all parties must respect the order and verdict of the Court. The Congress is for the construction of the temple without dismantling the mosque.

It was the responsibility of the Government of Uttar Pradesh to ensure that the orders of the Court were implemented and the construction activity on the acquired land was stopped. However, the situation was allowed to escalate to a point where the State Government expressed its inability to do anything and in fact requested that either the Home Minister or I should persuade the sants and mahants to stop the work. In view of the critical situation that had come about at Ayodhya, I had a meeting with the religious leaders on 23 July 1992. During the discussion, I drew the attention of the delegation to the serious situation created by the non-compliances of the Court orders by the Government of Uttar Pradesh. I also informed the delegation that I would be in a position to begin the process of dialogue only after the construction activity came to a halt. Finally, I requested the religious leaders to see that the work was stopped so that efforts to solve the Ramjanmabhoomi–Babri Masjid dispute could thereafter be proceeded with, in a time-bound manner. I also told them that once the work was stopped, I would revive the efforts initiated by the previous governments that had remained unfinished, plus the preliminary soundings I had been making for some time past.

The purpose of this exercise is to bring about an amicable settlement through negotiations. In case it becomes necessary, the litigation pending in various courts on the subject could be consolidated and considered by one judicial authority, whose decision will be binding on all parties. This would require a fairly elaborate exercise at the government level and appropriate submissions to the courts for their consideration. I expressed my belief that this exercise at the government level could be expedited and completed within four months. I found agreement on this approach.

The construction activity on the acquired land at the Ramjanmabhoomi–Babri Masjid complex is reported to have ceased on 26 July. I hope this will pave the way for arriving at an agreed solution of the problem and bring about an amicable settlement of this long-standing issue. I therefore appeal to all political parties and all sections of the people to help in strengthening the traditional values of religious tolerance and in maintaining peace, tranquillity and communal harmony.

Appendix V

Prime Minister's letter to leaders of political parties dated 27 September 1992

Dear—,

As you are aware, I had made a statement in both Houses of Parliament on 27 July 1992 on the Ramjanmabhoomi–Babri Masjid issue. In this statement, I had given, inter alia, an outline of the action proposed to be taken by the Government to resolve this issue through negotiations. The Cell announced by me has now completed its preparatory work of collecting the relevant documents and records and going through the mass of evidence presented by the two sides in the course of their negotiations held during the period December 1990–February 1991.

The stage has now been reached where the process of meaningful discussions can be resumed from the point where they got discontinued in February 1991. Representatives of both sides who had participated in the previous negotiations are being invited to a meeting on 3 October to determine the modalities of carrying on future discussions.

The informal consultations held so far have given me hope that there is a genuine and general desire for an early amicable settlement of the dispute. Since you are, no doubt, of the same view, your express support to the process of the negotiations will be of invaluable help, both psychologically and substantively. I am therefore writing to you for your kind information and help. I shall keep in touch with you on the progress of the negotiations.

Thanking you,
Yours sincerely,

Appendix VI

Prime Minister's intervention in the meeting of the National Integration Council on 23 November 1992

This is the third meeting of the National Integration Council in a little more than a year on the Ramjanmabhoomi–Babri Masjid issue.

We last discussed this issue on 18 July this year. Useful discussions were held, but we did not succeed in passing any resolution, in view of opposition from some of our friends here. We took note of the construction that was going on in violation of the orders of the court, in particular, the order passed by the High Court on 15 July 1992. By this order of 15 July, the High Court had restrained the parties from land which had been notified by the Government of Uttar Pradesh; for any construction on the land, prior permission from the court would need to be obtained. The Chief Minister of Uttar Pradesh assured the National Integration Council that his government was making sincere efforts to stop the construction.

Despite the assurance given by the Chief Minister, the construction activity did not stop. The situation was allowed to escalate to a point where the State Government expressed its inability to do anything, and requested that either the Home Minister or I should persuade the sants and mahants to stop the work. As you all know, I had a meeting with the religious leaders on 23 July. I am happy that they agreed to stop the *kar seva.* I promised that the process of negotiations, which had been initiated by the previous government, would be resumed and attempts would be made to find an amicable solution to the dispute through negotiations. I also said that, if necessary, the litigation pending in various courts on this issue would be consolidated and referred to a single judicial authority. I indicated that the government could complete this exercise leading to the reference in about four months' time. I also made a detailed statement in Parliament on 27 July covering these developments.

The first step in the resumption of negotiations was to examine the record of the previous negotiations, which were started by the government of Shri Chandra Shekhar in December 1990, and which continued till February 1991. Before restarting the dialogue we wanted to be clear as to who had said what on which issue during those negotiations, what were the areas of agreements and disagreements and what kind of evidence had been presented by either side. We found that the evidence was quite voluminous. This evidence has to be studied, classified, analysed and authenticated. All this work was done by the cell created in my office for Ayodhya affairs.

Another area which required a lot of painstaking effort related to the court cases. The original dispute concerned five title suits, which were consolidated and are being heard at Lucknow by a special bench of the Allahabad High Court. Then there were writ petitions challenging the acquisition of land by the Government of Uttar Pradesh in October 1991, petitions in the Supreme Court alleging violation of the court orders, apart from a large number of miscellaneous petitions covering various aspects of the controversy. The Central Government was not a part of either the civil suits or the contempt petitions. It had only been impleaded as a party in some of the petitions against the land acquisition, as the Land Acquisition Act is a Central Act, and the Constitutional validity of the Act was under challenge. Special arrangements had to be made at the High Court and the Supreme Court to obtain copies of orders and other papers in all these cases.

While this exercise was going on at the official level, I had been meeting a large number of individuals and delegations directly concerned with the dispute, as well as those who were interested in bringing the two sides to a negotiated solution. These consultations gave me valuable insights into the various facets of the controversy and the multitude of suggestions which had been thrown up for a possible solution.

Finally, at the end of September, we felt that we had done enough homework and now direct talks between the representatives of the Vishwa Hindu Parishad and the All India Babri Masjid Action Committee (the two sides who had participated in the 1991 negotiations) could be fruitfully resumed. The first meeting was held on 3 October under the chairmanship of the Home Minister. I am happy that our friends from the VHP as well as from the AIBMAC responded favourably to our invitation. My colleagues Shri Sharad Pawar and Shri P.R. Kumaramangalam agreed to help in coordinating these discussions. We also requested Shri Bhairon Singh Shekhawat, Chief Minister of Rajasthan and Shri Subodh Kant Sahay, both of whom had played a key role in the talks. On the eve of the talks, I also wrote to the heads of all the recognized political parties seeking their help and support to the resumed process of negotiations. I considered the step necessary as a problem like this requires concerted efforts not only by the government or by the parties directly involved in the dispute, but by all sections of society.

The meeting of 3 October was held in a cordial atmosphere. Fresh evidence and documents were given by both sides. Useful discussions took place and the respective positions of the parties acquired greater clarity. The process was carried further in the next meeting on 16 October. This meeting took an important step forward by agreeing on a cut-off date for presentation of evidence as also for comments on the evidence. I am happy to say that these cut-off dates were fully respected by both the sides. In between, we were also able to settle a controversy, continuing from the previous round of negotiations, about certain archaeological excavations conducted by Professor B.B. Lal, former Director General of the Archaeological Survey of India. The historians nominated by the AIBMAC wanted to see some material relating to these excavations. We were told that the normal practice in archaeology is not to make material available for inspection until the publication of the report. However, in deference to the sentiments of our friends, we decided to make a departure from this practice. The historians and archaeologists nominated by both the sides examined the material and gave their comments.

We had reached a stage where the work of presentations of evidence and offering comments on it was over. The positions of the two parties on the central issue had also been clarified in response to questionnaires addressed by them to each other. The negotiations appeared poised to enter a decisive phase and we had expected crucial decisions from the meeting scheduled for 8 November 1992. Unfortunately, in the meantime, a unilateral announcement of resumption of *kar seva* with effect from 6 December was made. The announcement created an atmosphere in which carrying forward direct talks did not appear feasible. With a great deal of disappointment, a decision was taken in the meeting of 8 November 1992 to postpone the talks.

Even after postponement of the direct talks, we continued our efforts to create an atmosphere so that the negotiations could be resumed. Several meetings were held at my level and at the level of my colleagues with leaders of the two sides. However, the sudden, utterly inexplicable and unilateral announcement of the *kar seva* programme from 6 December had vitiated the atmosphere and we were unable to arrive at any understanding. Next, we tried to obtain agreement on a reference to the Supreme Court. A number of alternatives regarding the issues to be considered by the Supreme Court were also discussed. We had hoped that this would be acceptable, because from time to time leaders of both sides had indicated that such a step would be looked upon favourably. Regrettably, however, even this failed to secure agreement.

The Supreme Court has been hearing certain contempt petitions with regard to the Ayodhya matter. The Court has considered it necessary for the Union Government to indicate its stand so that the Court may have the assistance of the Union Government in making such orders as would ensure enforcement of the earlier orders of the Supreme Court. Pursuant to this direction, the Solicitor General appeared in the Supreme Court today to make the necessary submissions as well as to give an assurance to the Court that the Union Government would take all necessary steps in furtherance of the directions of the courts to have their earlier order implemented. I understand that the Supreme Court has given time to the Government of Uttar Pradesh until day after tomorrow to spell out the concrete steps that they would like to take in this connection and that is where the matter rests.

This, then, is the background in which the present meeting of the National Integration Council has been called. We have before us the announcement of the resumption of *kar seva* with effect from the sixth of the next month. Our efforts to persuade the organizers to withdraw this announcement have not yielded any result so far. We have reports that the build-up for the *kar seva* in terms of recruitment of volunteers and movement of material has started and various plans are being announced.

I understand that the proceedings of the High Court in the land acquisition matter are in the final stage. Arguments have been concluded, only the order remains to be pronounced. Forcing the issue at this stage would be an open contravention of the discretion of the High Court and the Supreme Court.

As regards the construction of the temple, we all agree that a grand Ram temple should be constructed in Ayodhya. I had said as much from the Red Fort on Independence Day. I do not think that there is anyone here who would disagree with this basic proposition. The issues on which there are differences of opinion are the plan of construction, the safety of the existing structure and compliance with the court orders on the subject. With agreement on the basic issue of construction of a temple, it should not have been difficult to work out the remaining details given an attitude of mutual accommodation and respect for rule of law. Unfortunately, all our attempts have proved infructuous.

We have still not given up our attempts to try to find some workable solution. We would consider any possible option that respects the basic democratic values and constitutional principles. However, no violation of the law or of the orders of the Court shall be countenanced. There can be no compromises on this.

Subject to this, I would request those who are organizing the *kar seva* on the acquired land on 6 December to reconsider their decision and to desist from violating the law and the orders of the Court.

Finally, I request members of the NIC to discuss the matter and I look forward to their valuable suggestions.

Appendix VII

Extracts from important affidavits of the Government of Uttar Pradesh, 1991-92

October 1991 before the High Court in WP No. 3540 of 1991
. . . That the purpose for which the land has been acquired has been clearly indicated in the Notifications dated 7-10-1991 (Annexure No. 7) and 10-10-1991 (Annexure No. 8) issued under Sections 4 and 6 of the Land Acquisition Act respectively. The land has been acquited for the development of tourism and providing amenities to pilgrims at Ayodhya in district Faizabad. There has been no intention of the State Government to transfer it . . .

November 1991 before the Supreme Court in WP No.1000 of 1991
. . . That the purpose for which the land has been acquired has been clearly indicated in the notification dated 7-10-1991 issued under Sections 4 and 6 of the Land Acquisition Act respectively. The land has been acquired for the development of tourism and providing amenities to pilgrims at Ayodhya in district Faizabad. There has been no intention of the State Government to transfer it. Maps showing the position clearly on a smaller and bigger scale are attached herewith as Annexure Nos. 'C' and 'D' respectively.

That the State Government has not violated any order of the Court. In fact, there was no restrictive order against the State Government. Moreover the State Government has the statutory right to acquire any land in Uttar Pradesh, whether subject matter of a suit or not, for a public purpose . . .

. . . That the State Government has taken all necessary steps to protect the disputed structure . . .

January 1992 in the High Court in WP No. 3540 of 1991

That it may be mentioned as follows:

(a) Previously 55.6744 acres of land around and adjoining Shri Ram Janma Bhumi Sthal was acquired or granted for the purposes of Ram Katha Park. The land called Shri Ram Janma Bhumi Sthal was left out. No plan for development of Ram Katha Park could be completed without Shri Ram Janma Bhumi Sthal being included into it, as the Ram Katha Park was designed to be built around Shri Ram Janma Bhumi. With this end in view, the State Government has further acquired under the present notification 2.77 acres of land of Ram Janma Bhumi Sthal so that an integrated plan can be prepared for development of this land to provide amenities to pilgrims visiting Shri Ram Janma Bhumi and to develop at Shri Ram Janma Bhumi a tourist centre.

(b) The plan is now being prepared after the present acquisition in which a part of the land of Shri Ram Janma Bhumi will be left vacant for the renovation and reconstruction of the temple of Bhagwan Shri Ram Virajman there and its appurtenant facilities and conveniences through agencies decided upon by State Government.

(c) In view, however, of the pendency of litigation, the status quo relating to the disputed structures shall be maintained till the dispute is not settled by the court . . .

April 1992 in the High Court in WP No. 3579 of 1991

. . . This purpose of acquisition was, as specified in the declaration by the Government under Section 6 of the Land Acquisition Act vide notification No. 3838/41-33-86 dated Lucknow October 10, 1991 annexure CA-l, the public purpose of development of tourism and providing amenities to pilgrims at Ayodhya. The declaration is conclusive and cannot be questioned by the petitioners.

The allegation of mala fide intentions is denied. In fact the foremost thing to be done for achieving the object of developing tourism and providing amenities to pilgrims at Ayodhya, is the renovation and re-construction of the temple of Bhagwan Shri Ram Lala Virajman at Shri Ram Janma Bhumi, and the development of the adjacent area as Ram Katha Park. The first essential step to be taken in that direction is the clearance of the site of Shri Ram Janma Bhumi of the several structures and encroachments thereon. The next steps is the development of Shri Ram Janma Bhumi Sthal by the Government and in doing so the area of Shri Ram Janma Bhumi and some more land adjacent thereto would have to be kept in reserve for the renovation and reconstruction of the temple of Bhagwan Shri Ram Virajman there, and its appurtenances. All this development work is to be completed, according to the decision of the Government, from public funds in accordance with plans approved by the Government.

July 1992 in the High Court in WP No. 3540 of 1991

That in reply to the contents of paragraph 5 of the application it is stated that the terms of this Court's orders dated 25-10-1991 and of the Supreme Court's orders dated 15-11-1991 will appear from the perusal thereof and the orders of the Courts have not been violated by the opposite parties in any manner. The land had been acquired by the Notification dated 7-10-1991 for the development of tourism and providing amenities to pilgrims at Ayodhya in district Faizabad. The order dated 25-10-1991 of this Court permitted to make arrangements for the purposes notified which would include providing of amenities to pilgrims at Ayodhya. The State Government, therefore, undertook the levelling of the land for the aforesaid purpose. Every year people from all over the country visit Ayodhya during the month of Shrawan for Sawan Jhula. Sadhus and pilgrims have been congregating in the acquired land since time immemorial throughout the year and in greater number during Chaturmas and on other festivals in this very place, which is held to be holy . . .

(a) According to the information received from the District Administration, Faizabad a day or two before 9-7-1992 the construction at the shilanyas site including the canopy was removed by the pilgrims and the sadhus present at the site and as volutantary kar seva, on 9-7-1992 at the shilanyas site the laying of a platform was commenced. Large crowds had gathered there and the platform is now reported to be approximately of the size of 70 feet by 30 feet and is about 3 feet thick. Both the removal as well as the laying of the platform were undertaken by the pilgrims sadhus present at the site by way of kar seva at the place where the shilanyas was performed on 9-11-1989, without any objection by the State Government and the Central Government.
(b) Neither the Government nor the District Administration or any other Government officers is party to the laying of the platform which was being done by the pilgrims and sadhus.
(c) The UP Government is fully committed to the protection of the disputed structure. Full measures and arrangements have been made to ensure it. In addition, adequate police force have been deployed for the protection of the structure round the clock.
(d) The State Government has therefore taken all steps to ensure

that the structure stands fully protected and that no untoward incident taken place. It was not very clear about the nature and extent of the construction which had been done as voluntary kar seva at the shilanyas site after the canopy and the construction had been removed. There were huge crowds of devotees, pilgrims and sadhus at the site at all times of day and night. The platform which is being laid is being used during religious discourses for the devotees to sit on as otherwise, due to rains, the ground was slushy.

(e) It appears that no foundation itself was dug for laying the platform and the concrete seems to have been spread on the already levelled land.

(f) Any attempt to use force with a large assembled crowd of saint and sadhus, and minor children and other pilgrims might result in breach of peace, bloodshed, and loss of innocent lives. This might also have serious respercussions on the prevailing peaceful atmosphere in the State. It is likely to lead to large-scale violence in the country.

(g) That the platform which is now being put would be a great use to the pilgrims specially during the rainy season for the purpose of resting and seating large crowds for listening to the religious discourses and by its very nature an amenity for the pilgrims and by reasons of this, being only a platform is not a structure, nor a permanent structure in the sense in which it is used in the order of the Courts dated 25-10-1991 and 15-11-1991.

(h) The orders pronounced by this Court on 15-7-1992 were made available on 16-7-1992 to the State Government and the directions of the Government were communicated by the Chief Secretary to the Government of UP to the District Magistrate, Faizabad by the letter dated 16-7-1992. A copy of which is being enclosed as Annexure No. A-l to this counter affidavit, which was despatched by Special Messenger and reached the District Magistrate, Faizabad in the forenoon of 17-7-1992.

The District Magistrate, Faizabad was directed to take necessary steps to ensure compliance of the orders of this Court. The District Magistrate with the help of police without the situation breaking out into a law and order one but consistent with the due implementation of the order of this Court dated 15-7-1992 is taking all necessary steps. Meanwhile, several rounds of dialogues have been held by the District Magistrate and other officers with the saints, religious leaders and other social leaders . . .

9 July 1992 in the Supreme Court in WP No. 264 of 1992

. . . That as regards the contents of paragraph 6 of the writ petition the Notification and its contents arc admitted. The object of the acquisition is as stated in the Notifications. In the plan of development that is being finalized, a part of the land of Sri Ram Janma Bhumi is being left vacant for the renovation and reconstruction of the Temple . . .

14 September 1992 in the Supreme Court in Contempt Petitions 97 and 102 of 1992

7. In I.A. No. 3/1992 it was stated that Ram Janmabhoomi Nyas had started construction of a concrete platform on 9-7-1992. In additional affidavit dated 11-7-92 it was stated that Shri Ashok Singhal had given a call to the members of VHP to assemble at site for carrying out construction. In the Affidavit dated 14-7-1992 it was stated that construction of permanent nature is being built at the disputed site.

19.1 deny averments in the affidavits filed in support of the Contempt Petition that the Government took no steps or that the Government provided any direct or indirect help for the construction. The allegation that water tankers were supplied by the Municipality for construction activity or that Ministers of the UP Government participated in the construction activity are denied. The allegations that adequate security for protection of the disputed structure was not provided is also wrong and is denied. Consistent with the ground situation, all necessary measure have been taken for security of the disputed structure and for compliance with the order of this Hon'ble Court. It may be mentioned that provisions of section 144 Cr. P.C. could not be invoked because of possible apprehension of provocation to kar sevaks and sadhus and possibility of defiance of any order under section 144 Cr. P.C. by the large congregation which could have resulted in grave law and order situation. The allegation of the Government aiding or abetting the construction or of alienating the acquired land are denied . . .

25 November 1992 before the Supreme Court in IA No. 5

2. The State Government has been giving grave and anxious consideration to the situation arising from the call given for resumption of kar seva on the acquired land. The State Government agrees that the duty of preventing the violation of orders of the court lies on it and is its responsibility.

3. The State Government is however constrained to point out that the course suggested by the Central Government for preventing such violation will not be the appropriate course as it will necessarily involve the use of force. To prevent the congregation and flow of kar sevaks in 2.77 acres and to prevent the movement of construction machinery into the area can only be done by the use of police and para military forces.

4. In October, 1990 in a similar situation the Government sought to use the PAC and the para military forces, for the purpose of blocking the entry of kar sevaks across the Saryu Bridge and around the disputed structure and even the entry of people into UP but the result was that inspite of this effort people were able to overcome the police barricade and even have acccess to the disputed structure itself. As a result, there was loss of many lives and injury to many persons. Commission of Enquiry has been appointed.

5. The State of UP believes sincerely that the solution to the problem lies in negotiations and persuation and use of force or the alternative suggested by the Central Government should be resorted to, if at all, as a last alternative.

6. The State of UP therefore is of the firm view that in the first instance, efforts should be made for negotiations and persuasion.

7. The State of UP would therefore be seeking direct negotiation with the leaders of VHP and the leaders of the Dharam Sansad for the purpose. So that the solution for achieving the religious aspirations should be achieved without violating the orders of the court. If this were to be done, the State Government will need at least a week to report to the court the outcome of its negotiations with the leaders mentioned earlier.

8. The State submits that it would be in the interest of maintaining the majesty of judicial institution and peace and harmony in the country that the State Government should be given this time of a week for achieving the laudable end.

27 November 1992 in the Supreme Court in IA No. 5

. . . The process of negotiation with various parties has been initiated by the State Governmeat. The response has been positive. The letter of Swami Chinmayanand Ji, Member of Parliament, and a senior functionary of the Sri Ram Kar Seva Samiti, would confirm this. The State Government is now confident that as long as the Writ Petitions regarding acquisitions are pending and the interim orders of the High Court are in force no construction, permanent or temporary, will take place, though to allay the religious aspirations of the Ram Bhakats, kar seva other than by way of construction, as stated may take place.

4. That the State Government is confident that giving some more time will bring some positive results out of these talks.

5. The actual situation on 2.77 acres and in its vicinity has not deteriorated till now. There has not been any development on the ground which can be construed as being detrimental to the

observance of the orders of the Court. According to the report dated 26-11-1992 received from District Administration, Faizabad so far there has been no arrival of kar sevaks in Ayodhya and there is no congregation on 2.77 acres or around it. Also no fresh building material or construction machinery has arrived in Ayodhya in connection with the call for kar seva.

6. The State Government again submits that negotiation and persuasion is the best course of action to handle the situation.

7. The State Government is fully competent to present the violation of Court's order and the assistance of force offered by the Central Government is not necessary in the present circumstances. It may be mentioned that the present government of UP has an enviable regard of maintaining law and order in the State, particularly in maintaining communal harmony.

8. Even in July, 1992, the Government had succeeded in getting kar seva on 2.77 acre discontinued through negotiations and persuasion.

9. The State Government reiterates that it is fully committed to safeguard and protect the disputed Ram Janam Bhoomi Structure in Ayodhya. The State Government has been frequently reviewing security arrangements of the disputed structure and has been taking all necessary steps to ensure its safety. Entry to the disputed structure is carefully controlled and every person is checked before entry. Metal detectors and closed circuit TV are in operation. Road barriers are also used for controlling the crowd whenever necessary. Recently the State Government has decided to deploy additional 15 companies of PAC and additional police force for the security of the structure and for maintaining law and order.

10. Thus the State Government is fully competent to ensure the safety of the structure without any additional Central force.

11. The State Government submits that no development has taken place till now to warrant any anxiety or to doubt the competence of the State Government to deal with the situation.

According to the State Government there appears no need to entrust the prevention of violation of Court's order to any authority other than the State Government. If any other authority is so entrusted it will amount to abandonment of the course of negotiation/persuasion and is likely to lead to avoidable use of force.

12. That the State Government shall always act to fulfil its Constitutional obligations and requests this Hon'ble Court to ensure the most expeditious disposal of the land acquisition case pending before the High Court in Lucknow to strengthen the hands of the State Government in its handling of the religious groups.

28 November 1992 before the Supreme Court in IA No. 5

2. The State Government would like to place on record the further progress the negotiations have taken. The ongoing process of discussions and negotiations with the religious leaders and the leader of the VHP have been fruitful as a result of which Smt. Rajmata Scindia, senior leader and Trustee of the VHP has sent a letter to the Chief Minister of UP which is self-explanatory. The letter is annexed herewith and marked as Annexure I.

3. As already stated, the State Government is now confident that as long as the writ petitions regarding acquisition are pending and the interim orders of the High Court are in force no constructions, permanent or temporary, will take place, though to satisfy the religious aspirations of the Ram Bhakats, kar seva other than by way of construction as stated may take place.

4. The State Government is confident that there will be no movement of construction machinery or construction materials into the acquired land of 2.77 acres and therefore, the question of machinery or building material being moved from the site of the Lakshman Temple or Seshavatar Temple (which is adjacent to the acquired land) into the acquired 2.77 acres does not arise.

5. The State Government sincerely believes that if the religious aspirations of the people of this country who have faith in the Shri Ram Janmabhoomi by performing kar seva in the manner

mentioned above or without violating the orders of the court is to take place, there will be total peace and harmony reigning in Ayodhya. Of this the Government is certain, especially because of the hope created in the minds of the people that the orders of the Court will not indefinitely stand in the way of the legitimate objectives of the people. 5th December 1992 is Geeta Jayanti and 6th of December 1992 has been fixed for kar seva as being a very auspicious mahurt. In these circumstances it is submitted that no orders, whatsoever, are called for on the applications made by the petitioner i.e. IA No. 5 of 1992 so that justice may be done except to direct the High Court to deliver the judgment in the acquisition writ petitions most expeditiously, to strengthen the hands of the State Government in its handling of the situation.

Appendix VIII

Statements of important leaders of BJP/VHP during the build-up to the *kar seva*, November-December 1992

1. L.K. Advani

Date	Place	Statement
7-11-92	Bhubaneswar	Urged the Central Government not to put hurdles in the way of the construction of the RJB temple and warned that the people were prepared to wait indefinitely.
1-12-92	Varanasi	Said that *kar seva* would be started on 2.77 acres on 6 December at all costs. Opined that there was no legal hurdle to start *kar seva* on the acquired land and that Central Government should not create any obstruction in *kar seva* on 2.77 acres of land on 6 December. Appealed to *kar sevaks* to reach Ayodhya in large numbers and participate in *kar seva* on 6 December.
1-12-92	Kanpur	Stated that *kar seva* did not mean bhajans and kirtans and said that *kar seva* would be performed with bricks

		and shovels on the 2.77 acres of acquired land.
2-12-92	Mau	Stated that *kar seva* to be started from 6 December always meant 'shram seva' which may not amount to construction and the same would be decided in Dharm Sansad at Ayodhya (4/5 December). Blamed Congress-I for unsuccessfully trying to divide and weaken the RJB movement.

2. M.M. Joshi

16-11-92	Bhopal	Said that *kar seva* would begin in right earnest and any attempt to thwart it would invite unnecessary confrontation with the Centre.
1-12-92	Mathura	Appealed to the gathering to assemble at Ayodhya in large numbers for *kar seva* and to demolish the so-called Babri Masjid.
2-12-92	Bulandshahar	Expressed his determination that *kar seva* would be started on 2.77 acres plot from 6 December at the venue where it was stopped in July 1992. Criticized the Supreme Court for appointing an 'Observer' at Ayodhya and demanded that the Constitution of India be defined as per the wishes of general public.
2-12-92	Hathras	Accused PM of instigating Muslims and encouraging the BMAC to oppose the VHP and of trying to create schisms among the sants. Clarified that the nature of *kar seva* on 6 December

		would be decided by the sants and not by a court of law, as it was a matter of the religious sentiments of the people.
2-12-92	Meerut	Opined that at least the issue of the 2.77 acres of land could have been solved as it had nothing to do with the disputed structure. Alleged that the PM and his representatives had come up with new formulas but were never serious. Alleged that the Constitution had been violated by sending Central forces into UP without a demand from the State Government and also by appointing an 'Observer' at Ayodhya.

3. Sadhvi Ritambhara

23-11-92	Kanpur	Said Hindu Samaj was shocked when PM called the disputed structure a mosque. Blamed all the political parties who were favouring Muslims on RJB-BM issue only to consolidate their Muslim vote bank. Said RJB issue could not be resolved through negotiations. Added that this time *kar sevaks* were ready to sacrifice everything for RJB temple and they were prepared to face any eventuality. Appealed to all Hindus to participate in *kar seva* programme.
28-11-92	Nagpur	Warned the Central Government of dire consequences if the UP Government was dismissed and exhorted Hindu youth

		to be prepared to face any eventuality to uphold the glory and honour of Hinduism. Urged the Hindu youth, old men and women to be prepared for the 'battle'.

4. Ashok Singhal

19-11-92	Ahmedabad	Stated that PM was given four months to find a solution to the RJB issue but during Independence Day speech he stated that Masjid would remain where it was, thereby indicating that Ram temple should not be constructed at the birth place of Rama.
3-12-92	Ayodhya	Asserted that whether it was legal or illegal, VHP would follow the decision of the sants. The Supreme Court may take any action it liked on the report of the Observer.
4-12-92	Ayodhya	Said that the demolition of the disputed structure was a matter of secondary importance. Since the structure was a temple, they would confine themselves only to its renovation.

6. Vinay Katiyar

22-11-92	Faizabad	Declared that if the idols of Ram Lalla were removed from *garbha griha*, the Babri Masjid would be demolished and the debris thrown into Saryu river.
3-12-92	Faizabad	Said that as long as the idols of Ram Lalla were in the disputed structure, no damage was to be caused to the

		structure at any cost.
5-12-92	Ayodhya	Expressed apprehension that use of force against the *kar sevaks* might lead to widespread violence in the country.

6. Smt. Vijaya Raje Scindia

23-11-92	Patna	Said that the Babri Masjid will have to be demolished.
24-11-92	Patna	Appealed to the women to take part in the *kar seva* at Ayodhya from 6 December.
4-12-92	Orai	Addressing a gathering of *kar sevaks*, said that their fight was not against Muslims but against persons like V.P. Singh, M.S. Yadav and Chandra Shekhar. Called upon the PM not to create hurdles or his Government would meet the same fate as the earlier ones.
2-12-92	RJB/BM Complex	Disclosed that the UP CM was ready to face the dismissal of the UP Government for the cause of construction of the RJB temple and appealed to the *kar sevaks* to be prepared for the supreme sacrifice to this cause.

7. Uma Bharti

3-12-92	Faizabad	Reiterated the resolve for construction of RJB temple from 6 December from the point it was stopped in July 1992.

8. Giriraj Kishore

26-11-92	Delhi	Declared that *kar sevaks* would reach Ayodhya in a phased manner.

		Further said that around 15 lakh *kar sevaks* would participate this time.

9. V.H. Dalmia

9-11-92	Delhi	Declared that the RJB temple would be constructed in the same way it was demolished by Babur. Said *kar sevaks* were pressurizing the leadership that they should be called not to construct the RJB temple but to demolish the Masjid.

Appendix IX

Important communications/letters written by Home Minister/senior officers of the Central Government to the State Government of Uttar Pradesh from time to time in regard to Ramjanmabhoomi–Babri Masjid issue

S.No.	*Date* *Written by*	*Brief subject*	*Reply/Remarks*
I	ACQUISITION OF LAND		
1.	9.10.1991 HM	Apprehensions expressed by Shri Syed Shahabuddin on the acquisition of land in the RJB–BM complex.	
2.	11.10.1991 Addl. Secy. (NHA)	Land Acquisition Fax message asking for copy of notification site plan and other particulars of land being acquired.	UP Chief Secretary's reply dated 12.10.1991–furnishing a copy of the notification, plan and other particulars
3.	15.10.1991 HM	Reservations expressed by Shri Shahabuddin regarding land acquisition.	Chief Minister, UP, letter dated 22.10.1991 stating the purpose of acquisition of land.

S.No.	Date Written by	Brief subject	Reply/Remarks
II	DEMOLITION OF TEMPLES AND OTHER STRUCTURES ON THE ACQUIRED LAND		
1.	22.3.1992 HS	Fax message from HS regarding transfer of land to RJB Nyas and demolition of structures on acquired land.	Principal Secretary's (Home, UP) letters dated 23.3.1992 and 25.3.1992 received in this regard including the details of structures demolished.
2.	23.3.1992 HM	HM's letter regarding demolition of structures and transfer of land to RJB Nyas in violation of the spirit of the court orders.	CM's letter dated 24.3.1992 stating that the State Government has not taken any steps which in any way affect/violate the final orders of the court.

S.No.	Date Written by	Brief subject	Reply/Remarks
III	CONSTRUCTION OF WALL		
1.	23.2.1992 HM	Construction of new wall. Request to reconsider the construction of the wall in view of the prevailing tension.	CM's letter dated 10.3.1992 stating that the wall is being constructed for safety of the disputed structure.
2.	17.3.1992 HS	Reminder regarding construction of wall.	Chief Secretary's letter dated 28.3.92 stating that by the construction of the wall the orders of the Court are not violated and that the security of the disputed structure will be strengthened. The wall is not constructed on the acquired land.

S.No.	Date Written by	Brief subject	Reply/Remarks
IV	SECURITY ARRANGEMENTS AND COMPLIANCE WITH COURT ORDERS		
1.	15.10.1991 HM	For making adequate security arrangements—the State Government should not take any action which constituted a breach of the High Court's orders.	CM's letter dated 22.10.1991 stating elaborate security arrangements being made by the State Government.
2.	13.11.1991 HM	HM's letter regarding security arrangements—referring to State Government's assurance given in the NIC (meeting 2.11.1991) regarding the safety of the disputed structure.	CM's letter dated 15.11.1991 stating that adequate security arrangements have been made.
3.	26.12.1991 JSM	For implementation of the recommendations of the Central Experts Team.	
4.	26.12.1991 HM	For implementation of Central Experts Team.	

S.No.	Date Written by	Brief subject	Reply/Remarks
5.	2.1.1992 HS	Fax message dated 2.1.1992 from HS regarding removal of barricades–security arrangements.	Principal Secretary's (Home) letter dated 2.1.1992 stating that barricades could be restored at short notice.
6.	10.1.1992 HM	Central Government's concern regarding the security of RJB–BM structure and the need to strengthen the arrangements.	CM's letter dated 27.1.1992 stating that necessary steps for maintaining security have been taken by the State Government.
7.	17.5.1992 HM	Security arrangements and removal of barricades. Requested the State Government not to take any action which violates the spirit of the orders of the High Court and the Supreme Court.	CM's letter dated 27.5.1992 stating that all arrangements for the safety of the disputed structure have been made.
8.	29.5.1992 HM	Security arrangements and to protect the disputed structure from damage by water-logging etc. Request to maintain the status quo in accordance with the letter and spirit of the orders of the Court.	CM's letter dated 16.6.1992 stating that adequate measures have been taken and there is no threat to the structure due to water-logging, digging etc.

S.No.	*Date* *Written by*	*Brief subject*	*Reply/Remarks*
9.	30.5.1992 MOS (H)	Threat to the disputed structure due to digging, levelling etc. Request for security arrangements.	CM's letter dated 16.6.1992 stating that adequate measures have been taken and there is no threat to the structure due to water-logging, digging etc.
10.	7.7.1992 HM	Regarding threat to the disputed structure due to mob violence. The action of the State Government should not violate the letter or spirit of the Court orders.	CM's letter dated 9.7.1992 stating that adequate security measures have been taken to protect disputed structure.
11.	11.9.1992 HM	Preparation of fresh security plan and security measures of the disputed structures.	CM's letter dated 17.11.1992 stating that maintenance of law and order is a State subject and State has made adequate security arrangements.
12.	29.10.1992 HM	Preparation of fresh security plan and security measures of the disputed structures. Maintaining of law and order and the safety of the disputed structure during the coming religious festivals at Ayodhya. The State Government was also requested to ensure that nothing is done in violation of Court orders.	

S.No.	Date Written by	Brief subject	Reply/Remarks
13.	11.11.1992 HM	Emphasizes the need for a comprehensive review of the security plan for RJB–BM structure.	
14.	21.11.1992 HM	Expresses concern on mobilization of *kar sevaks*; emphasizes the necessity to comply with Court orders; points out implication of allowing *kar sevaks* to congregate and resume *kar seva* for the maintenance of law and order not only in Ayodhya and UP but in various parts of the country; reiterates the need to comprehensively review the security arrangements for the RJB–BM structure.	CM's letter dated 25.11.1992 stating that adequate security measures have been taken to protect the disputed structure; that his government is committed to its protection and that it is determined to discharge its responsibility under the Constitution.
15.	24.11.1992 JS (P)	Conveying the decision to deploy Central Para Military Forces to tackle the situation arising out of the proposed *kar seva*.	CM UP's letter to HM dated 25.11.1992 registering his protest about the deployment of Central Para Military Forces and stating that the disputed structure is fully safe.

S.No.	*Date* *Written by*	*Brief subject*	*Reply/Remarks*
			CM UP's letter to PM dated 30.11.1992 registering his protest over unilateral decision of deploying Central forces.
16.	1.12.1992 HM	Requesting to strengthen the security of the disputed structure.	CM UP's letter dated 2.12.1992 stating that adequate security measures are in force.
17.	1.12.1992 HM	Requesting for providing adequate cooperation to the Central Para Military Forces.	CM UP's letter dated 2.12.1992 informing about the alleged misbehaviour of the Central Para Military Forces and registering his protest over the 'unconstitutional' unilateral deployment of forces.
18.	3.12.1992 HM	Regarding health hazards and request for medical and sanitary facilities to the *kar sevaks* at Ayodhya.	CM's reply dated 5.12.1992 stating that adequate arrangements for providing medical facilities etc. have been made.

S.No.	Date *Written by*	*Brief subject*	*Reply/Remarks*
19.	3.12.1992 HM	Concern of the Central Government about the outbreak of communal disturbances. Assurance given to the State Government to provide any kind of assistance for maintaining law and order and maintaining communal harmony.	
20.	3.12.1992 HS	Fax message from HS to CS, UP, regarding detection of bombs and explosives and to provide Sniffer Dog Squads to the State authorities. (On 5.12.1992 these were made available.)	DG(P), UP requested HM to issue instructions to CGO at Faizabad for functioning of Bomb Squad under the supervision of District Police at Ayodhya.
21.	5.12.1992 EP	Strengthening the security arrangements of the disputed structure as the site of the proposed *kar seva* is in the immediate vicinity of the disputed structure. Apprehensions of using explosives/bombs to damage the disputed structure by the mischievous elements. People continuing deployed by the State is not sufficient to meet the security requirements	

S.No.	*Date* *Written by*	*Brief subject*	*Reply/Remarks*
		especially if any untoward development takes place. CPHFs stationed by CM may be requisitioned by group.	
V	CONSTRUCTION WORK (PLATFORM)		
1.	5.7.1992 HM	Regarding commencement of the work of the platform near the *shilanyas* site; to implement Court orders in letters and spirit.	CM's letter dated 12.7.1992 stating that adequate security measures have been taken and also there is no need to deploy more Central forces.
2.	16.7.1992 HM	Regarding suspension of ongoing construction work and to implement Court orders.	CM's letter dated 17.7.1992 stating that DM, Faizabad has been instructed to ensure compliance of Court orders.
3.	17.7.1992 HM	Regarding suspension of ongoing construction work and to implement Court orders.	CM's letter dated 21.7.1992 stating that the Court orders will be implemented and there is no danger to the disputed structure. Adequate police force has been deployed to protect the disputed structure.

S.No.	Date Written by	Brief subject	Reply/Remarks
4.	20.7.1992 HM	Regarding suspension of construction work and implementation of Court orders.	CM's letter dated 21.7.1992 requesting that efforts be made at the level of PM/HM to persuade sadhus to implement Court orders.

Appendix X

Letters from Chief Minister, Uttar Pradesh to the Central Government, November 1992

25 November 1992

Priya Sri Chavan,

Kripaya grih mantralaya ke fax sandesha sankhya 10012/J S (P)/92, dinank 24-11-92 ka sandarbh len, jiske dwara pradesh shasan ko suchit kiya gaya hai ki Ayodhya vivad par sambhavit stithi se nipatne ke liye pradesh mein kendriya ardh-sainik balon ki tainati ki jaa rahi hai.

Pichhle kuch dinoh se kai sthanon par ki jaane wali taiyari se pradesh shasan ko yeh spasht ho gaya tha ki kendra sarkar is prakar ki karyavahi ka nirnay le chuki hai. Is sandarbh mein, mein kahna chahoonga ki kanoon-vyavastha ka vishay pradesh sarkar ke uttardayitva mein ata hai. Is prakar pradesh sakar se bina vichar-vimarsh kiye kendriya balon ko pradesh mein tainat karna samvidhan, sanghiya dhanche ke siddhant tatha loktantrik manya paramparaon ke pratikool hai. Bharat sarkar ki is ektarafa karyavahi ke prati mein apni aapatti darj karta hun.

Jahan tak Ayodhya vivadit dhanche ki suraksha ka prashna hai, hum pahle hi kendra sarkar ko aashwast kar chuke hein ki pradesh is disha mein sabhi sambhav karyavahi karegi. Hum swayam Faizabad jile mein police tatha PAC bal mein vriddhi kar rahe hein. Yadi iske atirikt kendriya balon ki avashyakta hogi to aapko soochit kiya jayega.

Isi paripredkshya mein yeh bhi ullekhaniya hai ki shanti vyavastha se sambandhit ek gambhirtar samasya, arthat aatankwad, ke liye hum kendriya sarkar se nirantar aagraha karte rahe hein ki pradesh mein paryapt maatra mein kendriya balon ki kampaniyan uplabdh karayi jaayen. Kintu, khed ki bat hai ki grih mantralaya ne hamare anurodh par samuchit dhyan nahin diya iske viprit rajya sarkar ki sahmati bina aur mang ke bina Ayodhya mein anavashyak roop se bahut adhik sankhya mein bal ki tainati ki jaa rahin hein.

Aapka,

Kalyan Singh

26 November 1992

Aadaraniya Pradhan Mantri ji,

Ram janm bhoomi ka hal dhoondne ke liye aap ke dwara sambadhit pakshon se vartalap ka silsila aarambh kiya gaya. Kintu Vishwa Hindu Parishad va Dharm Sansad ki 6 December se karseva aarambh karne ki ghoshna ke bad aisa pratit hota hai ki kendra sarkar ne vartalap ka rasta chhodkar bal prayog se samasya ko suljhhane ki niti apnayi hai. Rajya sarkar se paramarsh athava sahmati athava mang ke bina hi ektarafa kendra sarkar dwara Uttar Pradesh mein kendriya balon ko bheja jaa raha hai. Kendra sarkar ka yeh kadam samvidhan, sanghiya dhanche ke siddhant aur manya loktantrik manyataon ke pratikool hai. Mananiya ucchtam nyayalay mein kendra sarkar ki or se jo samasya ka samadhan prastut kiya jaa raha hai, usmein nishchit roop se bal ka prayog nihit hai.

Pradesh sarkar ka yeh mat hai ki bal prayog se is samasya ka hal nahin ho sakta. Isse samasya hal to ho sakti hai kintu sulajh nahin sakti. Na hi bal prayog se yeh garanti di ja sakti hai ki yehi samasya punah khadi nahin hogi.

Mah July mein bhi aap dwara pradesh sarkar ke anurodh par Vishwa Hindu Parishad va dharmik netaon se batchit ki gayi thi. Pradesh sarkar ne bhi vartalap mein poora sahyog diya tha. Parinamswaroop bina bal prayog ke gat July mein samasya ka hai nikal aaya. Pradesh sarkar ka manna hai ki yadi imandari se pramanik tatha gambhir prayas kiye jaayen to vartalap se ab bhi is samasya ka hai nikal aayega. Aisa karne se na keval un karodon sradhhaluon, jo ki mandir nirman mein aastha rakhte hein, ki bhavanaon ko thes pahunchengi, apitu nyayalaya ki garima bhi bani rahegi. Bal prayog se jo anavahsyak jaan-maal ki kshati hoti hai vah bhi nahin hogi.

Aapse anurodh hai ki aap kripya sambandhit pakshon se varta jaari rakhen aur usi ke madhyam se is samasya ka samadhan dhoondne ka prayas karne ka kashta karen.

Sasamman,

Bhavadiya,

Kalyan Singh

30 November 1992

Aadaraniya Pradhan Mantri ji,

Pichhle kuchh dinon se kendra sarkar dwara Uttar Pradesh, vishesh roop se Ayodhya aur Faizabad mein bhari sankhya mein kendriya bal behja jaa raha hein. Is sambandh mein na to rajya sarkar dwara Ayodhya prakaran ke sambandh mein kendriya sarkar se kendriya balon ki koi mang ki gayi, na rajya sarkar se paramarsh kiya gaya aur na hi rajya sarkar se sahmati li gayi.

Abhi bhi badi sankhya mein kendriya balon ka Uttar Pradesh mein aagaman ka silsila jari hein. Kendra sarkar ka is ektarafa kadam samvidhan ki mool bhavna ke pratikool, sanghia dhanche par prahar, manya loktantrik paramparaon ke sarvadha virudh aur Uttar Pradesh ki mahan janta ke svatva tatha atma samman par kutharaghat hein.

Samvidhan ke andargat kendra aur rajya sarkaron ke adhikar

kshetron ko vistrut roop se paribhashit kiya gaya hein. Samvidhan ke satvem anuchhed ke anusar kanoon vyavastha banaye rakhna poori tarah rajya sarkar ki paridhi mein aata hein. Rajya sarkar yadi chahen athava avashyak samjhhen to is vishay mein kendra sarkar se sahayata ka anurodh kar sakti hein. Kintu Uttar Pradesh mein aisi koi stithi nahin hein. Kanoon-vyavastha chust aur durust hain tatha sampradayik sadbhav bana hua hein.

Samvidhan sammat sanghiya dhanche ke sucharu roop se chalte rahne ke liye yeh avashyak hei ki kendra sarkar aur rajya sarkaren apne-apne adhikaron ki simaon ke andar karya karen tatha ek doosre ke adhikar kshetron ka atikraman na karen.

Samvidhan mein paribhashit paridhiyon ka kendra sarkar athava pradesh sarkar dwara atikraman rashtra ki loktantrik vyavastha ke liye ghatak siddh ho sakta hein. Samvidhan kahta hai ki kendra sarkar ke liye yeh avashyak hain ki voh rajya sarkaron ki svayattada ki raksha karein aur kisi bhi tarah se adhik saktishali hone ke karan apni shakti ke durupyog dwara rajya sarkaron par anuchit dabav dalkar apni iccha thopne ka prayas na karen. Yadi samay rahti is pravriti par niyantran nahin kiya gaya to hamare sanghiya dhanche ko apurna kshati hogi.

Kendra sarkar ke grih mantralaya ne kendra bal bhejne ki is ektarafa karyavahi ke sandarbh mein ek sandesh bhejkar keval itna hi kaha hein ki yeh bal Uttar Pradesh ke vibhinn sthanon mein keval isliye bheja jaa raha hein ki yedi pradesh sarkar ko avashyakta hui to alp soochna par yeh bal tainati ke liye uplabdh ho jayega. Kintu yeh bal rajya sarkar ke nirdeshon ke adhin nahin rakha gaya jabki is sandesh se aisa pratit hota hein ki kendra sarkar svayam is baat ko svikar karti hein ki kendriya balon ki tainati pradesh sarkar ke anurodh par pradesh sarkar ke adhin karya karne ke liye ki ja sakti hein. Kya isse yeh samjhha jayen ki abhi kendriya bal vibhinn sthanon par keval bheje gaye lekin unki tainati nahin kiya jana tha.

Khed ka vishay hein ki Ayodhya mein kendriya balon ke adhikariyon aur unke adhinasth karmiyon ke acharan se eisa nahin lagta. Kuchh din pehle 'Rapid Action Force' ke commandos ne motor cyclon par apni nindaniya kartooton ka pradarshan karke Ayodhya mein janta ko aatankit kiya. Bal ke javan janta mein amaryadit vyavahar karte hein. Ayodhya mein stith police control room mein kendriya balon ke do upadhikshakon ne jakar vahan ke staff ko kaha ki abhi to keval control room dehkne aaye hein kintu do din baad vah swayam aakar is par kabja kar lenge. Iske atirikt kendriya balon ke adhikari press ko yeh kah rahe hein ki vah jiladhikari ke adhin kaam nahin karenge kyonki yeh to sirf ek takniki baat hein, apitu vastav mein pradesh sarkar ke adhin karya na karke vah swatantra roop se karya karenge.

Kendriya balon ke is avanchaniya aacharan se Ayodhya ki janta mein aatank tatha tarah-tarah ki bhrantiyan utpann ho rahi hein. Unke prati janta mein tanav parilakshit ho raha hein aur is baat ki sambhavana se inkar nahin kiya ja sakta ki kendriya balon ke acharan ke karan nikat bhavishya mein sthaniya janta va kendriya balon ke beech takarav ki stithi utpann ho jeyen. Yadi aisa hua to iski poori jimmedari kendra sarkar ki hogi.

Manyavar, mein aapse punah anurodh karoonga ki aisa karke sanghiya dhanche par prahar na karen aur loktantrik paramparaon ko nashtha na karen. Mujhhe aasha hein ki mere vicharon par dhyan dekar aap tatkal hi akaran tainat kiye gaye kendriya balon ko vapas bulane ke aadesh ki anukampa karenge.

Sasamman,

Aapka,

Kalyan Singh

Appendix XI

Letters from the Union Home Minister to the Chief Minister, Uttar Pradesh, 1-5 December 1992

D.O. No. 81011/1/92-Ay. II

Home Minister
India
New Delhi-110001
December 1, 1992

Dear Shri Kalyan Singhji,

Kindly refer to your D.O. letter No. 91/GI/VI-Sanipr/92 dated 25 November 1992 and your letter No. PM/122/CM/92 dated 30 November 1992 to the Prime Minister in which you have, inter alia, referred to the security of the disputed structure and have also stated that the Central Para Military Forces which have been stationed at suitable locations in Uttar Pradesh should be withdrawn.

I need hardly reiterate the extent of the concern of the Central Government in relation to the security of the Ram Janma Bhoomi–Babri Masjid structure. The Centre's concern stems from the fact that any damage to the structure, intentional or unintentional, can lead to serious repercussions on the communal front and the law and order situation in various parts of the country. It is for this reason that I have, on several occasions, drawn your attention to this important matter and have been requesting you to strengthen the security arrangements for the structure. I had also reiterated this Ministry's suggestion that a comprehensive review of the security plan for the RJB–BM complex needs to be undertaken by a team in which, apart from representatives of the State Government, representatives of the CRPF and the IB may also be included. I am unable to appreciate your disinclination to accept this suggestion. You will no doubt recall that the earlier security plan for the RJB–BM structure had been prepared by Central experts in 1990 and that plan had been found very useful by the State Government. Contingents of the CRPF placed at the disposal of the State Government have been deployed for the RJB–BM structure since a long time and have valuable experience in relation to the security of the structure. Thus, any input provided by these organizations into the security plan would be valuable. I, therefore, request you to reconsider your decision in this regard.

The security concern acquires an urgent dimension in view of the imminent kar seva from 6 December 1992. It is reported that about 25,000 kar sevaks have already arrived at Ayodhya and that the organizers are expecting that within the next few days the number could increase to as much as 100,000. Many of the representatives of the organizations are reported to be making statements designed to incite the kar sevaks. Some statements have reiterated that the kar seva will be held even in defiance of Court orders. Some veiled threats have been held out to the disputed structure especially if the kar seva is interfered with. There are disturbing reports of specially trained squads being arranged during the kar seva for purposes inimical to the security of the structure.

Against the above background, the security aspect needs even greater attention. We are not sure whether the measures being taken by the State Government would be adequate for the occasion. In particular, it is not clear to us if any contingency plan has been drawn up in case the kar sevaks undertake construction activity in violation of the Court orders, or if they turn violent if such activity is stopped.

You have been assuring us about the State Government's

commitment to the security of the structure. However, on the other hand, many of the security measures which were earlier in existence have been dismantled in spite of our requests that this should not be done. You have indicated that 15 more companies of the PAC have been deployed in Ayodhya. In our view, this force will not be adequate if, in the environment of religious frenzy, violence breaks out at Ayodhya. On the other hand, the deployed forces can be unnecessarily exposed to danger if they are not in sufficient number to meet the situation. We have, on earlier occasions, offered to make available Central forces to the State Government and have now even stationed them at nearby locations so that these can be made available at a short notice when required by the State Government. I would request you to kindly seriously consider this offer.

The matter relating to the security of the RJB–BM structure also came up during the proceeding in the Supreme Court today. The deficiencies in the existing arrangements from the security point of view which were pointed out by the Central Government were also taken note of by the Hon'ble Court and, in fact, it was suggested that these may be brought to the notice of the State Government. The State Government's counsel was asked by the Hon'ble Court to give constructive consideration to these suggestions. In deference to the Court's observations, these suggestions were immediately communicated to the State Government's counsel in the Court itself. The Court proceedings thus vindicate the Centre's continuous concern about the security of the RJB–BM structure. I hope the State Government will give its urgent and serious consideration to our suggestions with the view to avoiding serious repercussions for the law and order situation not only in Uttar Pradesh but also in the country.

With regards,

Yours sincerely,
S.B. Chavan

D.O. No. 81011/1/72-Ay. II

Home Minister
India
New Delhi-110001
December 3,1992

Dear Shri Kalyan Singhji,

In your letter No. PM/122/CM/92 dated 30th November 1992 you had raised certain issues relating to the Central Para Military Forces (CPMFs) in Uttar Pradesh. In this regard, I had written to you vide my letter dated 1 December 1992 indicating that the allegations relating to the misbehaviour and indiscipline among the ranks of para-military forces stationed in Uttar Pradesh are not true.

In your above-mentioned letter you have objected to the stationing of the CPMFs in Uttar Pradesh by the Central Government. In this connection, I would like to invite your attention to the fact that the Central Government had assured the Hon'ble Supreme Court on 23 November 1972 that it is prepared to render all necessary assistance to the State Government for enforcing the directions of the Hon'ble Court. It was in the background of the above undertaking before the Hon'ble Supreme Court that the CPMFs were ordered to move to suitable locations on 24th November 1992. The State Government of Uttar Pradesh was informed on the same day, and it was specifically intimated that the forces are being stationed at suitable locations in Uttar Pradesh so as to be available at a short notice if and when required by the State Government for deployment in connection with the security of the RJB–BM structure and the maintenance of law and order. I am sure you will agree that it would not have been possible to mobilize forces from all over the country at a short notice without some advance action, as above.

I would also like to invite your particular attention to the distinction between stationing and deployment of forces. There can be no doubt about the Constitutional and legal right of the

Union Government even to deploy the Central forces anywhere in the country in certain situations. I would like to inform you that in the present instance we have only stationed the forces in Uttar Pradesh. I am sure that you would not doubt the Constitutional and legal right of the Union Government to station or deploy in certain situations its forces anywhere in the country whenever called for.

It is our anxiety that the developments on account of RJB–BM dispute should not be allowed to lead to a situation of communal disturbances in the State of Uttar Pradesh or any other places in the country. Also no activity should be allowed that is contrary to Court orders or derogatory of judicial authority. Towards that end, the Central Government has, time and again, brought its concerns to the notice of the State Government and rendered such advice as has been thought appropriate. I hope that the State Government would give constructive consideration to the concerns and views expressed by the Central Government. The Central Government is prepared to render whatever assistance is required by the State Government for maintenance of law and order and ensuring compliance with Court orders.

With regards,

Yours sincerely,
S.B. Chavan

No. 81011/1/92-Ay-II

Home Minister
India
New Delhi-110001
December 5, 1992

Dear Shri Kalyan Singhji,

I have written to you on a number of occasions regarding the security of the RJB–BM structure. In your last letter dated 2

December 1992, you have once again reiterated the State Government's commitment to protect the structure. However, our concern in this regard continues and is heightened by the large collection of kar sevaks at Ayodhya for the proposed kar seva.

There are reports that the kar sevaks are in a restive and even belligerent mood and that many of them are resorting to extensive purchases of Trishuls which can even be used for offensive purposes. It is also learnt that some of them are hostile to the Central forces. It is further learnt that with the massive influx of kar sevaks, the number of devotees visiting the shrine has gone up considerably.

As I had written to you earlier, the security arrangements made by the State Government may not be adequate for the occasion, especially if any violence breaks out. It has been reported that the control at entry points between the outer and inner cordons is lax, because of which large batches of visitors are exerting heavy pressure to enter the disputed structure. Further, it is reported that massive crowds are gathering freely and unchecked in the sankeertan area. The crowd pressure, it is reported, resulted in damage to wooden barricades on 4 December 1992 and that there was the danger of people rushing to the shrine which could be stopped only by intervention of the police. Needless to say that the barricading needs to be strengthened considerably. Some other shortcomings in the security arrangements have been brought to the notice of the State Government through a Fax Message No. 81011/1 /92-Ay. II dated 4 December 1992.

In view of the prevailing situation and the fact that the site of the proposed kar seva and other activities will be in the immediate vicinity of the disputed structure, it is necessary to upgrade the security arrangements substantially. I would suggest that the State Government should examine this matter very carefully and take immediate measures to strengthen the security arrangements. The shortcomings mentioned in the message need to be addressed on top priority. The buildings overlooking the RJB–BM structure also need to be secured to prevent the possibility of any attempt being made from those buildings to damage the disputed structure.

The possibility of some mischievous elements using explosives to damage the RJB–BM structure cannot be ruled out. I am glad the State Government has accepted our offer to place at its disposal the services of Bomb Detection and Disposal Squad and Sniffer Dog Squad available with Central police forces. Necessary instructions in this regard have already been issued.

As you are aware, contingents of the Central Para Military Forces have already been stationed at various places in Uttar Pradesh so as to make them available at short notice, if required by the State Government, for the security of the disputed structure and maintenance of law and order in view of the call given for the kar seva. I understand that only about 23 companies including 4 companies of the CRPF are currently deployed for the security arrangements in and around the RJB–BM complex. It is felt that this strength may not be sufficient to meet the security requirements especially if any untoward development takes place. I shall be obliged if you can have this matter looked into personally.

With regards,

Yours sincerely,
S.B. Chavan

Appendix XII

Prime Minister's statement in Parliament on 7 December 1992 in relation to the situation at Ayodhya

On 3 December 1992, statements had been made in both the Houses of Parliament on the general situation at Ayodhya in the context of the proposed *kar seva*. Since then, the developments have taken place at a fast pace.

The Hon'ble Members are aware of the unsparing efforts made by the Central Government to help in finding an amicable settlement of the contentious Ramjanmabhoomi–Babri Masjid dispute. After my statement in Parliament on 27 July 1992, I had held wide-rangingconsultations with a large number of individuals and groups. These included discussions with representatives of the two sides, leaders of political parties, representatives from the media, religious leaders, and others. Even after the resumed negotiations were jeopardized by the unilateral and unfortunate call for the resumption of the *kar seva*, I made every effort to convince the leaders of the VHP and allied organizations of the unreasonableness of their stand and tried to make them agree to some acceptable solution. However, a very intransigent stand was taken by the VHP and allied organizations and instead of cancelling or postponing the *kar seva*, preparations were started for it.

As the House is aware, the Hon'ble Supreme Court has also been seized of this matter. The Central Government was called by the Supreme Court to indicate the manner in which it could assist in the enforcement of its earlier orders. During the hearing, the Central Government had assured the Court that it would be prepared to give to the State Government whatever assistance is required in furtherance of the directions of the Court. We had also conveyed that the Central Government will take such action as may be directed by the Hon'ble Court to secure the enforcement of its order. The Government of Uttar Pradesh had to give an assurance and undertaking to the Court that no construction activity, either permanent or temporary, will take place or will be carried out on the acquired land and no construction machinery or construction material will move into the acquired land as long as the interim order of the High Court is in force in the writ petitions pending before it relating to the land acquisition. The State Government further submitted that the *kar seva* would be a symbolic occasion for carrying on certain religious activities and will not be allowed to be exploited for any constructional activities, symbolic or otherwise. The Supreme Court also directed the State Government, as also the Central Government, to give due publicity to the fact that the proposed *kar seva* would not involve any construction activity or moving of any building material into the acquired land so that all *kar sevaks* get properly informed in this regard.

Even outside the Court, the Government of India repeatedly took up the matter with the Chief Minister of Uttar Pradesh requesting him to take measures to ensure that no activity is allowed that is contrary to the Court orders or derogatory of judicial authority. This concern of the Central Government was conveyed to the State Government time and again. Even in his recent letter of 3 December 1992, the Home Minister again repeated this request to the Chief Minister.

The security of the RJB–BM structure has been a matter of

continuing concern for the Central Government. The Home Minister had taken up this matter with the Chief Minister of Uttar Pradesh on innumerable occasions through meetings, discussions, letters, etc. In recent weeks alone, the Home Minister had written several letters to the Chief Minister in this regard. He had suggested to the Chief Minister that a comprehensive review of the security plan for the structure may be carried out in which the representatives of Central organizations should also be associated. However, this suggestion was not accepted by the State Government despite repeated requests from our side. Also, particular shortcomings in the security measures taken by the State Government were pointed out to the State Government. We had also informed the Chief Minister that according to our assessment the forces deployed by the State Government for security purposes at Ayodhya would not be sufficient to meet the security requirement, especially if any untoward development takes place or, if in the environment of religious frenzy, violence breaks out. The Central Government also brought the inadequacy of security arrangements to the notice of the Supreme Court on 30 November 1992, when the Supreme Court asked the State Government to give its constructive consideration to the suggestions made by the Government of India. The Home Minister also wrote to the Chief Minister that reportedly arrangements such as food, water supply, sanitary facilities, etc. were not adequate to meet the large assembly of *kar sevaks* and, therefore, measures should be taken to ensure that this does not give rise to any health hazard or outbreak of epidemic.

The Central Government had taken the precaution of stationing Central Para Military Forces at various places in Uttar Pradesh on 24 November 1992 itself in the proximity of Ayodhya so that these could be made available at short notice if and when required by the State Government for deployment in connection with the security of the disputed structure and maintenance of law and order. As many as 195 companies of the Central Para

Military Forces were stationed and they were equipped with every facility required to deal with any untoward development such as tear gas, rubber bullets, plastic pellets, over 900 vehicles, etc. The force included Mahila CRPF companies, NSG commandos, bomb disposal teams and sniffer dog squads. The intention was that this force should be utilized by the State Government with minimum loss of time. The Home Minister urged the Chief Minister to consider deploying the force in connection with the security arrangements at Ayodhya. However, instead of utilizing the force, the Chief Minister criticized our action in stationing the force and demanded its withdrawal. He went to the extent of challenging the constitutional validity of the Central Government's action. All that the State Government accepted was the service of bomb detection squads and sniffer dog squads and that too after the Central Government brought to the State Government's notice the possibility of threat by explosives to the disputed structure and urged the deployment of these squads. Despite the Chief Minister's strange and recalcitrant attitude, the Central Para Military Forces stationed near Ayodhya were kept on total alert so as to be made available to the state authorities if and when required. The Union Home Secretary reiterated this message to the Central Para Military Forces on the morning of 6 December 1992.

On 6 December 1992, the initial reports from Ayodhya indicated that the situation was peaceful. About 70,000 *kar sevaks* had assembled in the Ram Katha Kunj for a public meeting to be addressed by senior leaders of the Sangh Parivar. Five hundred sadhus and sants had gathered on the foundation terrace and preparations were made for the pooja. Between 11.45 and 11.50 hrs, about 150 *kar sevaks* managed to break the cordon on the terrace and started pelting stones at the police personnel. About 1,000 *kar sevaks* broke into the RJB–BM structure. About eighty *kar sevaks* managed to climb on the domes of the structure and commenced damaging them. Meanwhile, *kar sevaks* had damaged the outer boundary wall of the structure. By about 12.20 hrs, there were about 25,000 *kar sevaks* gathered in the complex while large numbers were milling around outside. At 14.40 hrs, a crowd of 75,000 was still surrounding the structure of whom many were engaged in demolishing it. By the late evening of 6 December 1992, the RJB–BM structure had been totally demolished. It is also understood that the Ram Lala idols from within the structure had been taken by the head priest ostensibly for safe keeping; later, the idols were reportedly reinstalled and a tin shed has been erected over them.

According to available reports, no action by the local police to prevent the damage to the RJB–BM structure was noticed. The CRPF stationed in the isolation cordon of the structure could not take effective action for want of orders from the State Government officers under whose command it was placed. The movement of additional police forces to Ayodhya was blocked by *kar sevaks* by using iron poles, overturned trollies, etc. All the railway dressings between Ayodhya and Darshan Nagar were locked by the *kar sevaks*.

Immediately on receipt of information regarding the attack by *kar sevaks* on the disputed structure, the Union Home Secretary contacted the State officers and suggested that in view of the situation which seemed to be getting out of the control of the state authorities, they should use the Central Para Military Forces stationed at Faizabad and nearby places who had already been instructed to be available to the State Government without loss of time. Subsequently, the state authorities requested for three battalions of Central Para Military Forces which were made available. However, when the force was moving from Faizabad to Ayodhya it was sent back by local magistrates stating that their orders were that no use of force should be resorted to. Later, the State Government requested for fifty companies of Central Para Military Forces and these were also made available. The Union Home Secretary and other senior officers in the Home

Ministry kept in constant touch throughout the afternoon with the state authorities drawing their attention to the developing situation in the RJB–BM complex and repeatedly urged for immediate action for effective deployment of the paramilitary forces. The Home Minister also spoke to the Chief Minister of Uttar Pradesh on telephone more than once.

In the face of these developments, the Central Government recommended to the President imposition of the President's Rule in the state of Uttar Pradesh and the dissolution of the State Legislative Assembly. The proclamation in this regard was issued last night.

Alert messages were sent out by the Home Ministry to all the State Governments and Union Territories requesting them to take necessary measures to prevent communal disturbances in other places.

The developments at Ayodhya culminating in the tragic destruction of the disputed structure have brought shock and pain to all of us. It is hard to believe that any responsible State Government could behave in this manner. Ours is a federal structure and in recognition of this fact, we reposed a certain amount of trust in the commitments and assurances given repeatedly by the State Government. I regret that the State Government betrayed not only our trust but the trust of the whole nation. It also dishonoured the solemn pledges it gave before the highest court of the land as also before a body such as the National Integration Council. I understand that even the Hon'ble Judges of the Supreme Court during the special hearing on 6 December 1992 evening, expressed shock and dismay over the total failure of the State Government in abiding by its assurances given to the Court.

Sir, the nation has been a witness to one of the most dastardly acts being committed since it achieved freedom, after making untold sacrifices. Those who had laid siege to the minds and conscience of the people of this country for some time mounted the final assault when they demolished the Babri Masjid in Ayodhya. This ancient land of ours has within its boundaries from centuries past symbols and faiths which have motivated countless people belonging to different faiths and persuasions. In fact, India is recognized by this underlying pluralism of faith, religion and conviction. Every temple is sacred, every mosque is sacrosanct, every gurdwara is a source of inspiration and every church is a place for communion with God. The communal forces represented in this instant case by the BJP–VHP–RSS combine have thought fit to violate this sacred trust which every Indian holds dear and close to his heart. Every effort was made to halt this mad rush to destruction. Every political and constitutional initiative was set in motion so that we could, with wisdom and tolerance, reconcile the irreconcilable. This is the only way a democratic and civilized nation can function. If any set of people choose to break out of this mould and arrogate to themselves the right to do what they want in pursuit of power at any cost, the nation will have to summon the courage to meet such a threat squarely and decisively.

My government will stand up and face these forces and I am sure Parliament and political parties actuated by patriotism and the people of India would support us. We have decided to take the strongest action possible under the law against those who incited people all over the country and brought crowds to Ayodhya and in their presence persuaded them to commit this heinous act. I want to make a solemn commitment that the law of the land will catch up with such persons, whoever they might be. The cancer of communalism, sectarianism and obscurantism has been plaguing the body politic of our country for some time. In the liberal and democratic functioning in the country, everyone has the right to promote and practise what he thinks to be his line of action. But it is not given to anyone in this country to take a stand which militates against the very basic concepts and ideals of our democratic and secular polity. Unfortunately some people and some political parties have chosen to break out of these confines and made a determined bid to poison the political, social and cultural stream of our great country. We have decided that no longer shall we allow such people and organizations to continue doing this at the cost of our country's future. Appropriate steps will be taken to bring the activities of such people and organizations to a halt and if they persist, they will have to face the consequences of their acts, including being banned.

Ours is a federal structure with a strong unitary Centre. We have consistently tried to promote an atmosphere in which all states and institutions function in cooperative spirit for the well-being of the people. Our intention is to continue this policy. But it must, however, be clearly understood that anyone who has aided and abetted the crime committed at Ayodhya will have to bear the consequences of their action. On this there can be no compromise whatsoever.

At this moment of national peril, I appeal to all sections of the House to stand unitedly because only in this manner can we preserve and protect not only our Constitution, but the future of this country. To the minorities of India who live in every corner of this sacred land I have only one message to give, the Congress will not and shall not default on its basic commitment to protect and preserve their rights, their lives and liberty. We will walk every extra step that is needed in fulfilling this commitment which has been given to them not only by the Constitution of this country, but also by our great leaders Gandhiji, Pandit Jawaharlal Nehruji, Lal Bahadur Shastriji, Smt. Indira Gandhiji and Shri Rajiv Gandhiji. Let no one mistake our resolve or determination under any circumstances.

The demolition of the mosque was a most barbarous act. The Government will see to it that it is rebuilt.

Regarding the land and the new Ram Temple, appropriate steps will be taken after the judgement of the Lucknow Bench of the Allahabad High Court is delivered on 11 December.

Appendix XIII

Prime Minister's intervention in the Lok Sabha on 21 December 1992

I am indeed grateful to the large number of Hon'ble Members who have participated in this discussion and made valuable contributions. The debate has rightly been exhaustive and many members were able to express themselves with anguish, with anger, with reason and with so much of patriotism that this debate, perhaps, will go down as one of the debates of the highest order in the history of Parliament.

I once again express my gratitude to them. The occasion itself is one of introspection, seriousness, gravity and, perhaps, an occasion where each one of us has to set our sights on the vision of the future.

This country has been a great country. It has risen to great heights, it has seen aberrations, but from every aberration it has come out stronger and not weaker. I do hope that this great tragedy, this act of betrayal and vandalism, which occurred on the 6th of December, will be obliterated as quickly as possible from the public mind. I wish to God that this happens. Even the slightest remnant of the memory of this would be harmful to the country and I would appeal to all sections of the people, all sections of the House to help in this process, the process of living down this shameful event of 6th December and prove to the world once again that this is just an aberration. Otherwise, the country is one full of harmony, full of brotherhood and this has been so for thousands of years; it will be so for many thousands of years to come.

It is rather strange that this discussion should come in the form of a no-confidence motion. The Bharatiya Janata Party has no confidence in the Government of India. Why? Because the Government of India reposed confidence in the State Government of the Bharatiya Janata Party. Maybe this is good justice meted out to the Government of India. I have to own that, I have to admit that. But how do we run this country? How do Centre–State relations run? On the basis of suspicion? On the basis of mistrust? How do we run the country, how do we run the governments of the states which are so inextricably linked with the Centre that they have to be running a three-legged race all the time? One cannot go in advance, one cannot run in advance, leaving the other behind.

In the National Development Council, in the National Integration Council, in the Chief Ministers' Conference, we have seen that every problem is so intractable if seen in isolation but becomes easy when seen comprehensively with the State Governments and the Centre sitting together and trying to sort this out. During the last one-and-a-half years the National Development Council has been functioning this way. Several sub-committees of the Council headed by Chief Ministers belonging to different parties have been constituted and they have been doing excellent work. There has been no dissension of any kind and the National Council on the whole has acquitted itself admirably as a result of this functioning. This is how a federal state has to function.

But is it possible, is it conceivable for the Central Government of any federation to even imagine that one of its units, a State Government, would keep giving affidavits, giving assurances, and finally violate these assurances in a manner that until the last moment cannot be detected? That is why my first reaction was that for all appearances it was pre-planned. There is going to be an inquiry. So I would not like to anticipate the results or the findings of the inquiry. But it was so planned, it cannot be an accident, it just cannot be an accident.

I have been arraigned, I have been criticized for believing. That is the only sin I seem to have committed. I agree. I plead guilty for believing a State Government. I have no compunction on that. But the point is that I believed it not only as head of the Central Government; I found that there was nothing else to do but to believe the assurance of the State Government. Was there any other way when the Supreme Court believed it? The Supreme Court after its hearing placed more reliance on the State Government, asked the State Government to come back with more affidavits, asked me at some point of time to keep out because they would like to try this State Government. They had full faith in the State Government. The Central Government is not a party before the Supreme Court or in the High Court for that matter. But I was called for a particular purpose. We said: 'We are prepared to help the Supreme Court in whatever manner the Supreme Court wants us.' That is all the role that we played. And ultimately on the sixth itself, the Supreme Court was shocked; what they said is revealing. I do not remember any State Government in a federal set-up having behaved this way. So, those who told me, tell me now, did we not tell you? Yes, they have been proved right. I was proved right in July. But it is not a question of who is proved right.

The question is, what has happened to the Constitution of India in this process? It lies shattered. What has happened to Article 356? It lies shattered. I would like constitutional experts to go into it. Where is it that the President of the Union finds that a situation has arisen whereby the governance of the State cannot be carried on according to the provisions of the Constitution? What is that precise point? We have dismissed State Governments many times. Most of the State Governments dismissed or removed have been Congress Governments belonging to the same party at the Central Government. It was easy to tender your resignation. We send advisers from here and the State Government gets the President's Rule. In the few cases where other governments were also dismissed, a similar procedure—not quite from the beginning with the resignation, but some other procedure—was followed. But in no case was the practical implication of Article 356 tested. You send the advisers. They take over at leisure any time, maybe one day late, maybe one day early. Here you cannot do a thing without dismissing the State Government. I send my troops, the paramilitary forces. I send them because I want them to be available to the State Government. At no point of time does the State Government tell me that they will not use them. But they do not use them. I have yet to come across a scrap of paper from Shri Kalyan Singh saying that he refuses to use paramilitary forces sent by the Centre. The Home Minister will bear me out. But he has not used them. Ultimately, on the last day when we say, 'Please use them, please use them, please use them,' the Home Secretary, sitting with the Chief Minister, says, 'It is so unfortunate—unthinkable and unfortunate.' (Interruptions)

Earlier, the Home Secretary spoke to Principal Secretary, Home, Government of Uttar Pradesh at the Chief Minister's residence asking him to persuade the Chief Minister to accept the assistance of the Central forces. The Principal Secretary, Home, Government of Uttar Pradesh said that he would requisition Central forces after consulting the Chief Minister. At no point of time was it refused. This is what I am trying to impress. When does that moment arise when we come to the conclusion that the governance of the state cannot be carried on according to the provisions of the Constitution? So, these are some of the difficulties. If only one word had been there in Article 356 which says, 'a situation has arisen . . .', if after that it could have been added—'or is likely to arise'—then the Governor gets, the President gets a greater leeway. But, then, one has to go into it in greater detail. This is the first time in the history of the Constitution, in the history of Article 356, when it has been put to a test as it was never put to before; it has not been able to stand up to the test. Never mind who used it, never mind who did not use it, howsoever you look at it you will find that there is a lacuna and that would have to be made good.

On the one side these are the reasons why I have to trust the State Government.

SHRI SRIKANTA JENA (Cuttack): Did you receive any IB report or not?

PRIME MINISTER: There is no variance between the IB report and what I have read. Then, three days before the date, the Governor of Uttar Pradesh writes in categorical terms that the Central Government should not, I repeat, should not, think of imposing President's Rule in the State. He also adds that if any such thing is contemplated, the safety of the Babri Masjid can become questionable. I have got the letter. These are on one side. On the other side is, of course, the advice tendered by more knowledgeable people.

SHRI CHANDRA SHEKHAR (Ballia): He is quoting Article 356. Is it not under 356 that if the Government of India is convinced, without a report of the Governor and without the report of the State Government that the Constitution is not being implemented there, it can take action? And action has been taken even without the Governor's report, on the information that the Government of India collected.

PRIME MINISTER: I agree, Chandra Shekharji, I am only trying to list out the circumstances under which the government of the state could not be conducted. That is all I have said. On the other hand, as I said, was the advice that these people might let us down, and some statements here and there, not from the government but from some leaders, saying that they would not do *kar seva* only by sweeping. These were the other things. I say in all sincerity that the government had to weigh the evidence on both sides and we came to the conclusion that it was not possible to impose President's Rule, in the face of all this, at the time at which it would have been of some use. And I would also like to add—I do not know whether I should say this—that the situation in Ayodhya was such that one had to be very careful, extremely careful. The Babri Masjid—that structure—was a hostage. On one side was the possibility of its being saved by negotiation, by further commitment of the State Government, on the other side, you had absolutely no time. It is not with *kudals* and those things, it could have been blown up in a matter of minutes, seconds, by one bomb of the size of a tennis ball, detonated from two hundred yards, if the State Government connived at it. This is what I said. This is like the mother stabbing the child, the mother poisoning the child. You do not expect it but when it happens no one can save it. This is my case.

SHRI EBRAHIM SULAIMAN SAIT (Ponnani): What about previous experiences?

PRIME MINISTER: That is what I say. In July I succeeded. You all heard me, heard my statement here in this House. We discussed it. It worked. I was taking the same line which I had elaborated in my statement. We had the cell. We got the discussions going. Two meetings were held in a very good atmosphere. The third meeting was to clinch the issue of reference. It was at that point that a spanner was thrown in the works and the whole thing came back to square one. This is the situation. History will judge, the people will judge. I am not really being dogmatic about it. My own party people had different views. I told the party that it is possible for Congressmen to have different views. Who is proved right, who is proved wrong, that is not the question. You take a decision, you stick to it, you defend it. If you win, you win, if you do not win, you do not win . . .

SHRI VISHWANATH PRATAP SINGH (Fatehpur): The Hon'ble Prime Minister's full case is that he totally trusted the

BJP government, the UP government, and he had no reason to mistrust it. And because he trusted fully, therefore this tragedy took place. May I remind the Hon'ble Prime Minister that we had put a question that if Kalyan Singh suddenly resigns, how will he manage the situation. He did say: We have an alternative programme and within minutes we can get into action and manage the situation. That means that it was there and prudently so—as any administrator should have alternative plans and not mere trust. We were given to understand that there are alternative plans if Shri Kalyan Singh resigns. The whole scenario, as it developed, is described here. May I know where has that alternative plan gone? What happened to that alternative plan?

PRIME MINISTER: Sir, when Shri Kalyan Singh resigned, it was too late to do anything. The time was very clear. Nothing could be done then except to dismiss the government, which was done.

What I am really trying to impress on the House is let us not go into who is right and who is wrong. I have borne all the criticism from friends and from other parties. I am only trying to place some facts. In spite of the facts there had been a betrayal. A betrayal is something which is never detected. A conspiracy is something which comes to light much later, when only hindsight functions. Indiraji would not have been assassinated, Rajivji would not have been assassinated if the knowledge about the conspiracy had been available earlier. This is one of those mishaps where it has happened. Nobody can say that he is impeccably right. No plan can be absolutely, hundred per cent foolproof.

You get everything but you do not get magistrates. Is it possible? I would like to ask where do you take magistrates from? If the State Government does not give you twenty magistrates who are needed, do you take magistrates from Delhi? Is it possible legally? Can any legal luminary tell me?

Therefore, if you go into the details—there is a Commission of Inquiry, which will go into it—I am only placing before you some rudimentary facts which need to be taken into account.

SHRI INDRAJIT GUPTA (Midnapore): One small question to the Hon'ble Prime Minister. Is it not a fact that the news that the demolition work on the mosque structure having begun reached you, reached the Government of India, by twelve noon? If so, why was the Cabinet meeting not called till six o'clock in the evening to decide what to do?

PRIME MINISTER: The first impulse of anyone who gets a report like this is to see that we save the mosque first. We asked them to make use of the forces; we went on pleading with them; we went on asking them to do it. That is all that was done.

SHRI SOMNATH CHATTERJEE (Bolpur): How long did the Government of India continue to have faith in the Uttar Pradesh Government? Was it till eight o'clock in the evening or till nine o'clock in the evening, when by this time the demolition work had gone on? Therefore what we have been most anxious to find out from the Hon'ble Prime Minister is that realizing that the betrayal had started, that he has been betrayed, how long did he continue to have trust in him? This is what is worrying us.

PRIME MINISTER: By 9.10 p.m. the President had signed the papers. By 7.30 p.m. or so, Shri S.B. Chavan took the papers to him. Those are the timings, if I remember right.

The inexorable logic of 6 December has started in right earnest, started with whatever time is necessary to take action. Action after action has been taken. Yes, this is a change in direction because it was warranted by the worst tragedy we could imagine and the new direction has been accepted, the challenge has been accepted, the battle has been joined. There is no need for us to go into history now. The need for us is to make new history and that is that for the first time after many years the secular forces of the country have come together, the secular parties with all their internal differences have come together. And we will forge ahead, we will see that secular credentials of this country are reestablished fully and what our great leaders through the Constitution and through their own example told us to do, we will do it to the hilt.

Mr Indrajit Gupta has raised a very relevant point. In fact, I was going to read the same Resolution, which he read from the Constituent Assembly. I had occasion to raise this in one of our party meetings. In a secular democracy, what is the place of non-secular parties or what should be the composition and the programme of parties participating in that democracy, is a question which needs a national debate. I want this debate, I want thinkers, I want leaders to come together because the time has come when we can easily see that there is irreconcilability in these forces. We tried to carry on for many, many years. Now we find that there is a party, which takes a religious issue as its main plank. I have nothing against a religious issue, I have nothing against religion, but a religious issue being brought into politics, election after election, cannot be accepted. This will have to be looked into and this will have to be effectively checked.

If there is a party which takes to arms, for instance, if the candidate of one party has an AK-47 and moves with it and, the other candidate has nothing, it is an unequal fight. If a party takes Ram as the spokesman of the party and effects the minds and hearts of people day in and day out, whereas the other party does not even utter this because it is a secular party, does not want to make use of that as an issue, now it is again an unequal fight and the Constitution does not, in my view, allow an unequal fight. The field has to be even for both teams. Those who are participating in the elections would have to participate on the basis of certain guidelines, certain principles which are common to all and which are defined very clearly in the Constitution. This will have to be looked into. This is fair to both of us. Let Ram remain where he remains, let us fight on the basis of other issues which are much more important from the point of view of the people and that is the only way of making the Constitution work in its right spirit. I appeal to the other parties who are thinking perhaps that this is going to be a permanent asset to them, it will not be a permanent asset to them. The people of India can see through this game very easily and very quickly; maybe in one election or the other, or in the next election. They will see through it and perhaps you will be wasting five years doing nothing except raising unnecessary slogans. So, I would like this to be gone into. I thank Mr Indrajit Gupta for having brought out that resolution. We will have to act on it; we will have to think about it. I will come, if possible to the House or to the leaders of the Opposition first, all leaders and perhaps for a general debate, a wider debate in the country, of how this aberration which has become rather menacing during this decade has to be set right. It started in a small beginning, but then it has permeated to more or less every party.

Today, when I say that something which has happened will have to be undone, there are eyebrows going up in all parties. I do not want this at all to happen in any party if we are secular, the vandal cannot be allowed to take advantage of the act of vandalism committed by him. It is quite clear to me. It has to be seen; how we see it, it is for all of us to consider. Everything is there for discussion. We will discuss all these things, find ways, as we were about to find the way, we will find a way once again. I assure that to all of you. I would like to once again appeal that today, the day of balancing pluses and minuses is over, we will have to go ahead with a programme.

So far as rehabilitation and reconstruction measures are concerned, I thought I should apprise the House of what has been decided. The Government of India has advised the State Governments to take strong action against officers who have been derelict in their duties in maintenance of law and order during the recent communal riots. At present, the scale of ex gratia assistance to victims of communal riots differs from state to state. The Government of India will see to it that assistance to riot victims is given on a uniform scale by all the State Governments so that next of kin of persons killed in riots could be paid Rs 1 lakh and those who are permanently incapacitated are paid Rs 50,000 each. For this particular incident, I would like to add that as a one-time exception, we would like to raise this amount to Rs 2 lakhs.

SHRI BASUDEB ACHARIA (Bankura): The Uttar Pradesh Government is paying only Rs 50,000.

PRIME MINISTER: We will talk to the Uttar Pradesh Government and between them and us we will see that it is paid.

A fund will be set up for repair and reconstruction of all places of worship which were damaged in the disturbances. In addition to the ex gratia relief in the case of death, grievous hurt or damage to the property, the Government of India will recommend to the State Government that the victims of recent communal riots may also be given the following assistance: employment to widows and wards wherein the earning member had been killed or permanently incapacitated, allotment of tenements and house sites to families rendered homeless, allotment of shops/space for kiosks to families to restart their business and bank loans for capital investment as also working capital for recommencement of industries and businesses affected in the riots. Similar measures will also be taken in the Union Territories. These are the steps that have been decided upon.

SHRI BASUDEB ACHARIA: What about the payment of wages to the workers during the period of curfew? This also should be taken into account.

PRIME MINISTER: Some of these suggestions have come from the Hon'ble Members. If more suggestions come and we find them feasible, we will also go into them.

SHRI SRIKANTA JENA (Cuttack): The Prime Minister spoke day before yesterday and assured the House to give a White Paper on Ayodhya issue. That has not been submitted. About the reconstruction of that structure, you have not said anything today. What is your response about reconstruction?

PRIME MINISTER: The Supreme Court has asked the

Government of India to submit its views on this particular subject within a time frame which they have fixed. We would like to examine all aspects of this and go to the Supreme Court and make our submissions. I would like to tell the Hon'ble Members that this is being looked into. (Interruptions)

SHRI INDER JIT (Darjeeling): The cause of media men who have suffered has not been referred to.

PRIME MINISTER: Sir, there is a specific term of reference in the terms of reference of the Commission of Inquiry in regard to what happened to media persons. We have meanwhile decided to give those whose equipment etc. were damaged, certain concessions they had asked for. So, the Commission of Inquiry will go in great detail into what happened to the media persons.

Appendix XIV

The Acquisition of Certain Area at Ayodhya Ordinance, 1993, dated 7 January 1993

Promulgated by the President in the Forty-third Year of the Republic of India.

An Ordinance to provide for the acquisition of certain area at Ayodhya and for matters connected therewith or incidental thereto.

Whereas there has been a long-standing dispute relating to the structure (including the premises of the inner and outer courtyards of such structure), commonly known as the Ram Janma Bhumi–Babri Masjid, situated in village Kot Ramchandra in Ayodhya, in Pargana Haveli Avadh, in tehsil Faizabad Sadar, in the district of Faizabad of the state of Uttar Pradesh;

And whereas the said dispute has affected the maintenance of public order and harmony between different communities in the country;

And whereas it is necessary to maintain public order and to promote communal harmony and the spirit of common brotherhood amongst the people of India;

And whereas with a view to achieving the aforesaid objectives, it is necessary to acquire certain areas in Ayodhya;

And whereas Parliament is not in session and the President is satisfied that circumstances exist which render it necessary for him to take immediate action;

Now, therefore, in exercise of the powers conferred by clause (1) of article 123 of the Constitution, the President is pleased to promulgate the following Ordinance.

Chapter I
Preliminary

Short title and commencement

1. (1) This Ordinance may be called the Acquisition of Certain Area at Ayodhya Ordinance, 1993.

(2) It shall come into force at once.

Definitions

2. In this Ordinance, unless the context otherwise requires,—

(a) 'area' means the area (including all the buildings, structures or other properties comprised therein) specified in the Schedule;

(b) 'authorized person' means a person or body of persons or trustees of any trust authorized by the Central Government under section 7;

(c) 'Claims Commissioner' means the Claims Commissioner appointed under sub-section (2) of section 8;

(d) 'prescribed' means prescribed by rules made under this Ordinance.

Chapter II
Acquisition of the area in Ayodhya

Acquisition of rights in respect of certain area

3. On and from the commencement of this Ordinance, the right, title and interest, in relation to the area shall, by virtue of this Ordinance, stand transferred to, and vest, in the Central Government.

General effect of vesting

4. (1) The area shall be deemed to include all assets, rights, leaseholds, powers, authority and privileges and all property, moveable and immovable, including lands, buildings, structures, shops of whatever nature or other properties and all other rights and interests in, or arising out of, such properties as were immediately before the commencement of this Ordinance in the ownership, possession, power or control of any person or the State Government of Uttar Pradesh, as the case may be, and all registers, maps, plans, drawings and other documents of whatever nature relating thereto.

(2) All properties aforesaid which have vested in the Central Government under section 3 shall, by force of such vesting, be freed and discharged from any trust, obligation mortgage, charge, lien and all other encumbrances affecting them and any attachment, injunction, decree or order of any court or tribunal or other authority restricting the use of such properties in any manner or appointing any receiver in respect of the whole or any part of such properties shall cease to have any effect.

(3) If, on the commencement of this Ordinance, any suit, appeal or other proceeding in respect of the right, title and interest relating to any property which has vested in the Central Government under section 3 is pending before any court, tribunal or other authority, the same shall abate.

Duty of person or State Government in charge of the management of the area to deliver all assets, etc.

5. (1) The Central Government may take all necessary steps to secure possession of the area which is vested in that Government under section 3.

(2) On the vesting of the area in the Central Government under section 3, the person or State Government of Uttar Pradesh, as the case may be, in charge of the management of the area immediately before such vesting shall be bound to deliver to the

Central Government or the authorized person, all assets, registers and other documents in their custody relating to such vesting or where it is not practicable to deliver such registers or documents, the copies of such registers or documents authenticated in the prescribed manner.

Power of Central Government to direct vesting of the area in another authority or body or trust

6. (1) Notwithstanding anything contained in sections 3,4, 5 and 7, the Central Government may if it is satisfied that any authority or other body, or trustees of any trust, set up on or after the commencement of this Ordinance is or are willing to comply with such terms and conditions as that Government may think fit to impose, direct by notification in the Official Gazette, that the right, title and interest or any of them in relation to the area or any part thereof, instead of continuing to vest in the Central Government vests in that authority or body or trustees of that trust—either on the date of the notification or on such later date as may be specified in the notification.

(2) When any right, title and interest in relation to the area or part thereof vest in the authority or body or trustees referred to in sub-section (1), such rights of the Central Government in relation to such area or part thereof, shall, on and from the date of such vesting, be deemed to have become the right of that authority or body or trustees ofthat trust.

(3) The provisions of sections 4, 5, 7 and 11 shall, so far as may be, apply in relation to such authority or body or trustees as they apply in relation to the Central Government and for this purpose references therein to the 'Central Government' shall be construed as references to such authority or body or trustees.

Chapter III
Management and administration of property

Management of property by Government

7. (1) Notwithstanding anything contained in any contract or instrument or order of any court, tribunal or other authority to the contrary, on and from the commencement of this Ordinance, the property vested in the Central Government under section 3 shall be managed by the Central Government or by a person or body of persons or trustees of any trust authorized by that Government in this behalf.

(2) In managing the property vested in the Central Government under section 3, the Central Government or the authorized person shall ensure that the position existing before the commencement of this Ordinance in the area on which the structure (including the premises of the inner and outer court yards of such structure), commonly known as the Ram Janma Bhumi–Babri Masjid, stood in village Kot Ramachandra in Ayodhya, in Pargana Haveli, Avadh, in tehsil Faizabad Sadar in the district of Faizabad of the state of Uttar Pradesh is maintained.

Chapter IV
Miscellaneous

Payment of amount

8. (1) The owner of any laud, building, structure or other property comprised in the area shall be given by the Central Government, for the transfer to and vesting in that Government under section 3 of that land, building, structure or other property, in cash an amount equivalent to the market value of the land, building, structure or other property.

(2) The Central Government shall, for the purpose of deciding the claim of the owner or any person having a claim against the owner under sub-section (1), by notification in the Official Gazette,

appoint a Claims Commissioner.

(3) The Claims Commissioner shall regulate his own procedure for receiving and deciding the claims.

(4) The owner or any person having a claim against the owner may make a claim to the Claims Commissioner within a period of ninety days from the date of commencement of this Ordinance:

Provided that if the Claims Commissioner is satisfied that the claimant was prevented by sufficient cause from preferring the claim within the said period of ninety days, the Claims Commissioner may entertain the claim within a further period of ninety days and not thereafter.

Ordinance to override all other enactments

9. The provisions of this Ordinance shall have effect notwithstanding anything inconsistent therewith contained in any other law for the time being a force or any instrument having effect by virtue of any law other than this Ordinance or any decree or order of any court, tribunal or other authority.

Penalties

10. Any person who is in charge of the management of the area and fails to deliver to the Central Government or the authorized person any asset, register or other document in his custody relating to such area or, as the case may be, authenticated copies of such register or document, shall be punishable with imprisonment for a term which may extend to three years or with fine which may extend to ten thousand rupees, or with both.

Protection of action taken in good faith

11. No suit, prosecution or other legal proceedings shall lie against the Central Government or the authorized person or any of the officers or other employees of that Government or the authorized person for anything which is in good faith done or intended to be done under this Ordinance.

Power to make rules

12. (1) The Central Government may, by notification in the Official Gazette, make rules to carry out the provisions of this Ordinance.

(2) Every rule made by the Central Government under this Ordinance shall be laid, as soon as may be after it is made, before each House of Parliament, while it is in session for a total period of thirty days which may be comprised in one session or in two or more successive sessions, and if, before the expiry of the session immediately following the session or the successive sessions aforesaid, both Houses agree in making any modification in the rule or both. Houses agree that the rule should not be made, the rule shall thereafter have effect only in such modified form or be of no effect, as the case may be; so, however, that any such modification or annulment shall be without prejudice to the validity of anything previously done under that rule.

Appendix XV

Reference to the Supreme Court under Article 143 of the Constitution, dated 7 January 1993

Whereas a dispute has arisen whether a Hindu temple or any Hindu religious structure existed prior to the construction of the structure (including the premises of the inner and outer courtyards of such structure), commonly known as the Ram Janma Bhoomi–Babri Masjid, in the area in which the structure stood in village Kot Ramchandra in Ayodhya, in Pargana Haveli Avadh, in Tehsil Faizabad Sadar, in the district of Faizabad of the state of Uttar Pradesh;

And whereas the said area is located in revenue plot nos. 159 and 160 in the said village Kot Ramchandra;

And whereas the said dispute has affected the maintenance of public order and harmony between different communities in the country;

And whereas the aforesaid area vests in the Central Government by virtue of the Acquisition of certain Area at Ayodhya Ordinance, 1993;

And whereas notwithstanding the vesting of the aforesaid area in the Central Government under the said Ordinance the Central Government proposes to settle the said dispute after obtaining the opinion of the Supreme Court of India and in terms of the said opinion;

And whereas in view of what has been herein before stated it appears to me that the question hereinafter set out has arisen and is of such a nature and of such public importance that it is expedient to obtain the opinion of the Supreme Court of India thereon;

Now, therefore, in exercise of the powers conferred upon me by clause (1) of article 143 of the Constitution of India, I, Shanker Dayal Sharma, President of India, hereby refer the following question to the Supreme Court of India for consideration and opinion thereon, namely:

Whether a Hindu temple or any Hindu religious structure existed prior to the construction of the Ram Janma Bhoomi–Babri Masjid (including the premises of the inner and outer courtyards of such structure) in the area on which the structure stood?

New Delhi
7th January 1993

President of India

Appendix XVI

Supreme Court Judgment, dated 24 December 1994

In the following pages, the proceedings of the Supreme Court are extracted regarding the following matters, viz.:

1. Under the heading 'Contempt', the Contempt proceedings against and punishment awarded by the Supreme Court to Shri Kalyan Singh, the then Chief Minister, Uttar Pradesh, for violation of the orders of the Court regarding giving protection to the Babri Masjid, on 6 December 1992, have been given; and

2. Under the heading 'Result', the order of the Supreme Court regarding the resultant legal position on the future of the Babri Masjid has been brought out in detail.

In the Supreme Court of India
Contempt

The gravamen of the charge in these contempt petitions is that Shri Kalyan Singh, the then Chief Minister of the State, in view of his ideological and political affinity with the Bharatiya Janata Party and the Vishwa Hindu Parishad and their commitment to the building of Sri Ram Temple, deliberately encouraged and permitted the grossest violation of the Court's orders.

The defence in substance, is that the constructions were initially of the nature of 'levelling operations' done by the State Government for enabling the Parikrama facilities for the pilgrims. However, later, the large congregation of sadhus who had assembled on the land took upon themselves to make the constructions and that even those constructions which were in the nature of a platform did not amount to permanent structures such as were prohibited by the order of the Court.

In the meantime, as we have been told at the Bar, there was a meeting at the national level of the Integration Council and the Chief Minister of the State as it appears from the affidavit of the Home Secretary of the respondent State dated 13-11-1991 made certain statements to the Council. These have been extracted in paragraph 3 of the affidavit and read thus:

The Chief Minister has made several statements at the National Integration Council meeting on 2–11–1991. On the basis of the statements, the resolution of the National Integration Council was passed on 2–11–1991. The resolution itself states:

The Council noted the following assurances given by the Chief Minister of Uttar Pradesh:

(i) All efforts will be made to find an amicable resolution of the issue;

(ii) Pending a final solution, the Government of Uttar Pradesh will hold itself fully responsible for the protection of the Ramjanmabhoomi–Babri Masjid structures.

(iii) Orders of the Court in regard to the land acquisition proceedings will be fully implemented; and

(iv) Judgment of the Allahabad High Court in the cases pending before it will not be violated.

We shall take it, and Mr Jaitley has no objection to our doing so, that the State of Uttar Pradesh remains bound by what has been stated in this paragraph and this shall be the obligation of the State of Uttar Pradesh to stand by our order of today which is made after taking into account the stand of the State of Uttar Pradesh as disclosed by the Chief Minister and reiterated in the affidavit of the Home Secretary. It shall, therefore, be taken as a representation to the Court on which we have made this Order.

The questions that therefore arise for consideration are:

(i) Whether the undertaking given by the Chief Minister before the National Integration Council which was in terms recapitulated and incorporated in the order dated 15–11–1991 of this Court could be said to be an undertaking given by the Chief Minister personally or was merely an undertaking on behalf of the UP Government;

(ii) Whether there was any construction of a permanent nature carried on the land in wilful disobedience of the orders of the Court;

(iii) Whether these constructional activities were carried on by or at the instance of the State Government or its authorities or were done in connivance with and assistance and encouragement of the State Government; or were they carried out in spite of all reasonable steps taken in that regard by the State Government and the Chief Minister to prevent the same; and

(iv) Whether the State Government and the Chief Minister were not liable for contempt for any alleged wilful disobedience of the orders of this Court.

The purport of the defence—as gatherable from the various affidavits and counter-affidavits filed from time to time—does not seem to dispute that constructions of a substantial nature were carried out on the land in the month of July 1992. Implicit in these admissions is that had these works and activities been carried out by the State Government and its authorities, there would be no doubt whatsoever that they constitute a flagrant violation of the orders of the Court. What was, however, sought to be pleaded was that the area in question, by a long religious tradition in Ayodhya, attracts a large number of pilgrims and particularly in the month of July which coincides with the period of 'Chaturmas' where a large number of sadhus congregate to celebrate 'Sarvadev

Anusthan'. It was urged that these pilgrim-sadhus embarked upon the construction of a cement concrete platform and that their number was so large that any coercive preventive action would have triggered off an adverse reaction which might have endangered the safety of the disputed 'Ramjanmabhoomi–Babri Masjid Structure' which was situated in the immediate vicinity and for whose protection the Government stood committed. In view of these conflicting considerations and of the risks involved in the operations, the Government felt compelled to abstain from any coercive steps to prevent the constructions by the pilgrims. We shall later advert to the merits and bona fides of this version. Suffice it to say here that at no point of time did the Chief Minister seek before the Court to be absolved of his undertaking in view of these alleged conditions. They are now put forward as a defence in the contempt action.

But it is necessary to say that in a Government of laws and not of men the executive branch of Government bears a grave responsibility for upholding and obeying judicial orders. It is perhaps worthwhile recalling what the Supreme Court of United States observed in William G. Cooper, Members of the Board of Directors of Little Rock vs. John Aaron where, in his concurring opinion Justice Frankfurter said:

'The use of force to further obedience to law is in any event a last resort and one not congenial to the spirit of our Nation . . . Violent resistance to law cannot be made a legal reason for its suspension without loosening the fabric of our society. What could this mean but to acknowledge that disorder under the aegis of a State has moral superiority over the law of the Constitution?

'The historic phrase "a Government of laws and not of men" epitomizes the distinguishing character of our political society. When John Adams put that phrase into the Massachusetts Declaration of Rights he was not indulging in a rhetorical flourish. He was expressing the aim of those who, with him, framed the Declaration of Independence and founded the Republic.

'Compliance with decisions of this Court, as the constitutional organ of the supreme law of the land, has often, throughout our history, depended on active support by State and local authorities. It presupposes such support. To withhold it, and indeed to use political power to try to paralyse the supreme law, precludes the maintenance of our federal system as we have known and cherished it for one hundred and seventy years.

'Lincoln's appeal to "the better angels of our nature" failed to avert a fratricidal war. But the compassionate wisdom of Lincoln's First and Second Inaugurals bequeathed to the Union, cemented with blood, a moral heritage which, when drawn upon in times of stress and strife, is sure to find specific ways and means to surmount difficulties that may appear to be insurmountable.'

Dicey, in his *Law of the Constitution* (10th Edn. pp. 193–94), said: 'When we speak of the "rule of law" as a characteristic of our country, (we mean) not only that with us no man is above the law, but (what is a different thing) that here every man, whatever be his rank or condition, is subject to the ordinary law of the realm and amenable to the jurisdiction of the ordinary tribunals. In England the idea of legal equality, or of the universal subjection of all classes to one law administered by the ordinary courts, has been pushed to its utmost limit. With us, every official, from Prime Minister down to a constable or a collector of taxes, is under the same responsibility for every act done without legal justification as any other citizen. The reports abound with cases in which officials have been brought before the courts, and made, in their personal capacity, liable to punishment, or to the payment of damages for acts done in their official character but in excess of their lawful authority. A colonial governor, a secretary of state, a military officer and all subordinates though carrying out the commands of their official superiors, are as responsible for any act which the law does not authorize as is any private and unofficial person.'

In these formative years of our nation-building, it is more

important than ever to recognize that in a pluralist society law is the greatest and the only integrating factor. Respect for law and its institutions are the only assurance that can hold a pluralist nation together. Any attempt to achieve solutions to controversies, however ideologically and emotionally surcharged, not on the basis of law and through judicial institutions, but on the strength of numbers, will subvert the fundamental values of our chosen political organization. It will demolish public faith in the accepted constitutional institutions and weaken people's resolve to solve issues by peaceful means. It will destroy respect for the Rule of Law and the authority of courts and seek to place individual authority and strength of numbers above the wisdom of law. This is courting disaster, fratricidal wars, civil commotion, and disruption of everything that we hold sacred. The highest cherished value of our nationhood, which is tolerance, will be distorted by such misguided enthusiasm.

Commenting on the possible purpose of this structure, Shri Prabhat Kumar himself says, 'However, according to the statements of those involved in the construction work it was intended to be the first step towards putting up of the "Singh Dwar" of the proposed "Ram Mandir" as and when the same would be constructed.'

This Court constituted a committee consisting of Shri S. Rai, Registrar General, Supreme Court; Professor K.K. Nayar, IIT Delhi and Professor Arvind Krishan, School of Planning and Architecture, New Delhi. In the report of the Committee, the nature and the extent of construction is described thus:

'The area built-up can be visualized as five north–south strips arranged from the east to the west. Areas and dimensions of the first four strips increase step by step from one another. The fifth strip is cut back both in area and dimension. There are three layers of concrete in the structure. The first layer is about 0.62 m thick and it covers the full area of 1060 sq. m except for a circular opening of 7.1 m diameter in the centre of the fourth strip. On the northern side, the top level of this layer of concrete merges with the ground. On all other sides this layer is only 10 cm below the ground level. The second layer is 0.6 m thick and has an area of 560 sq.m. including the circular opening. It is laid on the first layer over the strips 2 to 5 and with setbacks. Both these layers are fairly symmetrical about the east–west axis, except for small irregularities in the dimensions. The third layer is also 0.6 m thick but covers only a small area of 130 sq. m. Bulk of concrete is laid on the south-west region of the structure. In general, the second and third layers have poor surface finish. The concrete casting work is unfinished.

'However, if one desires, a modified form of a classical temple can be related to this configuration.

'As already stated in Paragraphs 2(a). 04.1 to 2(a). 04.4, the magnitude of the work is such that it could not have been carried out without the use of construction equipment such as water tankers, cement concrete mixers, concrete vibrators, earth-moving equipment etc.'

There is, therefore, no manner of doubt that substantial work, indeed very substantial work, involving tonnes of cement and concrete deployed with the help of constructional machinery was carried on at the site. The photographs produced by the complainant—which are not disputed—indicate the gathering of workers. A mere perusal of the photographs justifies an inference that the large workforce at the site does not consist of mere sadhus but justifies the inference that professional workmen had been deployed at the site.

We must, however, indicate that the report of the Expert Committee headed by Shri S. Rai, Registrar General, was of the month of August 1992. But the significance of the report as to the nature and extent of work and whether it could be related to the month of July is determined by the fact that on Uttar Pradesh Government's own admission the work had stopped on 26-7-1992. It is, therefore, permissible to relate the factual state of construction indicated in the Expert Committee's Report to what must be presumed to have been carried out in the month of July 1992 itself. We have no hesitation in finding that there was massive work undertaken and executed on the land in violation of the Court's orders.

The next question is whether these activities were carried on by a congregation of sadhus at the site and not by the State Government and despite Government's efforts. Apart from a glib suggestion that any attempt to prevent the work would have created a violent situation endangering the safety of the 'Ramjanmabhoomi–Babri Masjid structure' itself, nothing is indicated as to what was sought to be done at all to prevent constructional material coming in. There is no mention in any of the affidavits of any of the officers as to what reasonable measures the Government took to prevent the inflow of constructional material such as large quantities of cement, mortar, sand, constructional equipment, water tankers etc. that were necessary for the work. The report of the Expert Committee has indicated that constructional machinery was indispensable with regard to the nature and magnitude of the work carried out. While it is understandable that the prevention of the gathering of sadhus might have created some resentment, it is not understandable why large quantities of building materials were allowed to be brought on the land unless it be—and that must be the reasonable presumption—that the Government itself was not too anxious to prevent it. It is not merely positive acts of violation but also surreptitious and indirect aids to circumvention and violation of the orders that are equally impermissible. If reasonable steps are not taken to prevent the violation of the orders of the Court, the Government cannot be heard to say that violation of the orders were at the instance of others. The presumption is that the Government intended not to take such preventive steps. In the facts and circumstances of the case, we are unable to persuade ourselves to the view that the Government was helpless and the situation that had developed was in spite of all reasonable steps taken by the Government. Indeed there is no indication that the Government bestirred itself to take any steps, reasonable or otherwise, to prevent large-scale building material getting into the site. The Chief Minister having given a solemn assurance to the National Integration Council and permitted the terms of that assurance to be incorporated as his own undertaking to this Court and allowed an order to be passed in those terms cannot absolve himself of the responsibility unless he placed before the Court sufficient material which would justify that he had taken all reasonable steps and precautions to prevent the occurrence. Indeed, if such reasonable steps had been taken he could not be faulted merely because he did not do the best by the standards of others. In this case, we find no explanation at all apart from the fact that the sadhus had congregated in that place in large number, as to what steps the Government took to prevent the constructional equipment from getting into the site. If any reasonable effort had been made and evidence of that placed before Court, it must have been possible for the Court to assess the situation in the light of that explanation to find out whether such steps had been taken. In the absence, we are constrained to hold that the Government failed to take steps to prevent the grossest violation of the order of this court. We record a finding accordingly.

The State Government is, therefore, liable in contempt. A Minister or Officer of Government is also either in his official capacity or if there is a personal element contributing to contempt, in his personal capacity, liable in contempt.

We find that the undertaking given by Shri Kalyan Singh was both in his personal capacity and on behalf of his Government. There has been a flagrant breach of that undertaking. There has been wilful disobedience of the order.

It is unhappy that a leader of a political party and Chief Minister has to be convicted of an offence of contempt of court. But it has to be done to uphold the majesty of law. We convict him of the offence of contempt of court. Since the contempt raises larger issues, which affect the very foundation of the secular fabric of our nation, we also sentence him to a token imprisonment of one day. We also sentence him to pay a fine of Rs 2,000. The fine shall be paid within a period of two months. For the sentence of imprisonment a warrant will issue.

The contempt petitions are partly disposed accordingly.

In the Supreme Court of India
Result

Held:

Per majority

It is clear from the constitutional scheme that it guarantees equality in the matter of religion to all individuals and groups irrespective of their faith emphasizing that there is no religion of the State itself. The Preamble of the Constitution read in particular with Articles 25 and 28 emphasizes this aspect and indicates that it is in this manner the concept of secularism embodied in the constitutional scheme as a creed adopted by the Indian people has to be understood while examining the constitutional validity of any legislation on the touchstone of the Constitution. The concept of secularism is one facet of the right to equality woven as the central golden thread in the fabric depicting the pattern of the scheme in our Constitution. 'The purpose of law in plural societies is not progressive assimilation of the minorities in the majoritarian milieu. This would not solve the problem; but would vainly seek to dissolve it.' The true concept of secularism, and the role of judiciary in a pluralist society, as also the duty of the court in interpreting such a law, have to be kept in mind. (Paras 37, 38 and 39)

'Law in a Pluralist Society' by M.N. Venkatachaliah, J., relied on.

Subject to the protection under Articles 25 and 26, places of religious worship like mosques, churches, temples etc. can be acquired under the State's sovereign power of acquisition. Such acquisition per se does not violate either Article 25 or Article 26. The decisions relating to taking over of the management have no bearing on the sovereign power of the State to acquire property. The power of acquisition is the sovereign or prerogative power of the State to acquire property. Such power exists independent of Article 300-A or the earlier Article 31 of the Constitution, which merely indicate the limitations on the power of acquisition by the State.

Secularism is a part of the basic features of the Constitution. Article 25(1) protects the rights of individuals. Exercise of the right of the individual to profess, practise and propagate religion is subject to public order. Secularism is absolute; the State may not treat religions differently on the ground that public order requires it. The principle of secularism illumines the provisions of Article 15 and 16. (Paras 135, 143 and 144)

Secularism is given pride of place in the Constitution. The object is to preserve and protect all religions, to place all religious communities on par. When, therefore, adherents of the religion of the majority of Indian citizens make a claim upon and assail the place of worship of another religion and, by dint of numbers, create conditions that are conductive to public disorder, it is the constitutional obligation of the State to protect that place of worship and to preserve public order, using for the purpose such means and forces of law and order as are required. It is impermissible under the provisions of the Constitution for the State to acquire that place of worship to preserve public order. To condone the acquisition of a place of worship in such circumstances is to efface the principle of secularism from the Constitution. (Para 140)

If the title to the place of worship is in dispute in a court of law and public order is jeopardized, two courses are open to the

Central Government. It may apply to the court concerned to be appointed Receiver of the place of worship, to hold it secure pending the final adjudication of its title, or it may enact legislation that makes it statutory Receiver of the place of worship pending the adjudication of its title by the court concerned. In either event, the Central Government would bind itself to hand over the place of worship to the party in whose favour its title is found. (Para 141)

At the hearing, it was strenuously urged that the question of fact referred under Article 143(1) of the Constitution is vague, the answer to it is by itself not decisive of the real controversy since the core question has not been referred; and it also gives no definite indication of the manner in which the Central Government intends to act after the Special Reference is answered, to settle the dispute. It was urged that the question referred is, therefore, academic, apart from being vague, and it does not serve any constitutional purpose to subserve which the advisory jurisdiction of this Court could be evoked; that the real object and purpose of the Reference is to take away a place of worship of the Muslims and give it away to the Hindus offending the basic feature of secularism; and that, therefore, we should decline to answer the Special Reference. The learned Solicitor General who appeared for the Union of India was asked to clarify the stand of the Central Government on this point. Initially, it was stated by the learned Solicitor General that the answer to the question would provide the basis for further negotiations between the different groups to settle the controversy and the Central Government would then be able to decide the effective available to it for resolving the controversy. On being asked to further clarify the stand of the Central Government about the purpose of the Special Reference, the learned Solicitor General made a statement in writing on behalf of the Union of India on 14-9-1994 as under:

'Government stands by the policy of secularism and of even-handed treatment of all religious communities. The Acquisition of Certain Area at Ayodhya Act, 1993, as well as the Presidential Reference, have the objective of maintaining public order and promoting communal harmony and the spirit of common brotherhood amongst the people of India.

'Government is committed to the construction of a Ram temple and a mosque, but their actual location will be determined only after the Supreme Court renders its opinion in the Presidential Reference.

'Government will treat the finding of the Supreme Court on the question of fact referred under Article 143 of the Constitution as a verdict, which is final and binding.

'In the light of the Supreme Court's opinion and consistent with it, Government will make efforts to resolve the controversy by a process of negotiations. Government is confident that the opinion of the Supreme Court will have a salutary effect on the attitudes of the communities and they will no longer take conflicting position on the factual issue settled by the Supreme Court.

'If efforts at a negotiated settlement as aforesaid do not succeed, Government is committed to enforce a solution in the light of the Supreme Court's opinion and consistent with it. Government's action in this regard will be even-handed in respect of both the communities. If the question referred is answered in the affirmative, namely, that a Hindu temple/structure did exist prior to the construction of the demolished structure, Government action will be in support of the wishes of the Hindu community. If, on the other hand, the question is answered in the negative, namely, that no such Hindu temple/structure existed at the relevant time, then Government action will be in support of the wishes of the Muslim community.'

The dispute and its background are mentioned in paras 2.1, 2.2 and 2.3 of Chapter II of the White Paper quoted earlier. This is the backdrop in which the constitutional validity of Act No. 33 of 1993 and the maintainability of the Special Reference made under Article 143(1) of the Constitution of India have to be examined.

Validity of Act No. 33 of 1993

Broadly stated, the focus of the challenge to the statute as a whole is on the grounds of secularism, right to equality and right to freedom of religion. The challenge to the acquisition of the area in excess of the disputed area is in addition on the ground that the acquisition was unnecessary being unrelated to the dispute pertaining to the small disputed area within it. A larger argument advanced on behalf of some of the parties who have assailed the Act with considerable vehemence is that a mosque being a place of religious worship by the Muslims, independently of whether the acquisition did affect the right to practise religion, is wholly immune from the State's power of acquisition and the statute is, therefore, unconstitutional as violative of Articles 25 and 26 of the Constitution of India for this reason alone. The others, however, limited this argument of immunity from acquisition of which would result in the extinction of the right to freedom of religion itself. It was also contended that the purpose of acquisition in the present case does not bring the statute within the ambit of Entry 42, List III but is referable to Entry 1, List II and, therefore, Parliament did not have the competence to enact the same. It was then urged by learned counsel canvassing the Muslim interest that the legislation is titled heavily in favour of the Hindu interests and, therefore, suffers from the vice of non-secularism and discrimination in addition to violation of the right to freedom of religion of the Muslim community. It was also urged by them that the Central Government, after the Prime Minister's statement made on 7–12–1992, to rebuild the demolished structure (para 1.22 in Chapter I of the White Paper) rescinded from the same and the injustice done to the Muslim community by the act of vandalism and demolition of the structure at Ayodhya on 6–12–

1992. On behalf of the Muslim community, it is urged that the statute read in the context of the content of the question referred under Article 143(1) of the Constitution, as it must be, is a mere veiled concealment of a device adopted by the Central Government to perpetuate the consequences of the demolition of the mosque on 6–12–1992. The grievance of the Hindu opponents is that the mischief and acts of vandalism committed by a few are being attributed to the entire Hindu community, the majority of whom is equally hurt by, and critical of, the shameful act. They urge that this disapproval by the majority community is evident from the result of the subsequent elections in which the Bharatiya Janata Party was rejected at the hustings by the Hindu majority. They also submit that the fact of demolition of Hindu structures like the Ram Chabutra and Kaushalya Rasoi which stood since ages in the disputed site resulting in interruption of even the undisputed right of worship of Hindus within that area is being ignored. It is also contended that there is no justification for acquisition of any property in excess of the disputed area and, therefore, the acquisition at least of the excess area belonging, admittedly, to Hindus is invalid.

On behalf of the Central Government, it is urged that in the existing situation and in view of the widespread communal flare-up throughout the country on account of the events at Ayodhya on 6–12–1992, the most appropriate course, in the opinion of the Central Government, was to make this acquisition along with the Special Reference to decide the question which would facilitate a negotiated solution of the problem, and if it failed, to enable the Central Government to take any other appropriate action to resolve the controversy and restore communal harmony in the country. It was made clear that acquisition of the disputed area was not meant to deprive the community found entitled to it, of the same, or to retain any part of the excess area which was not necessary for a proper resolution of the dispute or to effectuate the purpose of the acquisition. It was submitted that an assurance of communal harmony throughout the country was a prime constitutional purpose and avoidance of escalation of the dispute in the wake of the incident at Ayodhya on 6–12–1992 was an essential step in that direction, which undoubtedly promotes the creed of secularism instead of impairing it. It was submitted that the charge levelled against the Central Government of discrimination against any religious community or of anti-secularism is wholly unwarranted.

Legislative Competence

The legislative competence is traceable to Entry 42, List III and the State of Uttar Pradesh being under President's Rule at the relevant time, the legislative competence of Parliament, in the circumstances, cannot be doubted. That apart, the pith and substance of the legislation is 'acquisition of property' and that falls squarely within the ambit of Entry 42, List III. The competing entry set up is Entry I, List II relating to 'public order'. 'Acquisition of property' and not 'public order' is the pith and substance of the statute.

For a proper consideration of the challenge based on the ground of secularism, it is appropriate to refer to the concept of secularism and the duty of the courts in construing a statute in this context.

The polity assured to the people of India by the Constitution is described in the Preamble wherein the word 'secular' was added by the 42nd Amendment. It highlights the fundamental rights guaranteed in Articles 25 to 29 that the State shall have no religion of its own and all persons shall be equally entitled to freedom of conscience and the right freely to profess, practice and propagate religion of their own choice. In brief, this is the concept of secularism as a basic feature of the Constitution of India and the way of life adopted by the people of India as their abiding faith and creed. M.C. Setalvad in Patel Memorial Lectures 1965, referring to the Indian concept of secularism, stated thus:

> The coming of the partition emphasized the great importance of secularism. Notwithstanding the partition, a large Muslim minority, constituting a tenth of the population, continued to be the citizens of independent India. There were also other important minority groups of citizens. In the circumstances, a secular Constitution for independent India, under which all religions could enjoy equal freedom and all citizens equal rights, and which could weld together into one nation the different religious communities, became inevitable.
>
> The ideal, therefore, of a secular State in the sense of a State which treats all religions alike and displays a benevolent neutrality towards them is in a way more suited to the Indian environment and climate than that of a truly secular State.
>
> Secularism, in the Indian context, must be given the widest possible content. It should connote the eradication of all attitudes and practices derived from or connected with religion which impede our development and retard our growth into an integrated nation. A concerted and earnest endeavour, both by the State and citizen, towards secularization in accordance with this wide concept alone can lead to the stabilization of our democratic State and the establishment of a true and cohesive Indian nationhood.

*

'Acquisition or requisitioning of property, except for the purposes of the Union, subject to the provisions of Entry 42 of List III.' List III, Entry 42:

In S.R. Bommai vs. Union of India, a nine-judge Bench referred to the concept of 'secularism' in the Indian context. Sawant, J., dealt with this aspect and after referring to the Setalvad Lecture, stated thus: (SCC pp. 147–48, para 151)

'As stated above, religious tolerance and equal treatment of all religious groups and protection of their life and property and of the places of their worship are an essential part of secularism enshrined in our Constitution. We have accepted the said goal not only because it is our historical legacy and a need of our national unity and integrity but also as a creed of universal brotherhood and humanism. It is our cardinal faith. Any profession and action which go counter to the aforesaid creed are a prima facie proof of the conduct in defiance of the provisions of our Constitution.'

Similarly, K. Ramaswamy, J., in the same decision stated: (SCC p. 163, para 178 and p. 168, para 183)

'Though the concept of "secularism" was not expressly engrafted while making the Constitution, its sweep, operation and visibility are apparent from fundamental rights and directive principles and their related provisions. It was made explicit by amending the preamble of the Constitution in the 42nd Amendment Act. The concept of secularism of which religious freedom is the foremost appears to visualize not only of the subject of God but also an understanding between man and man. Secularism in the Constitution is not anti-God and it is sometimes believed to be a stay in a free society. Matters, which are purely religious, are left personal to the individual and the secular part is taken charge of by the State on grounds of public interest, order and general welfare. The State guarantees individual and corporate religious freedom and deals with an individual as citizen irrespective of his faith and religious belief and does not promote any particular religion nor prefers one against another. The concept of the secular State is, therefore, essential for successful working of the democratic form of Government. There can be no democracy if anti-secular forces are allowed to work dividing followers of different religious faith flaying at each other's throats. The secular Government should negate the attempt and bring order in the society. Religion in the positive sense, is an active instrument to allow the citizen full development of his person, not merely in the physical and material but in the non-material and non-secular life.

'It would thus be clear that the Constitution made a demarcation between religious part personal to the individual and secular part thereof. The State does not extend patronage to any particular religion. State is neither pro-particular religion nor anti-particular religion. It stands aloof, in other words maintains neutrality in matters of religion and provides equal protection to all religions subject to regulation and actively acts on the secular part.'

B.P. Jeevan Reddy, J., in the same context in the decision stated thus: (SCC p. 233, para 304)

'While the citizens of this country are free to profess, practice and propagate such religion, faith or belief as they choose, so far as the State is concerned, i.e., from the point of view of the State, the religion, faith or belief of a person is immaterial. To it, all are equal and all are entitled to be treated equally. How is this equal treatment possible, if the State were to prefer or promote a particular religion, race or caste, which necessarily means a less favourable treatment of all other religions, races and castes? How are the constitutional promises of social justice, liberty of belief, faith or worship and equality of status and of opportunity to be attained unless the State eschews the religion, faith or belief of a person from its consideration altogether while dealing with him, his rights, his duties and his entitlements? Secularism is thus more than a passive attitude of religious tolerance. It is a positive concept of equal treatment of all religions. This attitude is described by some as one of neutrality towards religion or as one of benevolent neutrality. This may be a concept evolved by western liberal thought or it may be, as some say, an abiding faith with the Indian people at all points of time. That is not material. What is material is that it is a constitutional goal and a basic feature of the Constitution affirmed in Kesavananda Bharati and Indira Nehru Gandhi vs. Raj Narain. Any step inconsistent with this constitutional policy is, in plain words, unconstitutional. This does not mean that the State has no say whatsoever in matters of religion. Laws can be made regulating the secular affairs of temples, mosques and other places of worships and maths. (See S.P. Mittal vs. Union of India.)'

Ahmadi, J., while expressing agreement with the views of Sawant, Ramaswamy and Jeevan Reddy, JJ., stated thus: (SCC p. 77, para 29)

'Notwithstanding the fact that the words "Socialist" and "Secular" were added in the Preamble of the Constitution in 1976 by the 42nd Amendment, the concept of Secularism was very much embedded in our constitutional philosophy. The term "Secular" has advisedly not been defined presumably because it is a very elastic term not capable of a precise definition and perhaps best left undefined. By this amendment what was implicit was made explicit.'

It is clear from the constitutional scheme that it guarantees equality in the matter of religion to all individuals and groups irrespective of their faith emphasizing that there is no religion of the State itself. The Preamble of the Constitution read in particular with Articles 25 to 28 emphasizes this aspect and indicates that it is in this manner the concept of secularism embodied in the constitutional scheme as a creed adopted by the Indian people has to be understood while examining the constitutional validity of any legislation on the touchstone of the Constitution. The concept of secularism is one facet of the right to equality woven as the central golden thread in the fabric depicting the pattern of the scheme in our Constitution.

It is useful in this context to refer to some extracts from a paper on 'Law in a Pluralist Society' by M.N. Venkatachaliah, J., as he then was (one of us). Therein, he said:

'The purpose of law in plural societies is not the progressive assimilation of the minorities in the majoritarian milieu. This would not solve the problem; but would vainly seek to dissolve it. What then is its purpose?'

Again in the words of Lord Scarman *(Minority Rights in a Plural Society*, p. 63):

'The purpose of the law must be not to extinguish the groups which make the society but to devise political, social and legal means of preventing them from falling apart and so destroying the plural society of which they are members.

'In a pluralist, secular polity, law is perhaps the greatest integrating force. A cultivated respect for law and its institutions and symbols; a pride in the country's heritage and achievements; faith that people live under the protection of an adequate legal system are indispensable for sustaining unity in pluralist diversity. Rawlian pragmatism of "justice as fairness" to serve as an "overlapping consensus" and deep-seated agreements on fundamental questions of basic structure of society for deeper social unity is a political conception of justice rather than a comprehensive moral conception.

'What are the limitations on laws dealing with issues or pluralism? Law should not accentuate the depth of the cleavage and become in itself a source of aggravation of the very condition it intends to remedy.

'To those that live in fear and insecurity all the joys and bright colours of life are etched away. There is need to provide a reassurance and a sense of belonging. It is not enough to say: "Look here . . . I never promised you a rose garden. I never promised you perfect justice." But perfect justice may be an unattainable goal. At least it must be a tolerable accommodation of the conflicting interests of society. Though there may really be a "royal road to attain such accommodations concretely". Bentham alluded to the pursuit of equality as a "disappointment-preventing" principle, as the principle of distributive justice and part of the security-providing principle.'

Keeping in mind the true concept of secularism and the role of judiciary in a pluralist society, as also the duty of the court in interpreting such a law, we now proceed to consider the submissions with reference to the provisions of the enactment.

As earlier stated, worship by Hindu devotees of the idols installed on the Ram Chabutra which stood on the disputed site within the courtyard of the disputed structure had been performed without any objection by the Muslims even prior to the shifting of those idols from Ram Chabutra into the disputed structure in December 1949; in one of the suits filed in January 1950, the trial court passed interim orders whereby the idols remained at the place where they were installed in 1949 and worship of the idols there by the Hindu devotees continued; this interim order was confirmed by the High Court in April 1955; the District Judge ordered the opening of the lock placed on a grill leading to the sanctum sanctorum of the shrine in the disputed structure on 1–2–1986 and permitted worship of the idols there to Hindu devotees; and this situation continued till demolition of the structure on 6–12–1992 when Ram Chabutra also was demolished. It was only as a result of the act of demolition on 6–12–1992 that the worship by the Hindu devotees in general of the idols at that place was interrupted. Since the time of demolition, worship of the idols by a pujari alone is continuing. This is how the right of worship of the idols practised by Hindu devotees for a long time from much prior to 1949 in the Ram Chabutra within the disputed site has been interrupted since the act of demolition on 6–12–1992 restricting the worship of the idols since then to only one pujari. On the other hand, at least since December 1949, the Muslims have not been offering worship at any place in the disputed site though it may turn out at the trial of the suits that they had a right to do so.

The communal holocaust unleashed in the country disrupting the prevailing communal harmony as a result of the demolition of the structure on 6–12–1992 is well known to require further mention. Any step taken to arrest escalation of communal tension and to achieve communal accord and harmony can, by no stretch of argumentation, be termed non-secular much less anti-secular or against the concept of secularism—a creed of the Indian people embedded in the ethos.

The narration of facts indicates that the acquisition of properties under the Act affects the rights of both the communities and not merely those of the Muslim community. The interest claimed by the Muslims is only over the disputed site where the mosque stood before its demolition, the objection of the Hindus to this claim has to be adjudicated. The remaining entire property acquired under the Act is such over which no title is claimed by the Muslims. A large part thereof comprises of properties of Hindus of which the title is not even in dispute. The justification given for acquisition of the larger area including the property respecting which title is not disputed is that the same is necessary to ensure that the final outcome of adjudication should not be rendered meaningless by the existence of properties belonging to Hindus in the vicinity of the disputed structure in case the Muslims are found entitled to the disputed site. This obviously means that in the event of the Muslims succeeding in the adjudication of the dispute requiring the disputed structure to be handed over to the Muslim community, their success should not be thwarted by denial or proper access to, and enjoyment of rights in, the disputed area by exercise of rights of ownership of Hindu owners of the adjacent properties. Obviously, it is for this reason that the adjacent area has also been acquired to make available to the successful party, that part of it which is considered necessary, for proper enjoyment of the fruits of success on the final outcome to the adjudication. It is clear that one of the purposes of the acquisition of the adjacent properties is the ensurement of the effective enjoyment of the disputed site by the Muslim community in the event of its success in the litigation; and acquisition of the adjacent area is incidental to the main purpose and cannot be termed unreasonable. The

'Manas Bhawan' and 'Sita Ki Rasoi', both belonging to the Hindus, are buildings which closely overlook the disputed site and are acquired because they are strategic in location in relation to the disputed area. The necessity of acquiring adjacent temples or religious buildings in view of their proximity to the disputed structure area, which forms a unique class by itself, is permissible (See M. Padmanabha Iyengar vs. Govt, of AP and Akhara Shri Brahma Buta vs. State of Punjab). We approve the principle stated in these decisions since it serves a larger purpose.

However, at a later stage when the exact area acquired which is needed, for achieving the professed purpose of acquisition, can be determined, it would not merely be permissible but also desirable that the superfluous excess area is released from acquisition and reverted to its earlier owner. The challenge to acquisition of any part of the adjacent area on the ground that it is unnecessary for achieving the objective of settling the dispute relating to the disputed area cannot be examined at this stage but, in case the superfluous area is not returned to its owner even after the exact area needed for the purpose is finally determined, it would be open to the owner of any such property to then challenge the superfluous acquisition being unrelated to the purpose of acquisition. Rejection of the challenge on this ground to acquisition at this stage, by the undisputed owners of any such property situated in the vicinity of the disputed area, is with the reservation of this liberty to them. There is no contest to their claim of quashing the acquisition of the adjacent properties by anyone except the Central Government, which seeks to justify the acquisition on the basis of necessity. On the construction of the statute made by us, this appears to be the logical, appropriate and just view to take in respect of such adjacent properties in which none other than the undisputed owner claims title and interest.

It may also be mentioned that even as Ayodhya is said to be of particular significance to the Hindus as a place of pilgrimage because of the ancient belief that Lord Ram was born there, the mosque was of significance for the Muslim community as an ancient mosque built by Mir Baqi in 1528 AD. As a mosque, it was a religious place of worship by the Muslims. This indicates the comparative significance of the disputed site to the two communities and also that the impact of acquisition is equally on the right and interest of the Hindu community. Mention of this aspect is made only in the context of the argument that the statute as a whole, not merely Section 7 thereof, is anti-secular being slanted in favour of the Hindus and against the Muslims.

Section 7(2) of the Act freezes the situation admittedly in existence on 7–1–1993 which was a lesser right of worship for the Hindu devotees than that in existence earlier for a long time till the demolition of the disputed structure on 6–12–1992; and it does not create a new situation more favourable to the Hindu community amounting to conferment on them of a larger right of worship in the disputed site than that practised till 6–12–1992. Maintenance of status quo as on 7–1–1993 does not, therefore, confer or have the effect of granting to the Hindu community any further benefit thereby. It is also pertinent to bear in mind that the persons responsible for demolition of the mosque on 6–12–1992 were some miscreants who cannot be identified and equated with the entire Hindu community and, therefore, the act of vandalism so perpetrated by the miscreants cannot be treated as an act of the entire Hindu community for the purpose of adjudging the constitutionality of the enactment. Strong reaction against and condemnation by the Hindus of the demolition of the structure in general bears eloquent testimony to this fact. Rejection of Bharatiya Janata Party at the hustings in the subsequent elections in Uttar Pradesh is another circumstance to that effect. The miscreants who demolished the mosque had no religion, caste or creed except the character of a criminal and the mere incident of birth of such a person in any particular community cannot attach the stigma of his crime to the community in which he was born.

Another effect of the freeze imposed by Section 7(2) of the Act is that it ensures that there can be no occasion for the Hindu community to seek to enlarge the scope of the practice of worship by them as on 7–1–1993 during the interregnum till the final adjudication on the basis that in fact a larger right of worship by them was in vogue up to 6–12–1992. It is difficult to visualize how Section 7(2) can be construed as a slant in favour of the Hindu community and, therefore, anti-secular. The provision does not curtail practice of right of worship of the Muslim community in the disputed area, there having been de facto no exercise of the practice or worship by them there at least since December 1949; and it maintains status quo by the freeze to the reduced right of worship by the Hindus as in existence on 7–1–1993. However, confining exercise of the right of worship of the Hindu community to its reduced form within the disputed area as on 7–1–1993, lesser than that exercised till the demolition on 6–12–1992, by the freeze enacted in Section 7(2) appears to be reasonable and just in view of the fact that the miscreants who demolished the mosque are suspected to be persons professing to practise the Hindu religion. The Hindu community must, therefore, bear the cross on its chest, for the misdeed of the miscreants reasonably suspected to belong to their religious fold.

This is the proper perspective, we say, in which the statute as a whole and Section 7 in particular must be viewed. Thus the factual foundation for challenge to the statute as a whole and section 7(2) in particular on the ground of secularism, a basic feature of the Constitution, and the rights to equality and freedom of religion is non-existent.

The status of the Central Government as a result of vesting by virtue of Section 3 of the Act is, therefore, of a statutory receiver in relation to the disputed area, coupled with a duty to manage and administer the disputed area maintaining status quo therein till the final outcome of adjudication of the long-standing dispute relating to the disputed structure at Ayodhya. Vesting in the

Central Government of the area in excess of the disputed area is, however, absolute. The meaning of 'vest' has these different shades in Section 3 and 6 in relation to the two parts of the entire area acquired by the Act.

The question now is of the mode of adjudication of the dispute, on the final outcome of which the action contemplated by Section 6(1) of the Act of effecting transfer of the disputed area has to be made by the Central Government.

A construction which the language of the statute can bear and promote a larger national purpose must be preferred to a strict literal construction tending to promote factionalism and discord.

Maintainability of the Reference

In the view that we have taken on the question of validity of the statute (Act No. 33 of 1993) and as a result of upholding the validity of the entire statute, except Section 4(3) thereof, resulting in revival of the pending suits and legal proceedings wherein the dispute between the parties has to be adjudicated, the Reference made under Article 143(1) becomes superfluous and unnecessary. For this reason, it is necessary for us to examine the merits of the submissions made on the maintainability of this Reference. We, accordingly, very respectfully decline to answer the Reference and return the same.

Result

The result is that all the pending suits and legal proceedings stand revived, and they shall be proceeded with, and decided, in accordance with law. It follows further as a result of the remaining enactment being upheld as valid that the disputed area has vested in the Central Government as a statutory receiver with a duty to manage and administer it in the manner provided in the Act maintaining status quo therein by virtue of the freeze enacted in Section 7(2); and the Central Government would exercise its power of vesting that property further in another authority or body or trust in accordance with Section 8(1) of the Act in terms of the final adjudication in the pending suits. The power of the courts in the pending legal proceedings to give directions to the Central Government as a statutory receiver would be circumscribed and limited to the extent of the area left open by the provisions of the Act. The Central Government would be bound to take all necessary steps to implement the decision in the suits and other legal proceedings and to hand over the disputed area to the party found entitled to the same on the final adjudication made in the suits. The parties to the suits would be entitled to amend their pleadings suitably in the light of our decision.

Before we end, we would like to indicate the consequence of the entire Act had been held to be invalid and then we had declined to answer the Reference on that conclusion. It would then result in revival of the abated suits along with all the interim orders made therein. It would also then result automatically in revival of the worship of the idols by Hindu devotees, which too has been stopped from December 1992 with all its ramifications without granting any benefit to the Muslim community whose practice of worship in the mosque (demolished on 6-12-1992) had come to a stop, for whatever reason, since at least December 1949. This situation, unless altered subsequently by any court order in the revived suits, would, therefore, continue during the pendency of the litigation. This result could be no solace to the Muslims whose feelings of hurt as a result of the demolition of the mosque, must be assuaged in the manner best possible without giving cause for any legitimate grievance to the other community leading to the possibility of re-igniting communal passions detrimental to the spirit of communal harmony in a secular State.

The best solution in the circumstances, on revival of suits is, therefore, to maintain status quo as on 7–1–1993 when the law came into force modifying the interim orders in the suits to that extent by curtailing the practice of worship by Hindus in the disputed area to the extent it stands reduced under the Act instead of conferring on them the larger right available under the court orders till intervention was made by legislation.

Section 7(2) achieves this purpose by freezing the interim arrangement for worship by Hindu devotees reduced to this extent and curtails the larger right they enjoyed under the court order, ensuring that it cannot be enlarged till final adjudication of the dispute and consequent transfer of the disputed area to the party found entitled to the same. This being the purpose and true effect of Section 7(2), it promotes and strengthens the commitment of the nation to secularism instead of negating it. To hold this provision as anti-secular and slanted in favour of the Hindu community would be to frustrate an attempt to thwart anti-secularism and unwittingly support the forces which were responsible for the events of 6–12–1992.

The hearing left us wondering why the dispute cannot be resolved in the same manner and in the same spirit in which the matter was argued, particularly when some of the participants are common and are in a position to negotiate and resolve the dispute. We do hope this hearing has been the commencement of that process which will ensure an amicable resolution of the dispute and it will not end with the hearing of this matter. This is a matter suited essentially to resolution by negotiations which does not end in a winner and a loser while adjudication leads to that end; it is in the national interest that there is no loser at the end of the process adopted for resolution of the dispute so that the final outcome does not leave behind any rancour in anyone. This can be achieved by a negotiated solution on the basis of which a decree can be obtained in terms of such solution in these suits. Unless a solution is found which leaves everyone happy, that cannot be the beginning for continued harmony between 'we the people of India'.

'As 1993 began, communal violence returned to India, sparked by the controversy over a sixteenth century mosque said to stand on the ruins of an ancient Hindu temple honouring Lord Rama.' It may be said that:

> 'fundamentalism and pluralism pose the two challenges that people of all religious traditions face';

and

> 'to the fundamentalists, the borders of religious certainty are tightly guarded; to the pluralist, the borders are good fences where one meets the neighbour. To many fundamentalists, secularism, seen as the denial of religious claims, is the enemy; to pluralists, secularism, seen as the separation of Government from the domination of a single religion, is the essential concomitant of religious diversity and the protection of religious freedom.'

The present state may be summarized thus:

'At present, the greatest religious tensions are not those between any one religion and another; they are the tensions between the fundamentalists and the pluralist in each and every religious tradition.'

The spirit of universalism popular in the late nineteenth century was depicted by Max Muller who said: 'The living kernel of religion can be found, I believe, in almost every creed, however much the husk may vary. And think what that means: It means that above and beneath and behind all religions there is one eternal, one universal religion.'

Conclusions

As a result of the above discussion, our conclusions, to be read with the discussion, are as follows:

(a) Sub-section (3) of Section 4 of the Act abates all pending suits and legal proceedings without providing for an alternative dispute-resolution mechanism for resolution of the dispute between the parties thereto. This is an extinction of the judicial remedy for resolution of the dispute amounting to negation of rule of law; Sub-section (3) of Section 4 of the Act is, therefore, unconstitutional and invalid.

The remaining provisions of the Act do not suffer from any invalidity on the construction made thereof by us. Sub-section (3) of Section 4 of the Act is severable from the remaining Act. Accordingly, the challenge to the constitutional validity of the remaining Act, except for subsection (3) of Section 4, is rejected.

Irrespective of the status of a mosque under the Muslim Law applicable in the Islamic countries, the status of a mosque under the Mahomedan Law applicable in secular India is the same and equal to that of any other place of worship of any religion; and it does not enjoy any greater immunity from acquisition in exercise of the sovereign or prerogative power of the State, than that of the places of worship of the other religions.

The pending suits and other proceedings relating to the disputed area within which the structure (including the premises of the inner and outer courtyards of such structure), commonly known as the Ramjanmabhoomi–Babri Masjid, stood, stand revived for adjudication of the dispute therein, together with the interim orders made, except to the extent the interim orders stand modified by the provisions of Section 7 of the Act.

The vesting of the said disputed area in the Central Government by virtue of Section 3 of the Act is limited, as a statutory receiver, with the duty for its management and administration according to Section 7 requiring maintenance of status quo therein under sub-section (2) of Section 7 of the Act. The duty of the Central Government as the statutory receiver is to hand over the disputed area in accordance with Section 6 of the Act, in terms of the adjudication made in the suits for implementation of the final decision therein. This is the purpose for which the disputed area has been so acquired.

The power of the courts in making further interim orders in the suits is limited to, and circumscribed by, the area outside the ambit of Section 7 of the Act.

The vesting of the adjacent area, other than the disputed area, acquired by the Act in the Central Government by virtue of Section 3 of the Act is absolute with the power of management and administration thereof in accordance with sub-section (1) of Section 7 of the Act, till its further vesting in any authority or other body or trustees of any trust in accordance with Section 6 of the Act. The further vesting of the adjacent area, other than the disputed area, in accordance with Section 6 of the Act has to be made at the time and in the manner indicated, in view of the purpose of its acquisition.

The meaning of the word 'vest' in Section 3 and Section 6 of the Act has to be so understood in the different contexts.

(b) Section 8 of the Act is meant for payment of compensation to owners of the property vesting absolutely in the Central Government, the title to which is not in dispute being in excess of the disputed area which alone is the subject matter of the revived suits. It does not apply to the disputed area, title to which has to be adjudicated in the suits and in respect of which the Central Government is merely the statutory receiver as indicated, with the duty to restore it to the owner in terms of the adjudication made in the suits.

The challenge to acquisition of any part of the adjacent area on the ground that it is unnecessary for achieving the professed objective of settling the long-standing dispute cannot be examined at this stage. However, the area found to be superfluous on the exact area needed for the purpose being determined on adjudication of the dispute, must be restored to the undisputed owners.

Rejection of the challenge by the undisputed owners to acquisition of some religious properties in the vicinity of the disputed area, at this stage is with the liberty granted to them to renew their challenge, if necessary at a later appropriate stage, in case of continued retention by Central Government of their property in excess of the exact area determined to be needed on adjudication of the dispute.

Consequently, the Special Reference No. 1 of 1993(19) made by the President of India under Article 143(1) of the Constitution of India is superfluous and unnecessary and does not require to be answered. For this reason, we very respectfully decline to answer it and return the same.

The questions relating to the Constitutional validity of the said Act and maintainability of the Special Reference are decided in these terms.

These matters are disposed of, accordingly, in the manner stated above.

Index